Contents

Preface

This is not just another book on drinks. It is specifically tailored to meet the needs of students of liquor studies.

The new City and Guilds 717 syllabus, jointly prepared by members of the hotel and catering industry, the wine trade and college lecturers, covers a wider area than in the past. I have prepared the necessary information to the required depth in all areas of this syllabus. The book should also be ideally suited to people studying BTEC hotel and catering courses, HCIMA liquor studies, City and Guilds 707–1 and 2 courses 700/5 and 700/8 courses. I hope that it will prove to be a worthwhile and valuable addition to the student bookshelf.

It will also be of great use to those employed in the hotel, catering and liquor trade as an introduction to the subject and a handy reference.

Brian Julyan

Acknowledgements

William Blacklock, City and Guilds of London
Percival Brown, Heyman Brothers Ltd
John Cunynghame, G B Vintagers
Christopher Piper, Christopher Piper Wines
Devon Fire Service
Havana Cigar Information Centre
Italian Wine Centre
Phillips of Bristol
South West Electricity Board

Maps and sketches by Keith Bloor.

Sources

Debretts Correct Form
Dictionary of Wines and Spirits (André Simon)
Hotel and Catering Law by David Field
World Atlas of Wine by Hugh Johnson

Chapter One

The hotel and catering industry

Hotel and catering establishments

The hotel, catering and leisure industry may be divided into a number of different sectors.

Hotels These are establishments that provide accommodation as a major part of their business. They include large and small hotels, motels, guest houses, holiday camps and holiday complexes.

Restaurants These provide meals as their main business. Restaurant types include luxury, in-store, ethnic and European.

Industrial catering This is a service provided for employees of companies. The sector includes canteens and some more specialized restaurants such as directors' dining rooms. The catering may be operated in-house – that is, run by the company itself, which employs its own catering staff – or it may be provided by a contract catering company.

Hospital and welfare catering This sector includes hospitals, nursing homes, schools and prisons. Catering is required for staff as well as the people attending or living in these establishments. In the public sector, the catering may be run by the local authority or by contract caterers. Privately run establishments may employ a contract caterer or operate a service in-house.

Transport catering This covers the provision of food and beverages to people in transit, for example on British Rail (Travellers' Fare), cruise ships, ferries, commercial shipping, and airlines.

Public houses This sector comprises those with restaurants, those which provide only bar snacks and drinks, and those which provide only drinks. Those supplying only drinks are now few and far between.

Wine bars and cocktail bars These usually serve food as well as drinks.

Clubs Clubs may be licensed, unlicensed, registered and unregistered.

Contract catering Contract caterers do not themselves run establishments. They are employed by other companies to provide a catering service. Recently the scope of their operations has been widened to include establishments in the public sector such as hospitals, prisons, and army camps.

Conference centres These operate conferences, banquets and other functions. They usually also have shops, kiosks and restaurants.

Leisure complexes These are sometimes combined with conference centres. They offer various forms of sporting and leisure activities. They will include a variety of food service outlets, kiosks, shops and bars.

Fast-food outlets This sector includes high street fast-food restaurants and take-aways, cafés, snack bars, motorway cafeterias, in-store cafeterias and many speciality restaurants. Fast-food outlets are found in sports stadiums, leisure complexes, shopping precincts and virtually anywhere people require a very quick service.

The armed forces The various catering services are supplied by regular armed forces personnel,

1

the Naafi organization and contract caterers.

Educational establishments This sector includes the catering for private, public and local authority schools, colleges, polytechnics and universities, in both main buildings and halls of residence.

Careers in beverage service

As can be seen from the wide variety of sectors within the industry, there is a multitude of opportunities for both full-time and part-time employment in beverage sales and service. Careers may culminate in management and ownership. The following is a list of possible jobs within the industry:

Bar person
Cocktail bar person
Bars manager
Publican: public house manager, tenant, or proprietor
Commis du vin
Sommelier
Head sommelier
Station waiter (chef de rang) serving own customers with drinks
Station head waiter
Restaurant manager
Food and beverage manager
Restaurant proprietor

Professional associations

There are a great number of professional and technical associations related to beverage sales and service. The following is a shortened list of these associations, each with its abbreviated aims. A full and complete list is available from the Hotel and Catering Training Board.

The British Hotels, Restaurants and Caterers Association (BHRCA)
Aims: to give help and advice to its members on legal aspects, purchasing, staff training and day-to-day problems. It represents its members' views to the government.

British Institute of Innkeeping (BII)
Aims: to promote and maintain nationally recognized levels of professional competence among licensees and those directly involved in the supervision of public houses; to help members develop business skills, to assist them with training and to set and maintain standards.

City and Guilds of London Institute (CGLI)
This is a non-profit-making examining body which oversees the development and examining of technical courses, including many for the hotel and catering industry. Its certificates enjoy worldwide recognition.

Cookery and Food Association (CFA)
Aims: to assist in the education and training of young people, chefs and others connected with the catering industry.

Court of Master Sommeliers
This is the examining body for the Master Sommelier Diploma. Aims: to set and maintain standards of service of wines and other beverages, to improve the knowledge of sommeliers (wine waiters) and to improve their status.

Food and Beverage Managers Association
Aims: to promote and develop the professionalism, effectiveness and standing of those involved in food and beverage within the industry.

Guild of Professional Toastmasters
Aims: to set and maintain standards and to promote and protect the professional standing of toastmasters.

Guild of Sommeliers
Aims: to improve the professional status of the sommelier, to promote interest in the knowledge and service of wine and to arrange educational activities to this end.

Hotel and Catering Training Board (HCTB)
Aims: to encourage and develop training in the hotel and catering industry.

Hotel, Catering and Institutional Management Association (HCIMA)
Aims: to promote standards of good practice in catering and accommodation management; to advance education, training and research; to establish and maintain standards of competence for managers in the industry.

Institute of Masters of Wine
Aims: to promote a high standard of knowledge of wines and all subjects relating to the wine trade, and to promote a high standard of professional practice among its members.

National Association of Licensed House Managers (NALHM)
Aims: to secure for its members the maximum possible benefit in their terms and conditions of employment.

National Union of Licensed Victuallers
Aims: to protect and improve the interests and welfare of its members, and to give advice on business queries.

The Restaurant Services Guild
This body is affiliated to the Cookery and Food Association. Aims: to improve the status of restaurant service workers, to improve national standards of restaurant service, to promote career development and to act as an advisory body for craft education.

The Restaurateurs Association of Great Britain (RAGB)
Aims: to protect and promote the interests and welfare of its members and to represent their views to the government.

The Scottish Licensed Trade Association
Aims: to protect and promote the rights and interests of the licensed trade in Scotland.

United Kingdom Bartenders Guild
Aims: to set and maintain standards of bartending and to assist with education and training.

Wine and Spirit Education Trust
Aims: to set standards of knowledge, education and training for those engaged in the wine and spirit trade.

The catering industry in the national economy

The hotel and catering industry is Britain's third largest employer. It employs between 2.3 and 2.4 million people; this represents approximately 10 per cent of the national workforce.

Over £26 500 million per annum is spent in hotels, restaurants, public houses and other catering outlets; over £15 000 million of this is spent on alcoholic drinks, and over £8 500 million on eating out.

Of each £1.15 spent in the hotel and catering industry, 15p goes in value added tax and a further 12p in other taxes such as National Insurance and income tax, making a total of 27p; this is approximately 24p out of every £1 spent. All of this goes to the government.

From these figures it can be seen that the hotel and catering industry is of major importance to the economy of the UK.

Chapter Two

Preparation and maintenance
of bar and cellar

Tools and equipment for restaurant, bar and cellar

Bottle openers and corkscrews

Waiter's knife or waiter's friend
The points to look for in a good waiter's friend are an adequate number of coils on the screw, and as wide and long a screw as possible. The lever should hold its position when opened, not flop about. See Figure 2.1.

Wing screw
This is not convenient to carry in a waiter's pocket. In addition, it has no knife. See Figure 2.2.

Double-action screw
This is very good for removing old corks but is not convenient to carry in a waiter's pocket. It also has no knife. See Figure 2.3.

T-shaped wooden handled screw, single pull
This corkscrew is not very useful. It has no knife or lever. The cork extraction is uncontrolled, resulting in a loud pop as the cork is pulled. It is of no use for extraction of corks from bottles which have a sediment. See Figure 2.4.

Screwpull corkscrew
A very efficient modern American invention which only lacks a knife for cutting the capsule. It is less convenient to carry than a waiter's knife. See Figure 2.5.

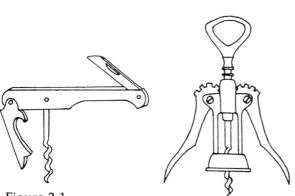

Figure 2.1
Waiter's Friend

Figure 2.2   *Wing screw*

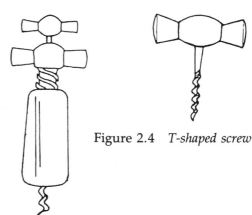

Figure 2.3   *Double-action screw*

Figure 2.4   *T-shaped screw*

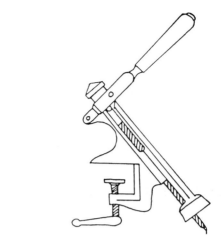

Figure 2.5 *Screwpull corkscrew*

Figure 2.6 *Bench corkscrew*

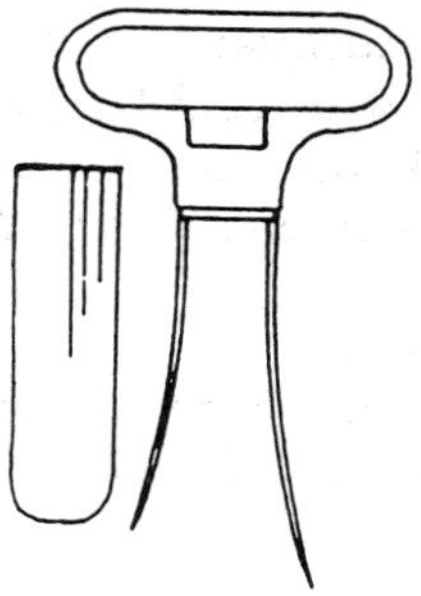

Bench corkscrew

This is ideal for a dispense bar or a wine bar. It is particularly useful in a dispense bar for function catering where set wines are being served. See Figure 2.6.

Broken cork extractor

This is used to remove a broken cork which has been pushed into the bottle. See Figure 2.7. The three wires of the extractor are inserted into the neck of the bottle until the claws are below the piece of broken cork. The wire or plastic ring is moved towards the handle so that the wires expand outwards. The extractor is then pulled out with the cork trapped between the wires and the claws. See Figure 2.7.

Extractor

The capsule of the bottle is cut in the normal way. The two pronged extractor is removed from its sheath. The two prongs are inserted between the cork and the neck of the bottle and twisted to remove the cork. See Figure 2.8.

Fruit knife and board

A small stainless steel knife is required for the bar for cutting oranges, lemons and other fruit to be used in drinks. There should also be a bar-board on which to cut this fruit. See Figure 2.9.

Figure 2.8 *Two pronged extractor*

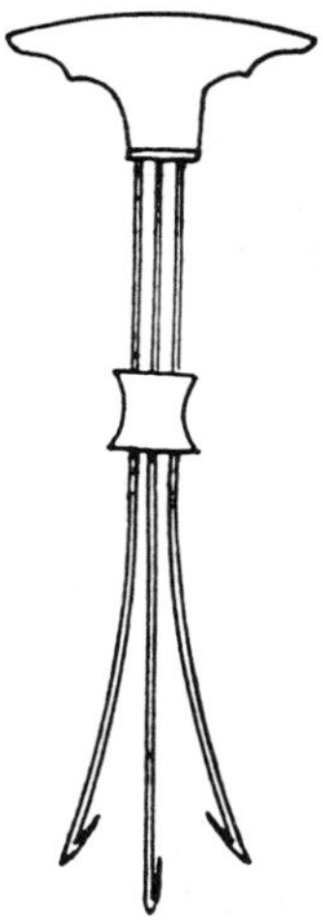

Figure 2.7 *Broken cork extractor*

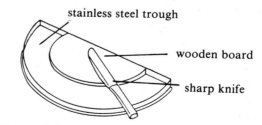

stainless steel trough

wooden board

sharp knife

Figure 2.9

Figure 2.10   *Squeezer*

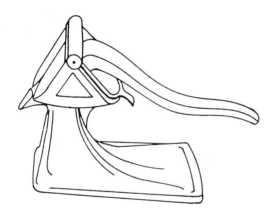

Figure 2.11   *Bar press strainer*

Fruit squeezers

There are two types of fruit squeezer in general use:

1 The small glass, plastic or stainless steel type (Figure 2.10).
2 The bar press or bench type, usually made from cast aluminium (Figure 2.11). These fruit squeezers are becoming increasingly popular in bars, wine bars and anywhere that fresh fruit juices are served.

Ensure that both types are clean before use and thoroughly washed and wiped after use.

Coasters

Bottles are placed on coasters to protect the table. They are made from metal (usually silver or stainless steel) and wood. See Figure 2.12.

Sometimes small card or paper mats, placed under glasses containing drinks, are called coasters. They often advertise the establishment or a product.

Optics

Optics include free-flow dispensers as used for some wines, non-stamped measures for vermouths, cordials etc. and government-stamped measures for spirits. Modern optics are non-drip. See Figure 2.13.

The government-stamped and sealed optical measures must not be tampered with (see Chapter 12).

To dispense a drink from an optical measure, a clean glass is pressed upwards against the bar or bars and held there until a full measure is dispensed. The glass is then removed and the optic refills. Use only clean glasses; never refill a

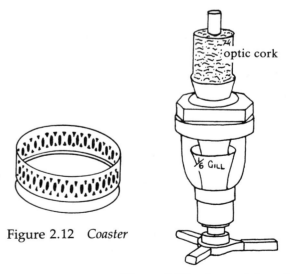

Figure 2.12   *Coaster*

Figure 2.13   *A non-drip optic*

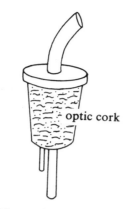

Figure 2.14
Thimble measures

Figure 2.15   *A pourer*

There is another type of syphon in which soda water can be made by injecting carbon dioxide into fresh water. Cordials may be added to the soda water. These syphons are mainly for domestic use.

Ice-making equipment

There are many ice-making machines on the market that are suitable for use in beverage sales and service. A machine should be chosen which will produce a sufficient quantity of ice for the needs of the operation. Cube ice is probably the most useful shape for beverages.

Ice crushers

Electric or hand-operated ice crushers will crush ice cubes or pieces of ice. Crushed ice is used for *frappés* and other drinks.

Cocktail shakers

There are two types of cocktail shaker.

used one for a customer, as this can cause cross-contamination.

Thimble measures

These are government stamped and must be kept scrupulously clean. Care must be taken to ensure that these measures are filled to the top when serving spirits. See Figure 2.14.

Pourers

Pourers are used on the tops of opened bottles of such items as vermouths, cordials, spirits and sherries (see Figure 2.15). In a busy bar this saves having to remove the bottle cap and replace it every time a drink is served from the bottle.

Pourers should only be used on fast-selling items; the product is open to the air and will deteriorate, even when the pourers have hinged caps. Pourers should be washed regularly.

Syphons

Syphons are used for the service of soda water. They should be kept in a cool place. Before using a new syphon, release a little over a sink, as the pressure is sometimes too high.

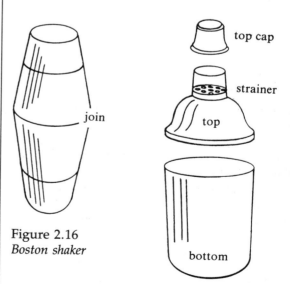

Figure 2.16
Boston shaker

Figure 2.17   *Standard shaker*

7

Boston shaker

This has two parts and is used in conjunction with a Hawthorn strainer (see later in this section). It is sometimes referred to as the professional shaker. It is the best type to use if the quantity to be mixed is large, but is equally good for a single cocktail. See Figure 2.16.

Standard shaker

This has three parts and a built-in strainer. It is shorter than the Boston shaker and is more suitable for smaller quantities. See Figure 2.17.

Blenders

Blenders are a type of liquidizer. They usually have two speeds, and may have an attachment for crushing ice. They should be washed out after use and dried. See Figure 2.18.

Always ensure the top is on the blender before switching it on.

Muddlers and spoons

A muddler is a stirrer, often made from plastic. It is served with long mixed drinks. Muddlers are often produced by drinks companies to carry advertising.

A bar spoon is usually made from EPNS or stainless steel. It is sufficiently long to be used with a mixing glass. The handle should have a flat top for crushing, e.g. sugar lumps for an Old-Fashioned. See Figure 2.19.

Mixing glass

The mixing glass is used for stirred cocktails such as a Dry Martini. Rinse it out before use to

Figure 2.18 *Blender*

Figure 2.19

Figure 2.20

ensure that there is no dust in it. Throw away the ice used for each drink; *never* re-use the ice. See Figure 2.20.

Hawthorn strainer

The Hawthorn strainer is used in conjunction with the Boston shaker and the mixing glass for the service of mixed drinks and cocktails.

It is usually made of EPNS or stainless steel. It has a coil around the outside edge which will compress when pushed into a Boston shaker or mixing glass to form a perfect fit for the strainer. See Figure 2.21.

Wine cradles

Wine cradles or baskets were designed to transport bottles of wine on their sides from the cellar to the point of decanting without disturbing the sediment in them. See Figure 2.22.

Many establishments use them, incorrectly, to pour the wine at the table. Although they may look decorative on the table, they are *not* designed for the service of wine, especially if the wine has sediment in it. As the cradle is

Figure 2.22   *Wine cradle*

tilted backwards and forwards for service the wine will wash up and down inside the bottle, disturbing the sediment and causing all but the heaviest particles to mix with the wine. The wine will become cloudy, and some will be wasted.

Decanters, carafes and water jugs

These should all be clean and highly polished in advance of service.

Decanters come in various shapes depending on the wine for which they are intended. Many establishments have all-purpose decanters. Decanters should have glass stoppers.

Carafes must be marked with the size, and are restricted by law to 25 cl, 50 cl, 75 cl, 1 l, 10 fl oz and 20 fl oz.

Water jugs may have a lip on them to prevent the ice from coming out with the water. However, this type of jug requires more care when polishing to ensure that the lip is polished properly. Water jugs should not be filled more than three-quarters full, otherwise it will be difficult to pour from them without spilling some of the water.

Funnels and strainers

Funnels are used in the bar and cellar to pour liquids from one container into another through a small hole. Strainers may be used with the funnels.

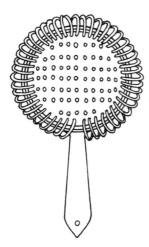

Figure 2.21   *Hawthorn strainer*

9

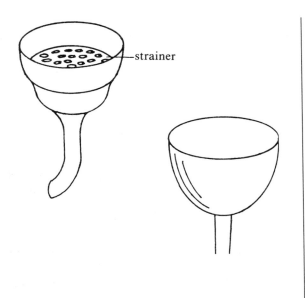

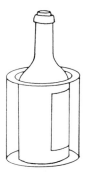

Figure 2.24

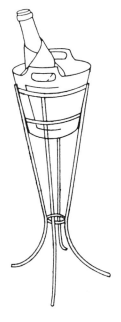

Figure 2.23
Decanting funnel and general-purpose funnel

Figure 2.25

The most obvious example is the decanting funnel, which is usually made from silver, EPNS, stainless steel or copper. This funnel usually has a built-in strainer in it, but it is often used in conjunction with a piece of muslin. See Figure 2.23.

Always wash and sterilize funnels and strainers after use.

Wine coolers

Wine coolers are insulated plastic cylinders which will keep wine cool for up to two hours. Most coolers do not actually cool the wine; it must be chilled in advance. Others do take small ice packs. See Figure 2.24.

Ice buckets

Ice buckets (also called wine coolers) are used to chill wines. If the bucket is placed on the table it

should be put on a plate or salver to prevent condensation spoiling the table. It should be filled with a mixture of ice and water to cover as much of the bottle as possible. A clean napkin should be draped over the top of the bucket so that the customer can wipe the bottle if he wants to serve himself.

Ice buckets are usually made from EPNS, stainless steel or aluminium. See Figure 2.25.

Beer dispensing equipment

Manual beer pumps
Manual pumping is the traditional method of raising cask-conditioned beer. The pump is mounted on and under the bar counter with the handle extending above the counter.

Carbon dioxide (CO_2) may be fed into the top of the cask as the beer is withdrawn to prevent bacteria in the air from coming into contact with the beer and spoiling it.

Free-flow or top pressure
This method is used to dispense keg beers and occasionally to serve cask-conditioned beer. A cylinder of carbon dioxide is connected to the keg; the gas pressure raises the beer to the point of dispense.

Electric cellar pump
This is used where long pipe runs or vertical lifts between the keg and the bar would necessitate using excessive pressure, which in turn would over-carbonate the beer. Only balanced CO_2 pressure is then necessary.

Beer meters
Beer meters may be used to dispense cask, keg or tank beers. They are government sealed and stamped and measure exactly half a pint each time the pump is operated. The Exemption Order 1965 allows these meters to be used with 'oversized' glasses.

All these systems should be cleaned out regularly with beer pipe cleaner fluid (see later in this chapter).

In-line coolers

In-line coolers may be provided for the cooling of keg beer. The beer pipes go through the coolers, which are adjusted to the correct temperature for each beer. The coolers are usually sited under the bar or shelving.

Lager beer should be served at 8.9–10.5°C (48–51°F). Bitter beers should be served at 12.2–13.9°C (54–57°F).

A certain amount of heat is given off by these coolers. However, they must not be used to dry towels or cloths as the air intake and vents may get blocked and a fire may result (see Chapter 12).

Cooling shelves

Cooling shelves are used to maintain bottles and cans of beers and minerals at the correct temperature for serving. They are discussed later in this chapter under 'Storage of beverages'.

Pressurized containers (kegs)

Kegs are supplied in various sizes according to the requirements of the brewery and the establishment (keg sizes are given at the end of the chapter).

Kegs should be kept in a cool place, and must not be left outside in the sun.

The gas pressure of keg beer is predetermined by the brewery. The pressure controls from the CO_2 cylinders which are connected to the kegs for service are pre-set on installation by the brewery or supplier, and should not require alteration. If there is a problem with the pressure, call in the service engineer.

Each beer has a specific pressure requirement. Do not try to use one brewery's connection equipment on another brewery's beers.

Pipe cleaning bottle

This is described later in this chapter.

Beer taps

These are used for the dispensing of cask-conditioned beers direct from the cask. They are usually made from brass. They must be brushed through and sterilized immediately after use and stored in the cellar tidy.

Shives and spiles

The shive is a wooden bung put into the hole in the top of a beer cask.

A soft spile is hammered into the shive. There is a sealing plug in the centre of the shive which

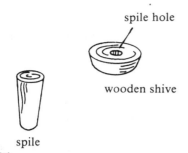

spile hole

wooden shive

spile

Figure 2.26

is forced out into the cask by the spile. A hard spile replaces the soft one before service.
See Figure 2.26.

Beer filters

Only filters which are used in conjunction with a filter paper should be used for beer. The filter paper must only be used once. Beer should only be filtered back into casks which are at least half full, to avoid disturbing the sediment in the cask. See Figure 2.27.

Wash all parts of the filter including the spile tube. Remove the bottom screw and replace it after cleaning. Sterilize the filter and put it away after use.

Stillions or thrawls

Stillions or thrawls are stands on which beer casks are 'stillaged' or 'thrawled' after delivery. This means that they are placed in the position for service, with the shive at the top and the tap hole at the bottom front. See Figure 2.28.

Tills

Bar tills are usually electronic and have till rolls incorporated in them.

The till should always be cleared by the management before and after each service. A key is required to clear the till. The cash in the drawer should be checked. Both the till reading and the actual takings should be recorded in a book.

The till drawer *must* be kept closed between each transaction.

If a mistake of over-ringing is made it should be noted on the till roll; it should *not* be corrected by under-ringing another transaction. Some establishments require over-rings to be

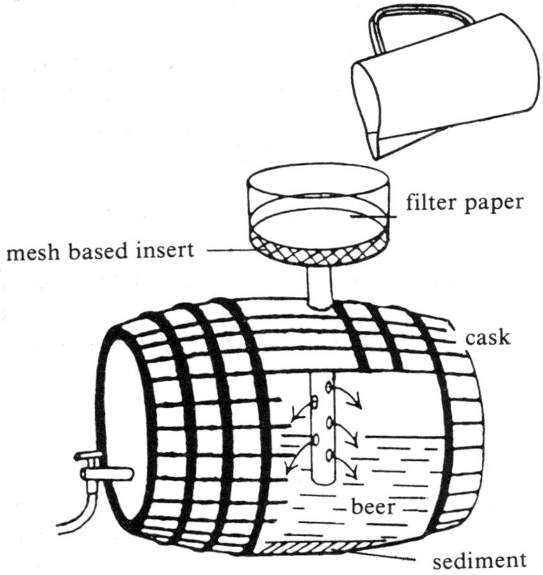

filter paper

mesh based insert

cask

beer

sediment

Figure 2.27

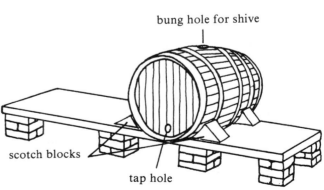

bung hole for shive

scotch blocks

tap hole

Figure 2.28 *Stillion or thrawl*

Figure 2.29   *Skip*

noted in a book and signed for by the bar supervisor or manager, but this is not common practice.

Skips

Plastic skips are placed in bars to hold empty bottles during service (Figure 2.29). Empty bottles should be placed in these skips, not thrown into them. Broken glass is very dangerous for the people who have to empty the skips at the end of service.

Cleaning equipment and materials

Equipment

Cloths
Various cloths are used in beverage sales and service:

Dish cloths should be kept clean. They should be washed out thoroughly, sterilized and then dried at the end of each service.
Swabs are another name for dish cloths or absorbent pads used for cleaning.
J cloths or other disposable cloths should be used where suitable (not on hot hotplates) and disposed of when worn.
Glass cloths should be made out of linen, not cotton, and they should be used to *polish* glasses. If glass cloths are used to dry glasses,

ensure that they are changed when damp; an over-damp cloth may well stick to the glass and cause it to break.

Brushes
Brushes used for cleaning equipment should be kept clean and sterilized daily to prevent bacteria and dirt being transferred from one item of equipment to another (cross-contamination).

Mops
Woollen mops are still used in many establishments for cleaning floors but are steadily being replaced by the more hygienic squeegee mops. Ensure that both types are left clean and sterile after use.

Vacuum cleaners
Always disconnect the vacuum cleaner before attempting to attend to any problem which it might have.
    Do not attempt to vacuum up bottle tops, wine capsules, tin tacks, nails or any piece of metal as these are likely to damage the vacuum cleaner.
    Empty the dust bag before it becomes too full.
    Ensure that the electric cable is sound, and that the wiring of the plug is checked regularly. Do not try to stretch the electric cable; use an extension lead.
    Keep the brush or beater cylinder free from accumulated cotton, string, etc. If there is any smell of burning rubber, or should the sound of the vacuum cleaner change abruptly, switch off immediately and investigate. This is usually a sign that something is preventing the brush or beater cylinder from revolving.

Glass washing machinery
Read and follow the manufacturer's instructions carefully. Ensure that the glass washer is emptied at the end of each service period. The practice of putting glasses through the

washing-up machine as well as crockery must be avoided as the glasses will invariably come out of the machine smeared.

Materials

Water
Be very careful not to scald yourself or another person with boiling water. Take care when cleaning cellar floors with very hot water that other people do not get scalded.

Ensure that taps are fully turned off and that they are not left to drip. In winter a dripping tap may cause the waste pipe to freeze up over-night.

Soap
Soap is generally used for hand washing in beverage service areas. There must always be a tablet of soap (or liquid soap dispenser) and a nail brush with all hand wash-basins. (Hygiene Regulations; see Chapter 12.)

Detergents
Use detergents in a diluted form as directed by the manufacturer. Use the correct detergent and the correct quantity for the job as directed. *Never* mix two or more detergents together as poison-ous and even explosive fumes may be given off.

Care should be taken when handling deter-gents, particularly in their undiluted states. If any concentrated detergent and in particular a caustic one comes into contact with the eyes or skin, liberally rinse with water and obtain medical attention.

Never put detergents into a container which is marked as another product, or one which could be mistaken for another product. *Never* use a drinking glass or cup to measure a required quantity of detergent; use a special container. Store detergents out of reach of children and in a safe place.

When using detergents, wear goggles and rubber gloves if recommended to do so by the manufacturer's instructions.

Abrasives
Abrasive powders are used for removing stub-born stains and dirt. They should *never* be used on silver or EPNS or other items which will scratch or mark.

Solvents
Care must be taken when using solvents. They must be used in the correct ratio for dilution as directed by the manufacturer. Use the correct solvent for the job.

Polishes
Before using a polish, ensure that the surface to be treated is clean and free from dust and dirt. If it is not, it should be washed thoroughly and dried before any polish is applied. Polish polishes; it does not remove dirt.

Bleach
As with detergents, care must be taken with bleach, especially in the undiluted state. It must be used diluted with water in the ratio as directed by the manufacturer.

If undiluted bleach comes into contact with the eyes or skin, wash off liberally with water. The same action should be taken if it is spilled on clothes.

Preparation of bar and restaurant for beverage service

Glassware

Polishing glassware
All glasses should be polished before they are placed in a bar or on a restaurant table for service. Dirty or smeared glasses are unhygienic and will also spoil the enjoyment of the bever-age.

If there is any sign of smear or dullness on the glass, hold it over very hot water and then polish it. This should produce a sparkling clean glass. If the glass still shows a smear or is otherwise soiled, put it to be washed. *Never* breathe on a glass to remove smears or marks.

To polish a stemmed glass, open the glass cloth out and hold it in both hands. Hold the bowl of the glass in one hand with the glass cloth, the thumb inside the glass and the fingers around the outside; hold the base of the glass with the other hand with the cloth. Rotate the glass, polishing all the surfaces of the glass both inside and outside. Don't grip the glass too tightly, as this might cause the stem of the glass to snap where it meets the bowl. If the glass is too small to put the thumb and cloth inside the bowl, just insert a small wad of the cloth and polish as before. Remember to polish the base of all glasses.

Always polish sufficient glasses for service.

Carrying empty glasses

During the *mise-en-place* or when transferring from one point to another, other than to the table, stemmed glasses may be carried upside down between the fingers.

When assembling the glasses in the hand, place them between alternate fingers of the upturned hand. Always ensure that the base of each glass is resting on the fingers, not on the base of other glasses; the glasses are then less likely to slip. Do not try to carry too many. Alternatively they may be carried upside down on a tray or salver.

When carrying empty glasses to the table, arrange them on a salver and place them on the table from the right of the customer in their correct position.

Setting glassware on the table

Always place the glasses on the table from the right-hand side of the customer when the customer is present (see Chapter 8). During the *mise-en-place* of a restaurant, place the glasses upside down on the table in their correct position.

Never place unpolished glasses on the table with the intention of coming back later to polish them. One or more are sure to be missed!

Ingredients

Fruit

Oranges and lemons should be cut in half lengthwise, sliced, and placed on a board or plate ready for service.

Some pieces of lemon zest should be prepared for Dry Martinis, dry vermouths and other drinks.

Frosting glasses

Frosted glasses are used for some cocktails and other special drinks to the requirements of the establishment. These are prepared by dipping the rim of the glass into a shallow dish containing lightly beaten egg whites, then into a shallow dish containing castor sugar. The sugar is sometimes coloured with vegetable colouring.

Crushing ice

An electric ice crusher may be available, and crushed ice is quickly and easily obtained with this machine.

Alternatively, crushed ice may be prepared by hand. Pieces of ice should be put into a clean cloth which is twisted tightly. This 'bag' should then be placed on a solid table and banged with a heavy object (preferably wooden) until the ice is crushed.

Fresh fruit juice

This is prepared by taking wiped fruit, usually oranges, lemons or grapefruit, cutting the fruit in half across the centre, and then placing each half into a bench fruit squeezer or pressing each half over the centre of a glass, plastic or stainless steel fruit squeezer.

Stocks

Rotation

Fresh stocks of spirits, beers, minerals and liqueurs must always be placed behind the existing stocks in a bar to ensure that they are used in strict rotation.

For wines which are kept on racks, an ordered system of rotation must be practised. For example, at the end of each service move all the remaining bottles of each bin number to the left of the racks before replenishing with new stock.

Condition

Some beers and wines require time to settle prior to service, e.g. Worthington White Shield, and red wines containing sediment. Sufficient stocks must be prepared in plenty of time to ensure that this can happen.

White, rosé and sparkling wines, lagers and some other bottled beers are best kept in a refrigerated cabinet or on a cooling shelf. Ensure that there are enough of these items at the correct temperature for service.

Red wines are served at a higher temperature than that of the cellar or wine store where they have been kept. Sufficient stock should be made ready elsewhere (e.g. the service area) to give the wine time to come up to room temperature (see Chapter 8).

Replenishment

During a busy service it is sometimes difficult to replenish stocks which have run out in the bar or restaurant, and this may cause the customers to have to wait. They will probably then be presented with a drink in the wrong condition. While fresh stocks are being brought up, customers are waiting to be served.

All this is business being lost. It is therefore vital that sufficient stocks are made ready before service.

Beverage lists

Beverage lists, like menus, are a prime marketing tool of any restaurant. They must be kept clean, well maintained and up to date. They must state clearly and correctly all the items which are available.

There must be sufficient beverage lists ready for immediate presentation to customers. In a restaurant the list should be presented to the customer at the same time as the menu (see Chapter 7).

Dirty and soiled lists present a scruffy image of the establishment to the customer.

Storage of beverages

Bottles of wine should be stored on their sides, labels uppermost. The cork is porous; it must be kept moistened by the wine, otherwise it will dry out and allow air to penetrate the bottle, which will spoil the wine.

Pasteurized wines, with plastic tops, often sold in litre bottles, are best kept upright.

Wines in storage should be kept at an even temperature, preferably at 11–13°C (52–56°F). Wines which are being kept ready for service in a dispense area should be at the following temperatures: red wines at approximately 18°C (65°F); white, rosé and sparkling wines at approximately 10°C (50°F). The exact temperature will vary according to the origin and age of the wine.

The ideal wine store or cellar will have little or no natural light, no draughts, no vibration, and little or no variation in temperature. It should be clean and easily accessible.

Spirits, liqueurs, syrups and cordials should be kept upright on shelves. This will prevent any leakage caused by a damaged capsule.

The temperature in a beer cellar should be maintained at 12.7–14.4°C (55–58°F), which is the correct temperature for the service of cask-conditioned beers. The best method of obtaining this temperature is to use thermostatically controlled cooling and heating units, cooling the cellar in hot weather and heating it in winter. Beer cellars must be kept scrupulously clean and should be washed down at least once per week (see later in this chapter).

Bottled and canned beers and minerals should also be stored at 12.7–14.4°C. A bottle cooling shelf behind the bar is convenient for storing these items at the correct temperature in sufficient quantities for service. Bottled and canned lagers should be served chilled at about 9–10°C (48–50°F). Cooling shelves work more efficiently when they are kept full. This prevents them icing up.

All beverage stocks must be used in strict rotation.

Clearing and cleaning the service area

Empty bottles, waste and ullages

Ullages are beverages that are not able to be sold, e.g. beer delivered in bottles which are empty or only partially filled, or wine which is unfit for service. These are kept for return to the supplier.

All empty returnable (deposit) bottles must be stored under lock and key and should be returned to the supplier when a delivery is made. Empty beer and mineral bottles are only returnable in full crates. These crates also carry a deposit so they must be looked after. They must be counted before being returned to the brewery, and a credit note received for them from the delivery man (drayman).

Empty wine, spirit and liqueur bottles do not carry a deposit and are therefore either disposed of in a glass crusher or compactor, or boxed up neatly and put out for the refuse collector to remove.

Equipment and service area

Equipment

Equipment must always be thoroughly cleaned after use and put away ready for service. When using it again it should be checked for cleanliness. Every piece of bar equipment should have its own set position, and all items must be put back in their correct places so that they are easily located when required.

Glasses usually require polishing, and other items such as funnels and mixing glasses should be rinsed out with water before use. Glasses should always be stored upside down in a bar. Extra stocks of glassware are best kept in the boxes in which they were delivered.

Stained decanters can be successfully cleaned by leaving them overnight filled with a mixture of hot water and a little washing-up machine powder. They must be thoroughly rinsed out the next morning.

Work area

At the end of service the service areas must be left clean and tidy. Work and service tops must be wiped down with a damp cloth and washed with diluted detergent if necessary. The floor of the bar work area must be swept and then washed, preferably with a squeegee mop.

Security of cash, stock and equipment

Floats should be checked when received and placed in the till. The drawer of the till should be kept closed between transactions. At the end of service the till should be read by a member of the management team. The cash should be counted and noted, and then put away in a locked safe. The key for the till should not be left either in the till or in the bar.

Stock should be kept in a locked store or cellar and issued by a member of the management team only on receipt of a signed requisition.

Requisitions should be made out as in Figure

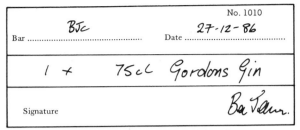

Figure 2.30 A completed requisition form

2.30. The line closing off the requisition will prevent any unofficial additions being made. *Never* leave an open unused line on a requisition.

A day-to-day stock control system should be in force for items such as wines. When deliveries are being received there must be a responsible person present to count the stock in and to check it with the delivery note. All items being returned, empty or otherwise, must be noted on a credit note.

Equipment should be locked away out of service hours, where possible, and an inventory of the equipment should be taken on a regular basis. Any equipment found to be missing at any time should be reported to the management.

Bars should have a security grille or screen in position when the bar is not in use. Only a restricted number of persons should hold a key to the grille.

Handling and changing beverages

Cask beers

Cask-conditioned beer is the traditional beer. It contains finings when delivered to an establishment. The cask should immediately be placed in the beer cellar on a stillion or thrawl, and scotched in a position with the bung hole at the top and the tap hole facing outwards (see Figure 2.28).

The temperature of the cellar should be 12.7–14.4°C (55–58°F).

A soft (porous) spile should be banged into the centre of the shive in the bung hole at the top of the cask within eight hours of delivery. If the beer begins to 'work' and a light froth appears on the top of the spile, leave the soft spile in until this stops. If the beer is quiet, or the frothing has stopped, a hard spile should be used to replace the soft one.

The keystone plug in the tap hole (or keystone bush) should then be wiped clean and a clean sterile tap (usually brass) hammered in with a rubber mallet. It is best to knock the tap into the cask with one solid blow, as this is less likely to disturb the sediment. The tap should be partially open to prevent air being forced into the cask and disturbing the sediment. Check the clarity, smell and flavour of the beer before connecting it up to the dispensing beer pipes.

The hard spile which is now in place must be loosened before service and tapped back again after service, otherwise it will be impossible to draw any beer.

A small quantity of beer should be drawn off from the pipes before opening each day. This can be returned to the cask through a filter. Sometimes CO_2 top pressure is used to eliminate air coming into contact with the beer in the cask as the beer is drawn off. In this case the gas spigot is screwed into the spile hole.

When approximately three-quarters of a cask of beer has been used it should be carefully tilted forward to enable most of the beer to be served. At the end of service the hard spile should be made firm.

Keg beers

Keg beers are ready for service on delivery. They are connected up to a CO_2 gas cylinder and service beer pipe. A gas reducing valve and a pressure gauge are attached to the pipes.

The pressure is set at the time of installation

and should be checked frequently. The beer supplier will state what the correct pressure should be. Too much pressure over-carbonates the beer, causing it to 'fob', i.e. to be too gassy and difficult to serve. Too low a pressure causes the beer to be flat.

Many dispensers have a flow adjuster on the tap which can be hand adjusted during service. This will regulate the size of the head on the beer.

Before changing a keg, switch off the gas supply.

Tank beers

The directions and instructions received from the supplier must be followed.

Bulk minerals

Bulk minerals come in two forms – pre-mixed and post-mixed.

Pre-mixed minerals are in a cylinder, usually of size 4 gallons or 20 litres. The mineral is ready for use in a similar way to a keg beer, and is dispensed through a free-flow tap or gun on the bar top.

Post-mixed minerals require an installation linking the water supply to the CO_2 gas cylinder and the syrup cylinder, which is of a similar size and shape to that used for the pre-mixed minerals. The water, syrup and CO_2 gas are brought together as required and dispensed through a free-flow tap or gun on the bar. Some suppliers seal their syrup containers to prevent adulteration, dilution or substitution with another brand. Other suppliers provide syrup in 5 litre plastic containers which are poured into the steel cylinders. The quality of the post-mixed type of mineral is dependent upon the quality of the local water supply.

When changing a bulk mineral container, switch off the gas before disconnecting.

Carbon dioxide

Carbon dioxide gas (CO_2) is available in 7 lb, 14 lb and 28 lb cylinders. The cylinders should be kept in a cool place, fixed to a wall in an upright position.

It should be remembered that gas expands with a rise in temperature. However, the cylinders are equipped with a safety bursting disc which will break if the pressure inside the cylinder becomes too great. This will cause a noisy release of all the remaining gas. If the cylinder is not properly secured to a wall it may be propelled round the cellar during this release. After release there would probably be a high concentration of CO_2 gas in the cellar atmosphere; this might be dangerous for somebody entering the area, as the gas would have replaced the oxygen in the air.

Optics

Optics should be washed out regularly. The corks should be checked to ensure that they are not breaking up, or allowing liquor to ooze out of the join between cork and bottle. New optic corks must be well soaked in water before they are put into use.

Separate optical measures should be kept for the different drinks, especially strongly flavoured ones. Special optics suitable for aniseed flavoured drinks are available.

After the last complete measure has been sold from a bottle on optic, it should be changed. When changing a bottle on optic, the optic and bottle should be released from the holder by grasping the optic and bottle neck with one hand and releasing the spring button securing the holder with the other hand. This hand should then be used to grasp the empty bottle. The empty bottle with the optic still attached should be stood upright on a work surface and the optic should be removed. Any small amount of liquor left in the optic will have run back into the bottle and this should be poured into the new bottle. The optic should then be placed into the neck of the new bottle firmly and the whole inverted and placed back into its holder, taking care to hold the optic in one hand and the full bottle in the other.

Government-stamped optical measures must never have their seal broken as this would make them illegal to use. This does not apply to non-stamped optics such as free-flow and cordial optics.

Clearing and cleaning the cellar area

Equipment

Kegs, casks and CO_2 gas cylinders do not carry a deposit but are expensive equipment. They should be stored in a secure place. They must be returned to the supplier on the next occasion a delivery is received; the items must be recorded on a return slip.

Empty cask-conditioned beer containers should have a hard spile knocked into the shive, and the tap hole should be sealed with a cork.

Carbon dioxide cylinders are given a five-year check-up, so it is most important to use them in strict rotation and to return empty ones as soon as possible after use to allow the supplier to have them maintained correctly.

Empty bottles should be sorted out and packed into their respective crates, either at the end of a service or during the preparation time on the morning of the next day. The crates should then be stacked in a secure area ready for collection by the drayman.

Walls, floors and ceiling

The walls and ceiling of a beer cellar should be whitewashed or painted in a light colour at regular intervals.

The atmosphere of a beer cellar encourages moulds to grow on the walls and ceiling, especially if the cellar is naturally damp. This will increase the chance of cask-conditioned beer becoming infected. In addition the cellar will acquire an unpleasant musty smell. Unnecessary wetting should therefore be avoided and ventilation should be provided as far as possible.

The cellar cooling air vents and intakes should be kept free of dust and dirt and any filters cleaned or replaced when necessary. It is best to have such a system on a maintenance contract. If this system should fail, call in the installation or maintenance firm.

The floor of a beer cellar must be kept clean and tidy at all times. The floor should be scrubbed and washed down at least once a week and where possible dried afterwards. While the floor is still damp a little diluted bleach or chloride of lime may be sprinkled over the floor; this will inhibit the growing of mould. Do not use strong-smelling disinfectants; they may spoil the beer.

No equipment must be left lying around on the floor, as this could prove to be a hazard to safety.

Drainage

The drains, gulleys and sump (if any) must be kept clean and fresh. If there is a sump, it must be scrubbed out at least once a week using bleach and chloride of lime. Ensure that the sump pump filter and grating are kept clean and in position.

Rubbish

Rubbish must not be allowed to accumulate or be left lying around. It can be a hazard to safety by being an obstacle to free passage or a possible source for a fire.

All rubbish must be properly binned outside the building in an area especially constructed for this purpose (and which can be cleaned and washed down), or compacted in a compactor, or burnt in an incinerator.

Cleaning and maintenance of beer dispensing equipment

Taps, pipes and pumps

Unsatisfactory or insufficient cleaning and maintenance of beer raising equipment can result in extra waste of beer through fobbing, unclean and hazy beer and breakdowns within the system.

Manual beer pump systems are cleaned by disconnecting the beer pipes from the cask tap and draining off any beer into a bucket. The pipe end should then be put into a bucket of clean water which is drawn through the system by operating the manual pump. The pipe end is then put into a plastic or stainless steel bucket of correctly diluted cleaning fluid, which is drawn through the whole system and left to stand for thirty minutes or as directed by the cleaning fluid/powder manufacturer. This is then well flushed out by drawing from a bucket of clean water. The pipe is then reconnected to the cask and beer is drawn through again, pushing out the water which is still in the pipe. The beer is then checked for appearance, smell and flavour. The manual pumps themselves should be dismantled and cleaned internally on a monthly basis.

Pressure systems are cleaned by first switching off the gas and disconnecting the connector head from the keg. Clean cold water should be put into a cleaning plastic 'bottle' provided by the brewery or supplier, which is then attached to the pipes by the connector head. The gas is switched on and water is drawn through the system by opening the serving tap, catching the beer and water in a bucket or other container. The pipes are disconnected from the water bottle and reconnected to another cleaning bottle containing diluted cleaning fluid. This is then drawn through the system and left to stand for thirty minutes or as directed by the cleaning fluid/powder manufacturer. The pipes are then connected to the clean water bottle

again and the system is thoroughly flushed out to remove all trace of the cleaning fluid. The pipes are now reconnected to the keg of beer and beer is drawn through, expelling the clean water. The beer is then checked for appearance, smell and flavour.

Large installations usually have a cleaning main with cleaning 'tees' situated on the walls round the cellar. This is then connected to a large plastic cleaning container. The beer pipes are connected to these tees and cleaned as for the pressure system described above.

The dispensing taps should be wiped down after every service period and the drip trays below them emptied away and washed. *Never* return the beer collected in these drip trays back into a cask or keg. This would contaminate the rest of the cask.

Cold shelves

When a cold shelf is beginning to show signs of icing up it should be switched off and completely emptied of bottles. When the ice has melted, any water which has not run down the drain pipe should be wiped up. The cold tray should be washed down and a little warm water poured down the drain hole. The tray should be *dried* and switched on again. The bottles should be wiped and replaced.

Refrigerated shelves become prematurely iced-up if the cold shelf is not kept filled up or if the temperature is set too low.

In-line coolers

In-line coolers are cleaned internally as a matter of course when the pipes are cleaned. At the same time, the outside of the coolers should be wiped down and any air intakes or outlet louvres wiped clean.

Other equipment

The corks, pegs and spiles used for cask-conditioned beers should be kept in plastic bags in the cellar tidy.

All items of equipment such as beer taps, dipsticks, beer filters, jugs and buckets must be washed and sterilized immediately before and after use.

All items of cleaning equipment such as brushes and dish cloths should be washed out after use and dried. They should be put away when not in use.

Sizes of bottles, casks and kegs

Beer and cider bottles

Nip	180 ml
Bottle	275 ml
Pint	568 ml
Litre	

Mineral bottles

Baby	113 ml
Split	180 ml
Non-returnables	various sizes

Beer casks

Pin	4.5 gallons
Firkin	9 gallons
Kilderkin	18 gallons
Barrel	36 gallons
Puncheon	54 gallons
Butt	108 gallons

The puncheon and butt are now rarely used.

Beer kegs

9 gallons
10 gallons
11 gallons
18 gallons
22 gallons
36 gallons

Spirit bottles

The standard bottle for spirits (except brandy) is 75 cl (26.4 fl oz). This gives 31.68 measures of 1/6 gill.

The standard brandy bottle holds 68 cl (24 fl oz). This gives 28.8 measures of 1/6 gill.

Miniatures, quarter-size and half-size bottles are also available, usually for off-sales. There is no standard capacity for miniatures, but they are normally between 3 and 5 cl.

Spirits are also available in sizes of 1 litre; 1.13 litres, the quart also called a Winchester (40 fl oz); 2.25 litres, the half-gallon, also called a tregnum; and 4.54 litres, the gallon.

Wine bottles

The standard size for a wine bottle will in time become 75 cl; at present many bottles contain only 70 cl. Correspondingly, half-bottles vary between 35 cl and 37.5 cl.

Some wines are available in 1 litre, 1.5 litre and 2 litre bottles. Some quality wines are also sold in magnums (1.5 litres or two bottle size). Some high-quality Bordeaux wines which are intended for keeping are bottled in impériales, which hold approximately 6 litres.

For the range of Champagne bottle sizes see Chapter 5.

Chapter Three

Wine production and selection

Definition of wine

Wine is the alcoholic beverage obtained from the juice of freshly gathered grapes, the fermentation of which is carried out in the district of origin according to local tradition and practice.

Wines may be red, white or rosé, and still or sparkling (Figure 3.1).

Still wine

Still wines are produced from black and white grapes in a fermentation which is allowed to complete naturally. Still wines may be divided into light and heavy wines.

Light wine

Light wine is the official name for a natural unfortified wine. It is also used to describe one lacking in body and low in alcoholic content.

The light wines of the world are described in Chapter 4.

Heavy wine

Heavy wine is an official term for fortified wine. It is also used to describe wines which have too much alcohol and fruitiness.

Fortified wine is made by adding grape spirit (brandy) to wine during or after the fermentation. If it is added during the fermentation it has the effect of stopping it, leaving the remaining sugar in the wine; this produces a sweet fortified wine, e.g. port. The fortification can be added after the fermentation has been completed, in which case dry or sweet wines may be produced, e.g. sherry. Apart from sherry, the majority of fortified wines are sweet.

Fortified wines are described fully in Chapter 5.

Sparkling wine

Sparkling wines are produced by allowing the natural carbon dioxide produced during fermentation to be retained in the bottle, or by the addition of carbon dioxide at a later stage.

Champagne and the production methods for sparkling wine are described in Chapter 5.

The production of wine

A number of factors contribute to the quality of wines:

1 The grape
2 The soil
3 Climatic conditions, location and aspect
4 Viticulture

Figure 3.1   *Types of wine*

23

5 The process of vinification
6 Other factors which are loosely termed the 'luck of the year'

The grape

Many varieties of grapes are used to produce wine. They are all based on the grafting of the scions of European varieties of the species *Vitis vinifera* on to American rootstocks *Vitis rupestris*, *Vitis riparia* and *Vitis berlandieri* (Figure 3.2). Grafting began in the nineteenth century because the louse *Phylloxera* attacked European rootstocks, and the practice has continued.

Alsace has traditionally marketed its wine under the name of the grape variety used in its production. Many more wines, especially those from the Americas, South Africa, Australia, New Zealand and some East European countries are being sold either under the name of the grape variety used or with the grape variety noted on the label.

The following sections set out some of the better known grape varieties. Although the character of the wine produced from these grapes will vary from region to region, the classic base usually remains, so the best known wines produced from these grapes have been listed.

White grape varieties
Chardonnay This is the classic white grape of Burgundy and Champagne. It produces wines full of flavour and crisp acidity. It is grown extensively in California, producing powerful full-bodied wines, and is becoming an important variety in Italy, Australia and New Zealand in particular. It thrives well on soil which is rich in calcium.

Chasselas The Chasselas is grown in the Loire valley, producing Pouilly-sur-Loire, and also in Switzerland.

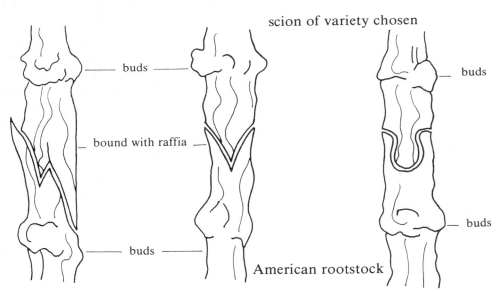

Figure 3.2 *Examples of grafting techniques*

Chenin Blanc This grape is grown extensively in the middle Loire regions of Anjou and Touraine. It is renowned for producing Vouvray and Saumur still and sparkling wines, and the sweet wines of Coteaux-du-Layon. It is now grown widely in Australia, California, South Africa and South America.

Gewürztraminer The wines are usually medium dry, spicy, full of fruit with a highly perfumed bouquet. The Alsatian wine of this name is the best known. It is grown in Australia, Austria, California, Germany, Italy and South Africa. In the Jura it is called Savignin and is used to produce the *vins jaunes* of this region.

Müller-Thurgau This is one of the main grapes used for German wines, producing wines which are slightly fuller than the Rhine Riesling, to which it is closely related.

Muscadet or Melon de Bourgogne This grape is the sole variety used in the production of Muscadet in the Loire valley. It produces crisp dry acidic wines.

Muscat The Muscat produces sweet wines and is used in many blends. Muscat-de-Beaumes-de-Venise and Asti Spumante are two of the best known wines from this grape. It is used in many German wines. On its own it has a raisin-like flavour and bouquet. Muscat d'Alsace is an exception in that it is a dry wine.

Riesling This is the classic white grape of Germany. It produces very high quality Hocks, Mosels and Alsatian wines. It is grown extensively throughout the wine-growing countries. Many of the so-called Rieslings grown in other countries are not the Rhine Riesling; the name is often applied to lesser grape varieties.

Sauvignon This grape produces dry fresh wines which are usually at their best within five years. Sancerre and Pouilly-Fumé are good examples of these light dry wines. They have a bouquet of blackcurrant leaves or wood, and a slight gooseberry taste; they are also described as grassy. Blended with the Sémillon grape it produces dry white Graves and the very sweet Sauternes and Barsac. It is also grown in Australia and California.

Sémillon This grape attracts the fungus *Botrytis cinerea* (giving *pourriture noble* or noble rot) and is blended with Sauvignon to produce Sauternes, Barsac and white Graves. It produces good wines in Australia, California and South Africa, and is being used to produce *Botrytis*-affected wines in Australia and California.

Sylvaner (Silvaner) This is used for Hocks, Mosels and Alsatian wines. The wines are less elegant than the Rieslings, and have a softer finish.

Black grape varieties
Cabernet Franc Blended with other grapes, it is used to produce claret (red Bordeaux). It also produces the rosé wine Cabernet d'Anjou and the red Chinon and Bourgeuil.

Cabernet Sauvignon This is the classic grape for claret. Blended with Cabernet Franc, Merlot, Petit Verdot and sometimes Malbec, it is responsible for all the great wines of the Médoc. It usually produces wines high in acid and tannin which will mature with age. It is an important variety in Australia, California, Chile and South Africa.

Gamay Gamay is the single grape variety of Beaujolais, producing a soft, light fruity wine which matures quickly and has a low tannin content.

Grenache This is a major grape variety of the South of France, and in particular in the lower Côtes du Rhône. It is the most important grape used in the blend for Châteauneuf-du-Pape. It produces a wine light red in colour and is the sole variety used for Tavel rosé and Lirac. It is

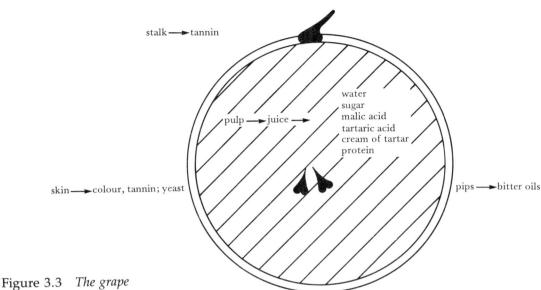

stalk ——► tannin

pulp ——► juice ——►

water
sugar
malic acid
tartaric acid
cream of tartar
protein

skin ——► colour, tannin; yeast

pips ——► bitter oils

Figure 3.3 *The grape*

used in California and Spain and other hot countries.

Merlot Merlot is an important grape in the production of Médocs and even more important for St-Émilion and Pomerol wines. It is grown in Australia, California, Italy, South Africa and Switzerland.

Meunier This is one of the three permitted grapes used for Champagne.

Nebbiolo Nebbiolo is an important grape variety in Piedmont, Italy. It produces Barolo and Barbaresco, and is used blended in many other wines.

Pinot Noir This is the classic grape of red Burgundy. It is the single permitted variety for AC Côte-d'Or red wines. It is also one of the three permitted varieties used for Champagne. It is grown world wide, in particular in Austria, California, Hungary and Switzerland.

Syrah (Shiraz) Syrah is the major grape variety of the northern Côtes du Rhône, producing Hermitage, St Joseph and Cornas. It is an important grape in the blend used for Châteauneuf-du-Pape. It is grown throughout the world and is very popular in Australia and South Africa. In South Africa it has been crossed with the Pinot Noir to produce the Pinotage grape.

Description of the grape
The grape is made up of four main parts (Figure 3.3):

1 The *pulp* produces the grape juice known as *must* in France and *mosto* in Italy and Spain. In the resulting wine, the juice provides the water content and the fruit flavours which come from the sugars and acids. It also supplies the sugar required for the fermentation process.
2 The *skin* of black grapes provides the colour and tannin in red wine. On the outside of the skin of a grape there are approximately 10 million wild yeasts, 100 000 wine yeasts and

100 000 bacteria, with acetobacter predominating.

3 The *pips* are not crushed in the vinification process, as they contain oils which are very bitter and which would spoil the wine.

4 The *stalk* is usually removed by an *égrappoir* before the grapes are crushed or pressed. Previously the stalks were left on the grapes for red wines, and this increased the tannin content of the wine.

The characteristics of the wine will vary according to the variety of grape used and the vinification process.

The soil

The vine will grow in any type of soil. However, it has been found that where it has to struggle for its existence in agriculturally poor soil it produces better wine grapes, because the vine will push its roots downwards, enabling it to pick up many more trace elements and minerals (see Figure 3.4).

Deeper roots make the vine less likely to be affected by severe winters. An example of this occurred in 1984–5 when, during the coldest winter recorded this century, the ground in Chablis was frozen to a depth of one metre from the surface. Although this is a dormant time for the vine, it does require to take in a certain amount of moisture. Thus, although damage was done to some of the younger vines, the majority survived.

Deep roots also enable vines to withstand long dry spells. However, in the very hot summers of 1975 and 1976 the water level in the soil fell below the roots of many of the younger vines, particularly in parts of Spain, causing them to die.

The topsoil should be well drained and fairly light. High-quality wines may be associated in particular with limestone (calcareous) and sandy/gravel soils, but good drainage is the most important factor.

Figure 3.4
Soil structure at Château Giscours in the Médoc

Climate and location

Vines grow best at latitudes of 30–50° north and 30–50° south.

The most northerly vineyards of Europe are in Germany, where the Ahr district is at latitude 50.5° north. South-west England is also at latitudes 50–51° north. However, because the German vineyards are situated in a large land mass away from the coast, they usually experience more hours of sunshine than the vineyards in England. In addition, the most northerly of the German vineyards are sited on south-facing slopes; this causes the vines to receive more concentrated rays from the sun. In some cases, as in the Mosel and parts of the Rheingau, light is also reflected from the rivers.

The Rheingau in Germany (see Chapter 4) has an excellent aspect, benefiting from the south-facing slopes, the reflected sun from the river Rhine, and the mist rising from the river early on summer mornings, allowing the vines to take in moisture through their leaves (Figure 3.5). Moreover there are often trees at the top of the slopes; these improve the humidity and, together with the slopes behind the vines, help to shield the crop from the cold north and north-east winds. At this point the river is very wide, and the expanse of water moderates any changes in temperature.

Climatic conditions are probably the most important factor in viticulture – next, of course, to the variety of grape. The average yearly temperature must not be below 10°C; the ideal average is 14°C.

Of all the climatic conditions, frost is the most feared. Frost in late spring will damage the new shoots, thus reducing the size of the crop. Various methods of combating the effect of late frosts are used. In Germany, Champagne and Chablis, oil stoves are set between the rows of vines to heat the air. It can cost as much as £1000 per week to protect 5 hectares of vines in this way. Another method is to spray the vines with water; the cold air will freeze the water, forming a coating of ice. The ice remains at freezing

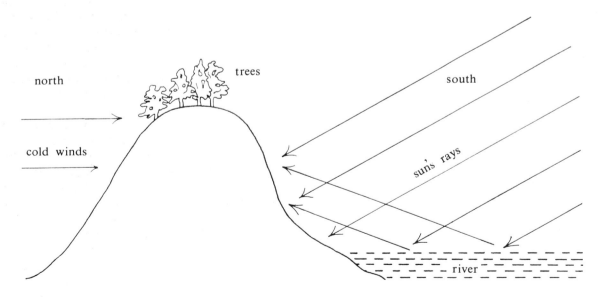

Figure 3.5   *Climate and location: the Rheingau*

point (0°C) during frosts, protecting the vine from air at lower temperatures. This is a process which has to be repeated. Large propellers are also used to disturb the air, as frost will only occur in still conditions. It is now thought that grass and vegetation produce a small amount of humidity which will attract frost, so recently vineyard owners have been keeping their rows of vines free from weeds!

Cold or wet weather at flowering time may cause *coulure*, which is the non-pollination of some of the blossoms, causing the grapes either to fall off or never to develop. Although this can greatly reduce the size of the crop, it will not affect the quality of the other grapes. *Milleran-dage* is another result of cold wet weather at flowering time, preventing the berries from developing.

The ripening period in the northern hemisphere is from June to September, and in the Southern hemisphere from November to February. A lack of sunshine during this period will produce grapes short of sugar. Too much rain towards the end of the ripening period will swell the grapes, raising the water content too much and thus weakening the resulting juice. Hail will damage the vines, sometimes seriously, and will split the grapes, causing unwanted moulds to form and the grapes to spoil. Heavy mists or rain at harvest time can ruin the whole year's work, preventing the grapes from being picked at the correct time.

If the winter is not cold enough, many diseases and pests will survive and produce problems in the following year.

Depending on the variety of grape, it is generally accepted that 85–100 days of sunshine are required from flowering to harvest. Rain puts the moisture into the grapes, while the sun ripens and sweetens them. A shortage of sunshine usually results in grapes high in acid and low in sugar; too much heat produces grapes high in sugar and low in acid, giving 'flabby' wines.

Viticulture

Before consideration of the vinification of wine, a mention must be made of the importance of viticulture – the growing of grapes for the production of wine. This requires deep study for full understanding, and it will only be touched on here. The type of pruning plays a large part in the quantity and thus the quality of the grapes produced. The methods of pruning are defined for each district and region by the applicable wine authority, e.g. in France by the Institut National des Appellations d'Origine (INAO). The vines and the soil must be looked after throughout the year, necessitating up to 18 visits to each vine in some districts for pruning, training the vine, spraying, hoeing or ploughing, picking and fertilizing.

Vinification

The vinification process is illustrated in Figure 3.6. The figure shows the essential difference between white and red wine production. For white wine, the grapes (white and/or black) are pressed immediately after harvest, and only the juice goes for fermentation. Sufficient yeasts run off with the juice for fermentation to take place. By contrast, for red wine the fermentation begins with the skins still present in the must; this practice is called *cuvaison*. The running wine (*vin de goutte*) is usually removed from the skins after a few days when sufficient colour and tannin have been extracted. The skins and other material are then pressed, and the resulting wine (*vin de presse*), high in tannin and colour, may be added to the *vin de goutte* depending on the style of wine required. The dry skins and pips, and also the stalks recovered from the early part of the process (the whole is called the *marc*), may be wetted and fermented again to produce a brandy of the region (e.g. Marc de Bourgogne in Burgundy), or used as a fertilizer. The *marc* from pressing

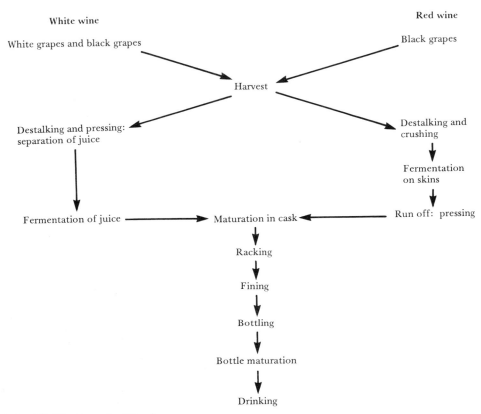

Figure 3.6 *Vinification of still wine*

for white wine is treated similarly. (See Chapter 6.)

Unfermented must contains perhaps 24 per cent sugar, together with malic acid, tartaric acid, cream of tartar, protein, tannin and colouring matter. After fermentation, the fermented must contains typically 11 per cent alcohol and 0.2 per cent sugar, together with carbon dioxide, malic acid, cream of tartar, protein, tannin, colouring matter and glycerol.

The alcohol formed in the production of wine is ethyl alcohol or ethanol (C_2H_5OH):

grape sugar (glucose)   ethyl alcohol   carbon doxide
$$C_2H_{12}O_6 + yeast = 2C_2H_5OH + 2CO_2 + heat$$

As mentioned earlier, there are myriad yeasts and moulds (bacteria) on each grape. If the wild yeasts and moulds are allowed to develop, the wine will be ruined. Wild yeasts will die when the alcoholic content reaches 4 per cent volume (% vol), whereas wine yeasts will continue to live to between 16 and 18% vol of alcohol.

Both the wild yeasts and the acetobacter, which is a wine-spoiling mould, are aerobic – that is, they require oxygen to live. Wine yeasts, however, are anaerobic – that is, they develop in the absence of oxygen. By adding sulphur dioxide to the unfermented must, the wine maker is able to prevent the development of wild yeasts and wine-spoiling moulds. The sulphur dioxide takes up any oxygen in the must and forms a film over the top, preventing any oxygen from getting through. This process is referred to as *sulphuring* the wine. The wine yeasts will cause fermentation to take place, quickly raising the alcoholic content above 4% vol and thus killing off the unwanted wild yeasts and bacteria.

Temperature is important to the fermentation process, as the wine yeasts will operate only between 5 and 30°C. It is essential to reach 4% vol of alcohol as soon as possible to ensure the destruction of the wild yeasts and acetobacter, but then a slower fermentation has proved to produce better quality wine. Many wine makers, particularly those in hot climates, cool their fermentation vats either by using double-skinned stainless steel vats with cold water circulating between the two skins or by running cold water over the vats. This temperature control has been especially important in the improvement of the quality of wines from countries such as South Africa and America. In cooler climates the reverse is sometimes the case. If the weather is bad and the temperature low during the fermentation, the vats may have to be heated.

Malolactic fermentation

This fermentation takes place after the alcoholic fermentation, and sometimes not until the spring following the harvest. It is the conversion of malic acid into lactic acid and a little carbon dioxide. If this takes place in the bottle it will make the wine slightly sparkling (*pétillant* or *spritzig*) and cause a small amount of sediment to form. Sometimes it will force the cork out of the bottle. This fermentation is usually carried out in vats or casks, either by the wine maker creating favourable conditions for this to occur, or by natural methods.

Malic acid is harsh and this process causes the wine to soften.

Macération carbonique

This is a modern system of controlling the speed of the fermentation. The fermenting vat is sealed but is fitted with a valve which allows the carbon dioxide to escape when a certain pressure is reached within the vat. This method of fermenting under pressure causes the colour pigment to be extracted very quickly, enabling the skins to be removed after a short time. This keeps the tannin content low and helps the production of a fast-maturing wine.

The method is used for the *nouveau* wines which have become highly popular in recent years.

The main characteristics of wine

Appearance and colour

Wine can be red, white or rosé. Whatever its colour, sound wine must be clear. If it is cloudy, either it contains sediment and has been shaken up, in which case it should be left to rest for 24 hours before decanting and serving, or there is something wrong with it. In both cases the wine should not be served.

As explained in the previous section, red wine is produced from black grapes, the skins of which are allowed to be present for all or part of the fermentation process. The colour ranges from purple through the various shades of red to brown. Young red wines are usually purple; old wines are reddish brown. The outer rim of the wine (*robe*) should be looked at to ascertain the colour (Figure 3.7). This will enable the connoisseur to judge the age of the wine.

White wine can be produced from black grapes, white grapes or a blend of the two. The red colouring pigment is contained in the skins of black grapes and not in the pulp or juice; therefore if black grapes are pressed and the juice is run off the skins straight away, white wine will result. White wine varies in colour from almost colourless through the shades of

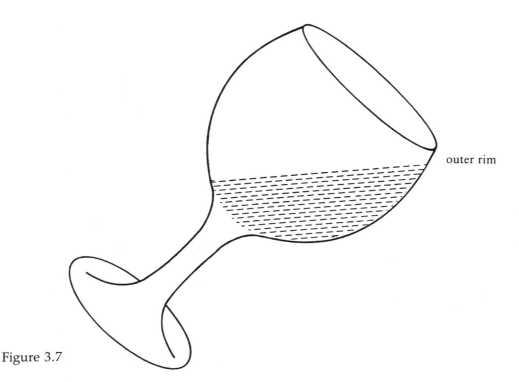

outer rim

Figure 3.7

yellow to gold. Some of the younger wines have a greenish tinge to them, while some of the older wines turn brown with age.

Rosé wine is made in several ways. The classic method is to commence the fermentation as for red wine, to remove the partly fermented juice from the skins after the correct degree of coloration has been achieved, and then to continue the fermentation off the skins. Another method is to blend a small quantity of red wine with a large quantity of white wine. A third method is to blend black and white grapes, with the fermentation taking place on the skins of the black grapes.

Pelure d'oignon is a term used to describe some rosé wines which have a russet brown tinge similar to that of an onion skin. It is also used to describe some old red wines which have acquired this colour with ageing.

Bouquet

The bouquet is the smell of the wine. It is very important in judging the characteristics and quality of a wine. It is generally accepted that (other than the label) the smell of a wine is the best indicator of its origin, its content, its age and its character. Wine should always smell like wine or, in tasting terminology, 'clean'. If the wine smells of vinegar, any decayed vegetables or cork, then there is something wrong with it.

Taste

The taste of the wine confirms the impressions formed by the wine's appearance and bouquet. The first thing which can be confirmed is the sweetness or dryness; then the acidity; the fruitiness; the tannin content, which often helps to indicate the age of red wines; and the 'weight' or 'body' of the wine in the mouth, which indicates the alcoholic content. Figure 3.8 shows the functions of the various parts of the tongue in detecting the characteristics of wine.

Ageing potential

Some wines, e.g. Beaujolais and Muscadet, are made for early drinking, which means that the wines will not improve with keeping for a long time: 'Old is not necessarily good.' These wines are made from grape varieties which produce wines full of fruit, low in tannin and early maturing. Red wines which are produced to age contain tannin; this is a preservative, and it falls out of the wine as it ages. Wines in this category are best from 'good' years – that is, years in which all the variable factors that contribute to quality combine to form an outstanding wine.

Full bodied or light bodied

Wines which are high in alcoholic content, i.e. 13% vol upwards, are classed as full bodied. The alcohol causes the wine to weigh heavy on the palate. The wine is also full in flavour. Light bodied wine is usually below 13% vol alcohol and lighter in flavour.

Sweet or dry

Sweet wine has a high sugar content. The sugar may remain in the wine after the fermentation has completed, e.g. Sauternes, or it may be added in sufficient quantity to produce a sweet wine. The addition of sugar is called *chaptalization* after the Dr Chaptal who developed this process.

Dry wine is low in sugar. This is usually arrived at by allowing the fermentation to use up the grape sugar (and any added sugar) in the fermentation.

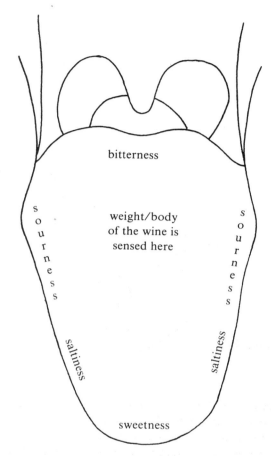

Figure 3.8
Functions of parts of the tongue in detecting characteristics of wine. Tannin is sensed by a dryness round the gums and the sides of the mouth

Quality categories: the wine label

France

Vin de table and *vin de pays*
Vin de table (table wine) is the lowest category of wine. It is meant for everyday drinking; it is not produced to be laid down, as it does not improve with age. Some *vin de table*, after

passing a tasting panel, can become the *vin de pays* of the region in which it was produced. *Vin de pays* (local or country wine) is therefore of a level slightly above *vin de table*, and is the lowest official category recognized by the French government. (*Vin de paille* is not to be confused with *vin de pays*. The best *vin de paille* is produced in the Jura; see Chapter 4.)

Vin délimité de qualité supérieure
This is an official category of French wine, and was introduced in 1949. It is a grading applied to wine in France which cannot obtain an *appellation contrôlée* (see next section). The area of production, types of vines permitted, production method, alcoholic content and yield are all subject to regulations. VDQS wines account for less than 5 per cent of French wine. It is generally accepted as being just below AC standard. Many wines which were previously VDQS have obtained AC status.

Appellation contrôlée
Appellation (d'origine) contrôlée (AC or AOC) may be applied to quality French wines which achieve certain standards and comply with regulations laid down for each area, region or district. The controls are organized by the Institut National des Appellations d'Origine (INAO). AC is a guarantee of origin of the wine, and the various *appellations* ensure other standards such as types of vine or vines permitted, yield, production methods, alcoholic content and character of the wine.

In some regions there are a number of ACs which could be applied to the wine. The Pauillac commune in the Haut-Médoc district of Bordeaux provides an example (see Figure 3.9):

Appellation Pauillac Contrôlée (1 on figure) This AC guarantees that the wine originated from the commune and meets the standards laid down for wine from the commune. The same

wine can be declassified and marketed under many other ACs, as follows.

Appellation Haut-Médoc Contrôlée (2 on figure) This guarantees that the wine originated from the Haut-Médoc and meets the requirements of this AC, which are slightly less specific than for Appellation Pauillac Contrôlée. The wine may be blended with wine from other communes in the Haut-Médoc. If the wine cannot meet these requirements, the following ACs are still available.
Appellation Médoc Contrôlée (3 on figure) This is the highest AC for wines from the Bas-Médoc which is north of Haut-Médoc. The requirements are also different for this AC.
Appellation Bordeaux Supérieur Contrôlée (4 on figure) This signifies that the wine comes from Bordeaux and has 1% vol of alcohol above the legal minimum for that style of Bordeaux wine.
Appellation Bordeaux Contrôlée (5 on figure) This guarantees that the wine originated in Bordeaux. It is the lowest AC available to a wine produced in Bordeaux.

Note A wine which has the name of the château, commune or district on the label must originate from that place even though it carries a lower *appellation* and does not therefore reach some of the other requirements of the higher *appellations*.

In some regions of France the AC may be given to groups of vineyards or even individual vineyards. The smallest vineyard in France to have its own AC is Château Grillet in Condrieu, Côtes-du-Rhône.

Some regional ACs are less definitive in their location. For example, in the Loire valley the AC for Muscadet wine defines the grape variety (Muscadet or Melon) which has to be grown within the specified district. The highest AC for Muscadet wine is Appellation Muscadet

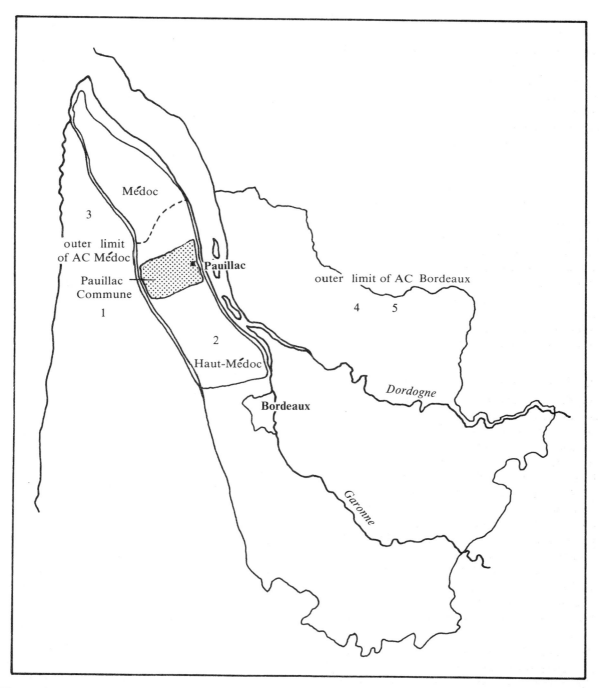

Figure 3.9 *Appellations of Bordeaux*

Sèvre-et-Maine Contrôlée, which is a region within the Muscadet district.

Germany

Tafelwein and Landwein
Tafelwein (table wine) is the lowest category of German wine. When this is made entirely from grapes which have been grown in Germany, it is sold under four *Weinbaugebiete* or wine regions (see Chapter 4); these wines are German table wines, *Deutscher Tafelwein*, and may state the vintage. When the wine is blended with wine from other EEC countries it is sold as *Tafelwein*, but must carry the words 'EEC table wine' on the label (*Wein aus mehreren Mitgliedstaaten der EWG*). *Landwein* is a higher-grade *Tafelwein* which must be sold as either *trocken* (dry) or *halbtrocken* (medium dry). There are 15 regions for *Landwein*, and these are different from both the *Tafelwein* and *Qualitätswein* bA regions.

Qualitätswein bestimmter Anbaugebiete
This is the second highest quality of the three categories of German wine. The official controls include measuring the amount of sugar in the must at harvest time, chemical analysis of the wine and a taste test. There are 11 *Anbaugebiete* (regions) specified for QbA (see Chapter 4), and a QbA wine must state on the label from which of these regions the wine originates. There are other regulations to which these wines must conform to be allowed to put the QbA classification on the label. These wines are permitted to be chaptalized. The name of the *Bereich* (district), *Grosslage* (collective) or *Einzellage* (vineyard) may be shown, plus the vintage (see Chapter 4). Each QbA wine carries an *Amtliche Prüfungsnummer* (control number).

Qualitätswein mit Prädikat
These wines are of superior quality. There are six *Prädikate* (distinctions or degrees of ripeness) which indicate details of the harvesting of the grapes and the sugar content of the grapes. No QmP wine is permitted to be chaptalized; all sweetness in the wine comes *naturally* from the grape. These wines may only originate from a single *Bereich* and the harvesting must be authorized by the local wine authorities. The label for these wines may show the same details as a QbA wine in addition to the *Prädikat*, and *must* show the *Anbaugebiete*.

The six *Prädikats* are as follows:

Kabinett Wines with this attribute are the least sweet of these quality wines. Before 1971 this name was used by the vineyard owners to indicate specially selected wines for their own use.

Spätlese This wine is made from late gathered grapes which have been left on the vine to ripen. These wines are a little sweeter and more expensive.

Auslese This wine is made from selected bunches of grapes which have been left on the vine and allowed to become *overripe*. Some will have been attacked by *Botrytis* to give *Edelfäule* (noble rot). These wines are sweeter and often produce a faint honeyed *nose* (bouquet). They should be used as dessert wines.

Beerenauslese This *Prädikat* means that specially selected berries (grapes) chosen from the ripest bunches, which have been affected by *Edelfäule*, have been used to make the wine. It is only made in outstanding years, and the quantity produced is very small and extremely expensive. It is very sweet, usually with a strong honeyed nose, and is a dessert wine.

Trockenbeerenauslese This literally means dried-up selected berries (grapes). Wine with this *Prädikat* is made only in exceptional years when *Edelfäule* has affected the grapes and they have been left to shrivel up on the vine. There is very little quantity, and it is an exorbitant price. It is strictly reserved for use as a dessert wine.

Eiswein This is made from overripe grapes

which have been left on the vine and caught by the frost, then picked at −6°C or less and pressed to separate the frozen water from the very sweet juice. This *Prädikat* may only be used in conjunction with another, e.g. Eiswein Beerenauslese.

Italy

Vino da tavola and vino tipico
Vino da tavola (table wine) is the lowest category of Italian wine. However, owing to the DOC laws there are some wines of outstanding quality which are only permitted to use this category. An example is Sassicaia. This wine is made in Tuscany from Cabernet Sauvignon grapes; however, Tuscany DOC does not recognize Cabernet Sauvignon as a permitted variety, so the wine is classified *vino da tavola*. *Vino tipico* (*vino da tavola con indicazione geografica*) (wine of an area) is a category of Italian wine similar in quality to *vin de pays* in France and *Landwein* in Germany.

Denominazione di origine controllata
The Italian wine law of July 1963 introduced three categories of Italian wine. The lowest of the three categories was abolished to meet EEC regulations, leaving two: DOC and DOCG.

DOC wines have controlled origin, grape varieties, methods of production, and characteristics of the district of origin. The first wines were granted DOC status in May 1966. The regulations which have to be complied with are similar to the AC regulations of France, and in some cases they are more strict. For example, if the specified limit of production by a grower is exceeded the total production is declassified, whereas in France only the over-production wine is declassified.

Denominazione di origine controllata e garantita
This category incorporates all the DOC controls and in addition guarantees the quality. DOCG appears on labels dated from 1985 onwards. All DOCG wines must be passed by a tasting panel.

EEC
Vin de qualité produit en régions déterminées is an EEC wine category, meaning quality wine produced in specific regions. The AC wines and VDQS wines of France qualify for VQPRD, but few put it on the label. The DOCG, DOC and *vino tipico* wines of Italy and the QbA and QmP wines of Germany can also use these letters on their labels.

Other information on the wine label

Vintage and non-vintage
'Vintage' with a date refers to the year in which the grapes were harvested. On its own it can also mean the gathering of the grapes. In France *millésime* and *récolte* are both terms on the label meaning the year of the vintage; in Spain *vendimia*, *cosecha*, or sometimes *año* plus the year, is used; and in Italy *vendemmia*, or sometimes *annata* plus the year.

There is a vintage every year, but the wine is not always sold under that year, particularly if it was a bad one. In this case the wine is usually blended with other years and sold as non-vintage wine (NV).

Bottling
French bottling terms include the following:

Mise en bouteille au château This means simply that the wine was bottled at the château named on the bottle. This is commonly used for Bordeaux wines and wines from other areas which have châteaux, like the Loire valley. The first château bottling was at Château Lafite in 1793.
Mise en bouteille au domaine: Mise du domaine These terms are used when the wine has been bottled on the estate or domaine. They

are used very often for quality Burgundy and Rhône wines and for wines of other areas that do not have large integral estates such as are found in Bordeaux. The estate may be made up of a number of vineyards in different communes but all under the same ownership.

Mise en bouteille dans nos caves This means bottled in the cellars. The cellars are usually those of the *négociant*, who will be named.

Mise en bouteille par Xyz Simply means bottled by the company or person Xyz.

Terms of other countries meaning 'estate bottled' include:

Erzeugerabfüllung or *aus eigenem Lesegut* (Germany)

Messo in bottiglia nel'origine or *imbottigliato del produttore all'origine* (Italy)

Embottelado or *engarrafado de origen* (Spain)

Engarrafado no origen (Portugal)

Sweetness and dryness

	Dry	Medium	Sweet
France	*sec*	*demi-sec/ demi-doux*	*doux*
Germany	*trocken*	*halbtrocken*	
Italy	*secco*	*amabile/ abboccato*	*dolce*
Spain	*seco*	—	*dulce*
Portugal	*séco*	—	*adamado/doce*

Colour

	Light red	Red	Dark red
France		*rouge*	
Germany		*Rotwein*	
Italy	*chiaretto*	*rosso*	*nero*
Spain		*tinto*	
Portugal	*clarete*	*tinto*	

	White	Rosé or pink	
France	*blanc*	*rosé*	
Germany	*Weiswein*	*Schillerwein, Weissherbst, Rotling*	
Italy	*bianco*	*rosato*	
Spain	*blanco*	*rosado*	
Portugal	*branco*	*rosado*	

Sparkling wine

The appropriate terms are covered in Chapter 5.

Fortified wine

Terms for fortified wine are also in Chapter 5.

Ordinary wine

Ordinary wine is rarely bottled. In France this is *vin ordinaire*, in Italy *vino ordinario* and in Spain *vino corriente*.

Chapter Four

Wines of the world

The wine-producing countries of the world are shown in Figure 4.1. They are grouped at latitudes 30–50°C north and south.

France

France remains the foremost country in the world in its diversity and experience of wines. The harvest is also large; for example, in 1985 it produced 68.6 million hectolitres, of which 16.5 million were *appellation contrôlée*.

France's wine-producing regions are as follows (see Figure 4.2):

Main regions
Alsace
Bordeaux
Burgundy
Champagne
Loire
Rhône

Lesser regions
Bergerac
Côtes de Duras
Jura
Jurançon
Madiran
Monbazillac
Languedoc/Roussillon
Provence

Alsace

The region of Alsace stretches from Strasbourg in the north to Mulhouse in the south (Figure 4.3). It runs along the eastern slopes of the Vosges mountains foothills close to the German border. It is subdivided into the Bas-Rhin and the Haut-Rhin, although this has little significance for the sommelier or the customer as the wines are not sold under these names. Riquewihr and Ribeauville are the best known vineyard towns, and Colmar is the business centre for Alsace wines.

Although wines have been made in Alsace since the fourth century, the wines as we know them today only go back as far as 1945. Alsace has been occupied by Germany for some of its history and it was not until the end of the Second World War that the vineyards were replanted with the noble grape varieties which are used now. Germany had previously allowed only lesser grape varieties to be grown in Alsace, in order to protect its own fine wine industry.

The wines are made by very natural methods and are not so highly fined or filtered as, for example, German wine. The majority of Alsatian wine is still white wine, but there is a little *vin rosé*, *vin gris* and *vin rouge*, all made from the Pinot Noir grape. There is also some sparkling wine.

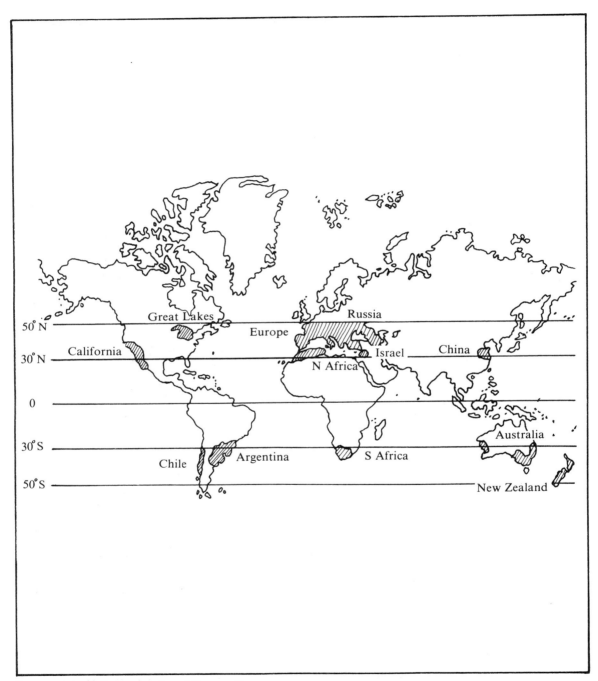

Figure 4.1   *Wine countries of the world*

Figure 4.2 *France*

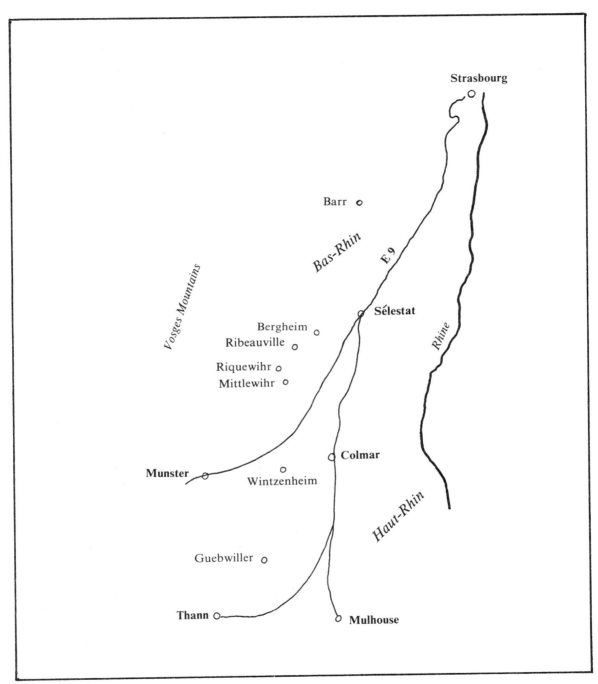

Figure 4.3   *Alsace*

Classification

AC Alsace Crémant This appellation for semi-sparkling wine was granted in 1976. The wine is fermented in the bottle as for Champagne but is only half the normal pressure for Champagne. It is sold in Champagne-style bottles.

AC Vin d'Alsace and AC Alsace Both of these have a minimum alcoholic content of 8.5% vol and must be made from a permitted grape variety or a blend of two or more.

AC Alsace Grand Cru This is a new classification of certain vineyards as *grand cru* vineyards. These wines must have a minimum of 11% vol alcohol and be made from *one* of the eight permitted varieties of Alsatian grapes.

AC Edelzwicker This is a wine made from a blend of noble grape varieties.

Grapes and wine characteristics

The wines of Alsace are usually sold under the name of the grape rather than the name of a vineyard, although some do state the origin on the label as well. If the wine is sold by the grape name the wine *must* by law be made from 100 per cent of that grape.

The six noble varieties are as follows:

Riesling Perhaps the best Alsatian wine, very dry, good strong fruity nose, a little fuller than

German Rieslings. It is an excellent complement to hors-d'oeuvres, oysters and fish dishes.

Gewürztraminer Full fruity flowery bouquet, dry, spicy and strong flavoured – the most distinctive bouquet and flavour of all these wines. It is excellent with pâté de foie gras and will stand up to dishes such as quails' eggs with spinach, and smoked mackerel. It is also favoured by some for desserts and cheese.

Tokay d'Alsace or Pinot Gris Full bodied, slightly 'sharp' yet smooth and dry. Soon to be called Tokay Pinot Gris.

Muscat d'Alsace Less spicy than Gewürztraminer, dry with a musky flavour, also suitable for service with dessert or cheese.

Pinot Blanc Dry well-balanced wine, suitable whenever white wine is requested.

Sylvaner The most widely grown grape in Alsace. As is usual for this grape variety the wine is dry, light and fruity, but softer than the others named.

The two non-noble varieties are:

Pinot Noir High in fruit, low in tannin, much lighter in body than Pinot Noir wines from Burgundy. This wine is made by leaving the maceration of the must on the skins for three to four days and the stalks are usually left in to give some tannin to the wine.

Chasselas Wine produced from the Chasselas grape in Alsace is rarely sold as such and is not exported because it is not as high a quality as the other exported Alsatian wines. It is normally used locally for house or carafe wines.

Alsatian wines are shipped in slender flutes (tall green bottles, as for Mosel wines). They are usually suitable for drinking between one and four years old. They are dry and exceedingly fragrant, all of them having at least a slight spiciness about their bouquet and flavour.

The German practice may be followed of leaving the grapes on the vine in a good year with a warm autumn to allow the grapes to become overripe. The wines then have the words *vendage tardive* (late harvested) added to the label. This produces a sweeter wine of generally a very high quality, high alcohol and excellent honeyed bouquet. These wines are excellent value for money.

Sélection de grains noble is a term used for grapes which have been left on the vine to become overripe and which have been individually picked. This is similar to Beerenauslese wines from Germany. These grapes are usually attacked by *Botrytis* to give *pourriture noble* or noble rot.

Bordeaux

The best quality wines of this region (see Figure 4.4) are produced from blends of grapes. The main black grape varieties are Cabernet Sauvignon, Cabernet Franc, Merlot, Malbec and Petit Verdot. The main white grape varieties are Sauvignon, Sémillon and Muscadelle.

The red wines of Bordeaux are known in English as claret, the white wines simply as white Bordeaux or Bordeaux *blanc*. An example of the AC system applied to a Bordeaux wine has been given in Chapter 3.

The top quality districts of Bordeaux are:

Médoc
Graves
Sauternes
Barsac
St-Émilion
Pomerol

The lesser quality districts are:

Cérons
Premières Côtes de Bordeaux
St Croix du Mont
Loupiac

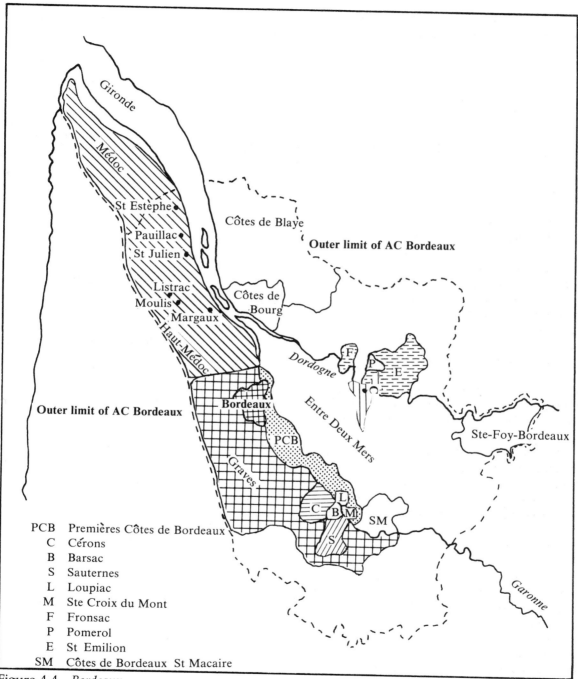

PCB Premières Côtes de Bordeaux
  C Cérons
  B Barsac
  S Sauternes
  L Loupiac
  M Ste Croix du Mont
  F Fronsac
  P Pomerol
  E St Emilion
 SM Côtes de Bordeaux St Macaire

Figure 4.4   Bordeaux

Entre-Deux-Mers
Ste-Foy-Bordeaux
Fronsac
Côtes de Bourg
Côtes de Blaye

Médoc
This district is subdivided into two; Haut-Médoc and Médoc. These two appellations may only be used for red wines.

The Haut-Médoc produces all the top wines of this district. It comprises 16 communes, the top six of which are Pauillac, Margaux, St Estèphe, St Julien, Moulis and Listrac. Each of these six communes has its own *appellation*. The tendency with Médoc wines is to concentrate on the 61 wines classified in 1855 and to forget the rest. These wines were graded into the five growths (*crus classés*) on the basis of the prices they had achieved during the previous few years. There are, however, many excellent

wines classified as *crus bourgeois* which are sometimes as good as some of the *crus classés* wines. In 1973 Château Mouton-Rothschild was upgraded from *second cru* to *premier cru*. The classifications of Bordeaux wines are given in Appendix 1.

The red wines of the Médoc vary in quality but they are all made from the grapes listed above. Most of them have a predominance of Cabernet in them, but the actual percentage varies from château to château. The main cause

for the differences in the wines is the soil, the best coming from well-drained soil with plenty of stones in it, close to the Gironde. The wine is usually left in oak casks until it is one and a half to two years old, fined, then bottled.

The top châteaux make wines in good years which will continue to improve in the bottle for 20 years upwards. They have a high tannin content, strong flavour and good acid content which will mellow over the maturation period. The bouquet of these wines is often said to resemble blackcurrants and cedar wood. Throughout the Médoc many wines are produced, and a large number of these are made to be ready for drinking within five years.

Graves
Better known in this country for its dry white wines, it also produces some very fine red wines from a blend of Cabernet Sauvignon, Cabernet Franc and Merlot. These red wines are produced in the northern half of the Graves district. The finest red Graves is Château Haut-Brion, which was classified in 1855 in the first growth of the Médoc. The red Graves are slightly drier than the Médoc wines.

The Graves wines were classified in 1959. Fifteen châteaux were classified, six for red and white wines, seven for red wine only and two for white wine only. (See Appendix 2.)

Sauternes/Barsac
Sauternes district produces some of the very best of the world's sweet white wines. The best Sauternes are made from grapes which have been attacked by *Botrytis cinerea* (giving *pourriture noble*). Sauvignon and Sémillon are the two varieties of grapes used, and it is the Sémillon which is left on the vines to be attacked by noble rot. This is a minute fungoid growth which causes the grapes to shrivel up, reducing the volume of must and imparting a honeyed bouquet to the finished wine.

There are five communes in the district: Sauternes, Fargues, Bommes, Preignac and Barsac. Wines produced in the commune of Barsac can be sold under the AC of either Sauternes or Barsac. The wines of Barsac, like those of Sauternes, are luscious and sweet with a tremendous concentration of flavour and colour. The alcohol must be 13% vol for these ACs.

The best of these wines are matured in cask for up to three years. They are then matured in bottle for as long as 30 to 40 years. They must be kept away from light and in cool surroundings, otherwise the wine will become *maderisé* (slightly bitter, like Madeira; maderized).

The 1855 classification graded the top châteaux into three growths. Château d'Yquem was graded alone as the *premier grand cru* or first great growth; 11 others were made first growths, and another 13 second growths (see Appendix 3).

St-Émilion
This district produces red wines of superb quality. The wines are blended from Cabernet Sauvignon, Cabernet Franc and Merlot. However, the predominant grape is the Merlot, not the Cabernet as is the case in the Médoc. The Merlot grape produces a softer wine which will mature quicker than the Cabernets, so these wines are usually expected to be ready for drinking a little earlier than their counterparts in the Médoc.

There are eight communes entitled to the AC St-Émilion, and there are a further six which can add St-Émilion to their names. These wines were classified in 1954 and again in 1984 (see Appendix 2).

Pomerol
Adjacent to St-Émilion, this district produces similar red wines, with the Merlot grape again forming as much as 80 per cent of the blend with Cabernet. It is slightly softer than St-Émilion and is often ready for drinking after five years, with the best maturing up to 12 to 15 years. The wines are of a high quality and have a slight truffle smell.

Cérons
Cérons is a commune of Graves but has its own AC. The wines are more like Sauternes and Barsac.

Loupiac and St Croix du Mont
These two districts are in close proximity to

Sauternes and Barsac, and produce similar but lesser wines. Each has its own AC.

Premières Côtes de Bordeaux
This long narrow district following the northern bank of the Garonne produces styles of wine related to those on the southern bank of the river. Red wines are produced in the north (nowhere near the quality of those produced in the Médoc), medium dry to dry wines in the centre, and sweet white wines in the south opposite Cérons, Barsac and Sauternes.

Entre-Deux-Mers
This is the largest district of Bordeaux and produces a large quantity of ordinary quality red and white wines, the white wines varying from sweet to dry.

Ste-Foy-Bordeaux
This small district is situated on the extremity of the Bordeaux appellation boundary in the north-eastern corner of Entre-Deux-Mers. It produces sweet and dry white wines and a small amount of red wine.

Fronsac
Fronsac produces fruity red wines after the style of Pomerol and St-Émilion, of a slightly lower quality.

Bourg and Blaye
Bourg and Blaye both produce red and dry white wines of average quality, but Blaye specializes in dry white wine while the district of Bourg is best known for its red wines, made mainly from the Cabernet. The wines from these districts are only of average quality.

Burgundy

The Burgundy region is long and narrow, spreading through the four *départements* of Yonne, Côte-d'Or, Saône-et-Loire and Rhône (Figure 4.5). The six districts of Burgundy are:

Chablis (Yonne)
Côte de Nuits (Côte-d'Or)
Côte de Beaune (Côte-d'Or)
Côte Chalonnaise or Région de Mercurey (Saône-et-Loire)
Côte Mâconnaise (Saône-et-Loire)
Beaujolais (Rhône)

The method of classifying Burgundies is a complicated one, but it is sufficient to know that some vineyards and plots are classified *grands crus* and others *premiers crus*. The wines made in these places still have to meet the criteria laid down by the INAO. The quality wines of Burgundy are sold under the name of the *climat*

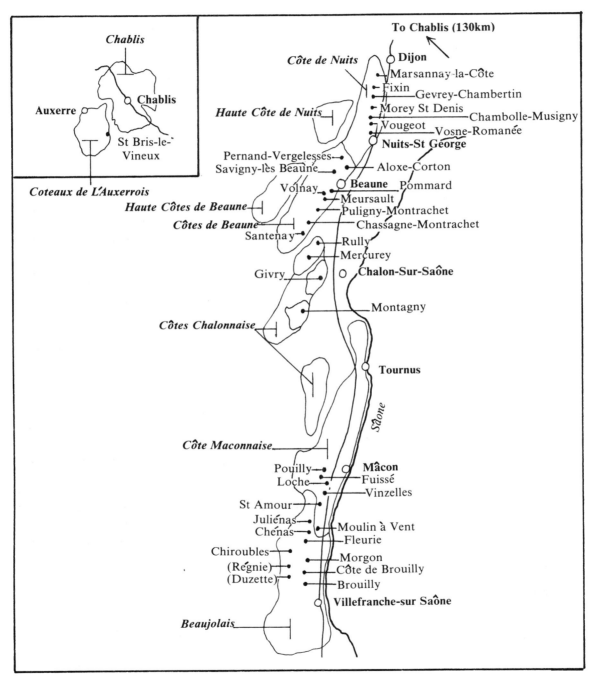

Figure 4.5 *Burgundy*

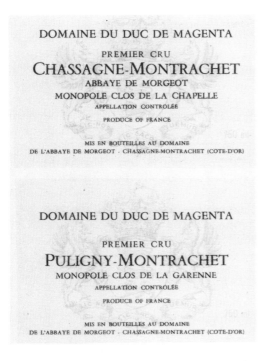

(vineyard or commune), or under the name of the district AC, e.g. Mâcon. Lower grade wines can take the AC Vin de Bourgogne, or Bourgogne Grand Ordinaire, which are both regional ACs. Other ACs are *AC Bourgogne Passe-tout-grain* (red and rosé 9.5% vol), a blend of a minimum of one-third Pinot Noir and the rest Gamay; and *AC Bourgogne Aligoté* (white 9.5% vol), made from the Aligoté grape with or without Chardonnay.

A further complication in Burgundy is caused by people owning very small parcels of land within vineyards, so that *négociants* are necessary to buy up wines and to blend them to make sufficient quantities to market. The wine is often very dependent on the *négociant*, so the name of the *négociant* on the label can be most important.

Chablis

This district is situated 130 km north-west of Dijon round the town of Chablis. The soil is very calcareous and is mixed with clay. It produces the dry white wine called Chablis, and this is classified as a white Burgundy. There is just one grape variety permitted for Chablis – the Chardonnay.

There are four AC for Chablis:

AC Grand Cru Chablis (11% vol)   This comes from only seven vineyards: Les Vaudésirs, Les Clos, Les Grenouilles, Les Preuses, Bougros, Valmur and Les Blanchots. The names of these vineyards may be included in the AC.

AC Chablis Premier Cru (10.5% vol)   This comes from 12 major vineyards. Some of the best of these are Mont de Milieu, Vaillons, Montée de Tonnerre, and Fourchaume. The name of the vineyard may also be included on the label.

AC Chablis (10% vol)   This is a good wine from a large number of vineyards classified for this AC.

AC Petit Chablis (9.5% vol)   This is the lowest AC for Chablis, but still a quality wine.

All Chablis are dry white wines, and are an excellent accompaniment to oysters, crab, lobster, smoked salmon and other shellfish and fish dishes.

VDQS Sauvignon de St Bris

This wine comes from a small cluster of villages south-east of Chablis, about 13 km from the town of Chablis. It is made from the Sauvignon grape, and is a dry white wine similar in style to the Sauvignon wines from the central vineyards of the Loire.

Côte de Nuits

This district is approximately 19 km long and rarely exceeds 0.5 km wide. It runs along the eastern-facing slopes of a range of hills from Fixin in the north to Corgoloin in the south. The Côte de Nuits produces almost all red wines from Pinot Noir. They are of a very high quality and are greatly sought after. They are full bodied and full of fruit, but require some years (depending on the vintage) to become perfectly balanced.

Between Dijon and Fixin there is a village called Marsannay where good quality rosé wine is produced under the AC Marsannay-la-Côte (and AC Bourgogne Rosé de Marsannay) and made from Pinot Noir.

Some of the best ACs in the Côte de Nuits are:

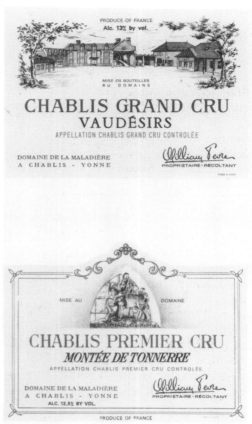

Climats AC	Commune AC
La Chambertin, Chambertin-Clos-de-Bèze	Gevrey-Chambertin
Bonnes-Mares	Morey-St-Denis
Musigny, Bonnes-Mares (Musigny also produces a little white wine)	Chambolle-Musigny
Clos-de-Vougeot	Vougeot
Richebourg, La Tâche, Les Échézeaux	Vosne-Romanée
Les St-Georges	Nuits-St-Georges

Côte de Beaune

This district runs south-west from just south of Corgoloin to just south of Chagny. It meanders along the slopes of the hills and has nearly double the amount of land growing vines to that of the Côte de Nuits. Red and white wines of excellent quality are produced using the Pinot Noir for red and the Chardonnay for white wines. The red wines are generally slightly lighter in colour and body than the Côte de Nuits wines. They do not usually continue to improve with age for as long as the Côte de Nuits reds. The white wines are all dry, and are outstanding wines with great depth of fruit and flavour.

Some of the best ACs in the Côte de Beaune are:

Climats AC
Le Corton (red, some white), Le Charlemagne (white)
Les Marconnets (red)
Le Montrachet (white)
Chevalier-Montrachet, Bâtard-Montrachet (white wines only)

Commune AC
Ladoix (red and white)
Aloxe-Corton (red and white)
Pernand-Vergelesses (red and white)
Savigny (red, some white)
Beaune (red, some white)
Pommard (red)
Volnay (red)
Meursault (white, some red)
Puligny-Montrachet (white, some red)
Chassagne-Montrachet (red and white)
Santenay (red, some white)

There is also the AC Côte de Beaune Villages (only red wines).

Hospices de Beaune
Nicolas Rolin and his wife opened a home for the old and infirm in 1443. Funds were needed so local vineyard owners were canvassed and an auction was set up from which a percentage of the sales would go to the upkeep of the Hospices. The auction takes place on the third Sunday of each November of the current year's wines. There are now 29 plots owned by the Hospices. All the wines (together with the Marc de Bourgogne, see Chapter 6) sold at this auction have the words 'Hospices de Beaune' on the label.

Chalonnais
Starting from below Chagny down to north of Tournus, the vineyard area of this district is only small. It has four main communes:

Rully, producing mainly white wines which are more often made into sparkling wines.
Mercurey, immediately below Rully, producing mainly red wines, some of good quality and similar in style to Côte de Beaune reds.
Givry, further south, producing nearly all red wines, and similar to Mercurey.

Montagny, which produces white wines only, made from the Chardonnay grape. These wines are continually being improved and are now very popular and can be of excellent quality.

Mâconnais
This area runs from just above Tournus to below the Pouilly-Fuissé vineyards, a distance of 48 km. In the main, average quality red and white wines are produced. Some excellent whites are situated below Mâcon around Pouilly and Fuissé; the soil at this point has a high proportion of limestone in it which is ideal for the Chardonnay grape. St-Véran is a relatively modern AC for wines just outside the Pouilly villages, and is often a good quality white wine.

Note The Chardonnay grape takes its name from a small village just south of Tournus, and the Chasselas grape from the small village of that name, also in the Mâconnais close to Fuissé.

Beaujolais
Similar in size to the Mâconnais, Beaujolais has far more land under vines and accounts for nearly half the viticultural area of Burgundy AC wines. There is an indeterminate border between the southernmost part of the Mâconnais and the northern extremity of the Beaujolais district. Granite hills start in the

extreme north, from which comes the very best Beaujolais, known as the *crus* Beaujolais. Two of the *crus* Beaujolais villages are in fact situated in the Mâconnais.

The red wines of Beaujolais are made from the Gamay grape, and Beaujolais *Blanc* from the Chardonnay.

The nine *crus* Beaujolais are:

St Amour
Juliénas
Chénas
Moulin-à-Vent
Fleurie
Chiroubles
Morgon
Brouilly
Côte de Brouilly

These are all AC that can be used on the label. It is generally expected that a tenth cru, Régnié, will be confirmed by the 1988 vintage. At present this is under review by the INAO.

AC Beaujolais Villages (reds 10% vol, whites 10.5% vol) Alternatively, AC Beaujolais plus the name of the village of origin. There are 39 villages allowed to produce wine under this AC, all of which are in the northern half of the district in the granite hills.

AC Beaujolais Supérieur (reds 10% vol, white 10.5% vol)

AC Beaujolais (reds 9% vol, white 9.5% vol) These two AC are used for wines from anywhere in the district.

Beaujolais Nouveau (AC Beaujolais) This wine is made by the *semi-macération carbonique* method, which extracts flavour and colour quickly under pressure produced by the carbon dioxide given off by the closed fermentation. This wine is virtually a rosé wine with a purple tinge to it. Light and fruity, it is at its best when served cool. It is released for sale on the third Thursday in November.

La Confrérie des Chevaliers du Tastevin

This is the Burgundy wine brotherhood which has its headquarters in the Château de Clos de Vougeot. It was set up in 1933 and concerns itself with maintaining the high standards of Burgundian wines and with their promotion. Some wines have their seal on the bottle to show that the wine has been passed by their tasting panel.

Burgundy wines with food

The dry white wines of Burgundy are noted for being greatly suited as an aperitif or as an accompaniment to shellfish and other fish dishes, as well as to lightly flavoured entrées such as chicken vol-au-vent and escalope of veal. The red wines are admirable with most meat dishes and are suited for continuation with the cheeseboard.

The Côte-d'Or Burgundies generally need some bottle age to make them ready for drinking, but the length of time will vary from vintage to vintage and wine to wine. For example many 1980 reds were ready for drinking in 1985, whereas the 1978 wines required further ageing as they were still improving.

Beaujolais *crus* are often at their best after five years and sometimes longer, but the lesser Beaujolais are best drunk young, after one to five years.

The great white wines vary. Chablis and Pouilly-Fuissé are often ready after two or three years, with the more powerful Côte de Beaune whites generally requiring longer. It is a matter of taste with white Burgundies; the wines definitely change their character as they age, becoming almost buttery and nutty.

Champagne

The Champagne region and its wines, and the methods used for producing sparkling wines in general, are covered in Chapter 5.

Loire

The River Loire is 960 km long, rising in the Ardèche in the south of France and running north close to the west side of the Rhône wine region and the Beaujolais district of Burgundy. It flows a further 140 km to where its own celebrated Central Vineyards begin at Pouilly and Sancerre, and then on through Orléanais, Touraine and Anjou to the sea beyond Nantes (Figure 4.6).

The main districts of the Loire, with their subdistricts are as follows:

Central Vineyards Pouilly-sur-Loire, Sancerre, Reuilly and Quincy.
Touraine Vouvray, Bourgeuil and Chinon.
Anjou Anjou, Saumur, Savennières and Coteaux-du-Layon.
Nantais Muscadet, Muscadet Sèvre-et-Maine, Coteaux de la Loire and Coteaux d'Ancenis.

These districts between them produce nearly every style of wine: dry crisp white wines from Muscadet, Sancerre and Pouilly; rosé wines from Anjou; light red wines from Touraine; sparkling wines from Touraine, Vouvray and Saumur; sweet dessert wines from Vouvray and Coteaux-du-Layon; and full-bodied red wines from Chinon and Bourgeuil.

Central Vineyards

Pouilly-sur-Loire There are three AC for this district. The best wines are made entirely from the Sauvignon grape and can be sold either as Pouilly-Blanc-Fumé or Blanc-Fumé-de-Pouilly. The third wine is made from the Chasselas grape and is called Pouilly-sur-Loire. Do *not* confuse these wines with Pouilly-Fuissé, which is produced in the Mâconnais from the Chardonnay grape.
Sancerre Sancerre is known for its excellent dry white wines, again made entirely from the Sauvignon grape. However, it also produces a small quantity of red and rosé wines from the Pinot Noir grape.

The white wines from the two subdistricts of Pouilly and Sancerre are best drunk young (up to five years old). They have a bouquet resembling the green wood or leaves of the blackcurrant bush; this is not to be confused with the blackcurrant bouquet and taste of wine made from the Cabernet Sauvignon grape.
Quincy and Reuilly These are lesser districts of the Loire and produce wines similar to those of Pouilly. They are both made from the Sauvignon grape.

Touraine

This province produces light red, white and rosé wines under the regional AC of Touraine. Within Touraine there are some smaller districts which produce higher quality wines.

Vouvray This is a delimited district of eight communes. The wines are made entirely from the Chenin Blanc grape, which can be made into dry, semi-dry or sweet wine, and still, slightly sparkling or sparkling wine made by the Champagne method (see Chapter 5). The wines are very fruity and are generally made to be at their best within five years, but some of the best wines will continue to improve for a long time.
Bourgeuil and Chinon These two subdistricts produce red wines from the Cabernet Franc grape. The best commune is St-Nicolas-de-Bourgeuil, which has its own AC. The best of these wines are full of fruit and have a slight taste of raspberries, while others have an earthy palate. Most of them are ready for drinking after two to three years.

Anjou

This is another large district producing red, white and rosé wines under the regional AC of Anjou. The best of the dry whites are made from the Chenin Blanc grape and the best of the reds and rosés from Cabernet Sauvignon and

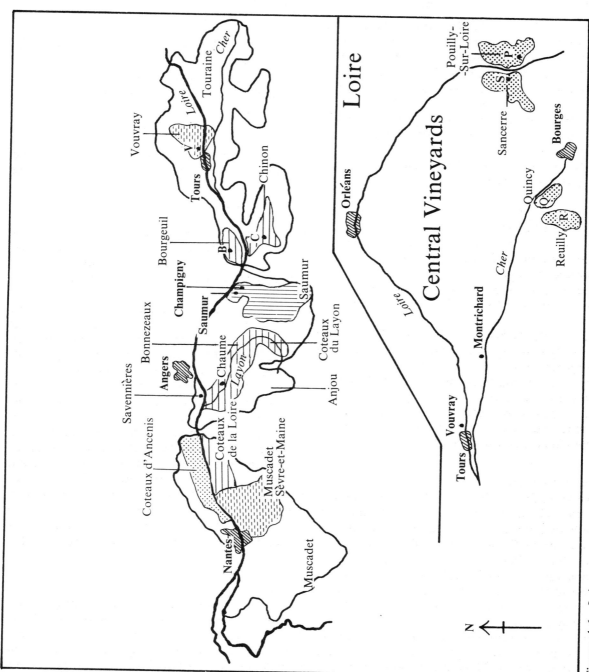

Figure 4.6 Loire

Cabernet Franc, although there is quite a quantity of Gamay grapes grown and sold under the AC Anjou-Gamay.

Anjou is probably best known for its rosé wines. The best are made from the Cabernet and sold under the AC Cabernet-d'Anjou-Rosé, while the majority are made from the Groslot, Cot and Gamay grapes and sold as AC Rosé-d'Anjou or Anjou Rosé.

There are three subdistricts in Anjou which produce very individual wines:

Saumur This subdistrict has an abundance of limestone caves and produces still and sparkling dry white wines of very good quality from the Chenin Blanc grape. The sparkling wines are often made by the Champagne method. Red and rosé wines are also produced, the best from the Cabernet grapes and coming from Champigny just south of the town of Saumur.

Coteaux-du-Layon This area produces red, white and rosé wines, much of the rosé wines being sold as Anjou Rosé or Rosé de Cabernet. The outstanding wine of this subdistrict is its sweet white dessert wine made from the Chenin Blanc, which in a good year will be equal to Sauternes, Barsac and the *Auslese* wines of Germany. Two outstanding vineyard areas producing these sweet wines are Quarts-de-Chaume and Bonnezeaux, which have their own *appellations*.

Savennières This is a commune on the north of

58

the river just south of Angers; it has its own AC. The soil is quite different from that of the surrounds, and it produces a very fine dry white wine from the Chenin Blanc grape.

Nantais

Nantais encompasses Muscadet and Muscadet Sèvre-et-Maine, Coteaux de la Loire and Coteaux d'Ancenis.

The main wine from this region is Muscadet, named after the grape from which it is made. This is the local name for the Melon grape. The best of this wine comes from the AC Muscadet Sèvre-et-Maine, and the next best is AC Muscadet-des-Coteaux-de-la-Loire. Sometimes these wines are sold *sur lie*, which means they have been matured on their lees, imparting an extra flavour to the wine. Muscadets are at their best young and fresh, and admirably complement shellfish and other types of fish.

Another wine produced here is the Gros Plant, named after the grape (which is also called the Folle Blanche). This wine is of a much lower quality and is sold as VDQS Gros-Plant-du-Pays-Nantais. It is dry and tart and most of it is drunk locally.

Rhône

From Vienna in the north to Avignon in the south there is an abundance of excellent vineyards, producing mainly red wines with some white, rosé and sparkling wines. The region falls into two distinct parts (Figure 4.7). The northern half is a narrow strip located on steep granite hillsides following the course of the Rhône. There is a gap of 40 km between this and the bottom half of the district, which is spread out over flatter countryside and a wider area.

The Syrah grape, known as the Shiraz in other parts of the world, is the main black grape of the northern half, although this is sometimes blended with one or more other varieties. The Voignier is the white grape of the north, and is often used in the production of these red wines.

The northerly red wines, e.g. Côte Rôtie, St Joseph, Crozes-Hermitage, Hermitage and Cornas, improve in bottle often up to ten years, but they are usually drunk too young. They all have their own ACs. However, the classic white wines of Condrieu and Château Grillet (the smallest AC in France) are usually at their best when drunk young. They are golden in colour, dry and spicy. St Péray produces white wine and sparkling wine made by the Champagne method. Die, which is a small area to the east of the main district on the river Drôme, produces a sparkling wine from the Clairette grape called Clairette de Die.

The southern half of the Rhône district is dominated by Châteauneuf-du-Pape, but there are a great many other wines produced in this subdistrict. There are many permitted grape

59

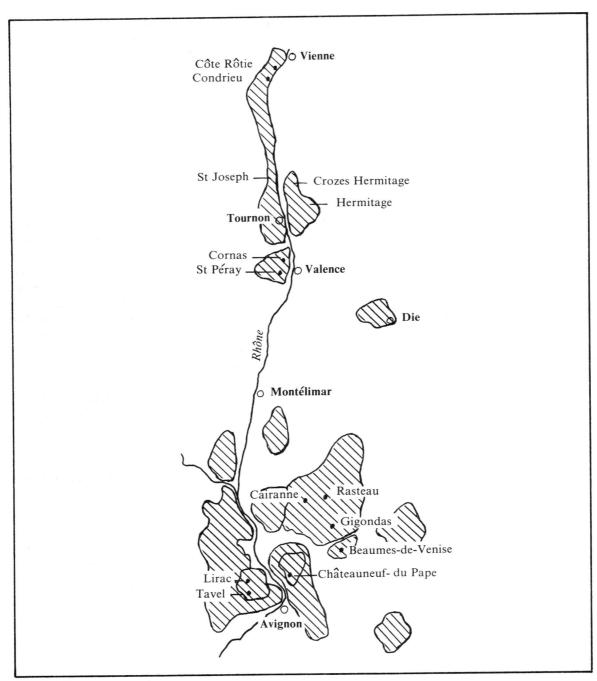

Figure 4.7   *Côtes du Rhône*

varieties, with Grenache, Carignan, Syrah and Cinsault being the most important black grapes. The wines are usually blended from many grape varieties. Much of the wine is made into AC Côtes-du-Rhône-Villages, and more still into AC Côtes-du-Rhône.

AC Gigondas has a majority of Grenache grape in its blend and is similar to Châteauneuf-du-Pape.

Rasteau and Muscat-de-Beaumes-de-Venise AC wines are naturally sweet and are produced by adding grape spirit (brandy) to the fermentation to arrest it (as in port production). This ensures that plenty of unfermented sugar remains in the wine, producing a sweet wine of 14–15% vol alcohol of tremendous fruit and flavour. These wines are dessert wines suitable to be served with the sweet course or drunk on their own.

Tavel is a strong dry rosé wine of 11–13% vol which is more of a *pelure d'oignon* (onion skin) colour. Lirac produces a similar rosé wine, and red and white wines also.

The Châteauneuf-du-Pape subdistrict takes its name from the ruined summer palace of the Pope. The wines are nearly all red, being made from blends of up to 13 grape varieties. The ground is covered in 'pudding stones' – large smooth rounded stones which help to drain the ground, act as storage heaters to warm the vines at night, and also prevent the soil underneath

from drying out. These wines are strong, robust and high in alcohol (minimum 12.5% vol).

All the red wines of the Rhône district are high in alcohol and suitable for serving with roasts and dark meat dishes. The southern wines are also excellent with stronger dishes, such as game and strongly flavoured stews.

Other wine-producing regions of France

Bergerac AC

The region is similar in size to Entre-Deux-Mers and is divided by the river Dordogne. Adjoining Bordeaux region, its wines are predictably similar in style, but have far less quality. In the north of the region, which adjoins St-Émilion, the wines are generally red, being made from Cabernet and Merlot grapes. In the south the wines are more often white and made from the Sémillon and Sauvignon, the same as for Sauternes.

Monbazillac AC

This small region is in the centre of Bergerac, producing wines similar to Sauternes but of a much lower quality.

Côtes de Duras AC

This is an extension of Entre-Deux-Mers to the east, producing a fuller style of wine.

Madiran

Situated in the French Pyrenees, it adjoins the south-western corner of the Armagnac region. It produces a strong full-bodied red wine and a small amount of white wine, which may be sweet or dry.

Jurançon

This is situated further to the south-west again, in the French Pyrenees south and west of Pau. The grape varieties are not used elsewhere but

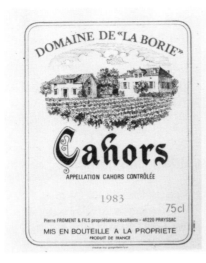

produce a distinctive spicy dessert wine high in alcohol.

Cahors

Situated south-east of Bergerac, this small region obtained AC status in 1971 for its strong, deep-coloured red wines which are high in tannin. They require time to mature and are usually at their best after eight to ten years.

Languedoc/Roussillon

These regions together are by far the largest producer in both cultivated area and quantity of wine, but sadly the wine is generally of ordinary quality. Vast quantities of red wines are made, and this is a prime reason for the so-called EEC wine lake. Some good and very good wines are produced, but these are in the minority.

Blanquette de Limoux AC Still, semi-sparkling and sparkling white wines are produced, but it is the sparkling wines made from the Chardonnay, Chenin and Mauzac grapes which are the best. The soil is heavy with limestone and the wines are produced for sparkling by the Champagne method.

Minervois VDQS and Corbières VDQS are sound wines, mainly red, and are above the general standard of this district.

Fitou AC Situated between Corbières and the Mediterranean, this small area produces some good red wines which are strong and dark.

Costière du Gard VDQS is in the eastern part of the district, producing red wines which are strong and rough.

Provence

Provence is noted for its large output rather than the quality of its wine, but the wines have been improved over the years and four ACs have been awarded to this district. Provence is best known for its rosé wines. AC Bandol and AC Cassis are the red wines from this district that are best known in the UK.

Jura

For such a small district a large number of different styles of wine are produced. Two of them are most unusual. One is the AC Château-Chalon, a *vin jaune* bottled in a squat, square bottle called a *clavelin*. It is made by leaving the white wine made from the Savagnin (Traminer) grape in vats which are never topped up for a minimum of six years. A *flor* settles on the wine as in sherry production, producing a *vin jaune* which is similar in many respects to an old sherry.

The other is the *vin de paille*, which was originally made from grapes that had been laid out on beds of straw to dry before fermentation. They are now put on wire netting or wicker trays. (Switzerland is also known for its *vin de paille*.) The wine is high in alcohol (14–16% vol) and very sweet, and gold to amber in colour.

Vin Fou, a refreshing sparkling wine, is also made here. AC sparkling wines in this region must be made by the Champagne method.

Germany

The wine-producing region of Germany is situated in the south-west quarter of West Germany (Figure 4.8). It is the most northerly wine region of Europe and crosses latitude 50°N, above which it is not normal elsewhere for grapes to fully ripen. However, it is in these borderline districts that some of the finest white wines are produced. Germany is known for its quality white wines; there is a little red produced, which is only of average quality.

Wine categories and labelling

The wines are produced and sold under the German Wine Law, which came into force in 1971 and which has had minor adjustments made to it since. The law set out the names under which wines can be sold and the terminology permitted for use on the wine label. The wines are divided into four categories (see Chapter 3): *Tafelwein, Landwein, Qualitätswein bestimmter Anbaugebiete* (QbA) and *Qualitätswein mit Prädikat* (QmP).

The four main *Weinbaugebiete* (regions) used for *Deutscher Tafelwein* are:

Rhein and Mosel (covers *Anbaugebiete* 1–8; see below)
Main (*Anbaugebiete* 9)
Neckar (*Anbaugebiete* 10)
Oberrhein (part of *Anbaugebiete* 11)

Deutscher Tafelwein may only be sold under one of these *Weinbaugebiete*. There are 15 *Landwein* regions permitted, but these are little known in the UK.

There are 11 *Anbaugebiete* (wine-growing areas) for *Qualitätswein* (QbA and QmP):

1 Ahr
2 Hessiche Bergstrasse
3 Mittelrhein
4 Mosel-Saar-Ruwer
5 Nahe
6 Rheingau
7 Rheinhessen
8 Rheinpfalz
9 Franken
10 Würtemburg
11 Baden

All *Qualitätswein* (bA and mP) must bear one of these names on the label. The following may also appear:

Bereich This is a district within an *Anbaugebiete* spanning many parishes and vineyards which all produce wine with similar characteristics, e.g. Bernkastel and Nierstein.
Grosslage This is the name for a collection of vineyard sites, e.g. Rosengarten for the vineyards surrounding Rüdesheim in the Nahe, Schwarze Katz for those surrounding Zell on the river Mosel, and Erntebringer for the vineyards round Johannisberg in the Rheingau.
Einzellage This is an individual vineyard site. The names of these sites are only permitted to be used on the label of *Qualitätswein* bA and mP. An example is Maximin Grünhause Herrenberg. The village of Maximin Grünhause is

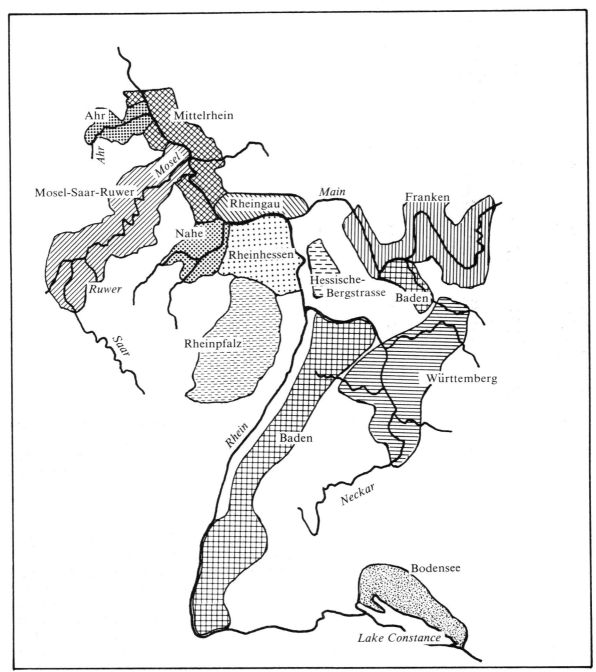

Figure 4.8 *German wine-growing areas*

situated in the *Grosslage* of Romerlay, which is part of the *Bereich* of Saar-Ruwer. This *Bereich* is in the *Anbaugebiet* of Mosel-Saar-Ruwer, which in turn is part of the *Weinbaugebiet* of Rhein and Mosel.

The majority of these quality wines are named after the *Bereich*, *Grosslage* or *Einzellage*, adding the letters -er; e.g. Bernkasteler.

Grape varieties

There are nearly 40 grape varieties permitted to be used in Germany. The most important of these are Riesling, Müller-Thurgau and Silvaner (Sylvaner). These are followed by Bacchus, Elbling, Gewürztraminer, Kerner, Morio-Muscat, Rülander (Pinot Gris) and Scheurebe. The

most notable black grape for the red wines is the Spätburgunder (Pinot Noir).

To name a single grape variety on the label, the wine must contain a minimum of 85 per cent of that grape.

Wine characteristics

The six *Prädikats* (degrees of ripeness) for QmP have been described in Chapter 3.

It was at Schloss Johannisberg in 1775 that the secret of *Spätlese* was first discovered. At harvest time, a courier was sent to the Bishop at Fulda, then in charge of the vineyard, to obtain permission to harvest the grapes. The courier fell ill *en route*, and arrived back at Schloss Johannisberg so late that the crop seemed to be ruined as the grapes were 'rotting' on the vines.

see text on page 79

However, the grapes were picked and made into wine which, to everyone's amazement, resulted in the best ever produced. This was caused by the action of *Botrytis cinerea* (giving *Edelfäule* or noble rot) on the grapes.

Auslese, *Beerenauslese* and *Trockenbeerenauslese* are dessert wines and are unsuitable with most dishes other than perhaps sweets and cheeses. They are normally drunk on their own.

German wines which are to be made into very dry wines will be called *trocken*, and those to be made into semi-dry wines will be called *halbtrocken*. Both *Kabinett* and *Spätlese* wines are occasionally produced in this way, although this is quite unusual.

Rheingau

This small area is on the slopes of the hillsides overlooking the Rhine from just north of Assmanshausen to the confluence with the Main. The vineyards face south and receive extra sunshine reflected from the broad expanse of the river (see Chapter 3). They are protected from the cold north winds by the hills. The main grape variety (nearly 80 per cent) is the Riesling. Location, soil and grape combine to produce outstanding white wines.

Schloss Johannisberg and Schloss Vollrads are two of the best single vineyards named after their estates. The villages of Johannisberg,

Rudesheim, Rauenthal, Hattenheim and Hochheim are perhaps the best known.

Assmanshausen is at the northerly end of the area nearest to the Mittelrhein. It is different from the other Rheingau villages as it produces more red wines than white wines; 60 per cent of the vines are Spätburgunder, and nearly 40 per cent are Riesling.

All Rheingau wines are sold in elongated brown bottles.

Rheinhessen

This is a much larger area situated opposite the Rheingau on the south and west sides of the Rhine, extending down from Bingen and Mainz in the north to just below Worms. The main grape variety is Müller-Thurgau, closely followed by Silvaner; these two account for two-thirds of the grapes grown in this area, with only about 5 per cent of Riesling. However, the very best wines are produced from the Riesling.

Liebfraumilch is the main wine produced in this area (see below) with Niersteiner Spiegelberg and Niersteiner Gutes Domtal (both *Grosslagen*) being the next in quantity. Nackenheim, Oppenheim, Nierstein and Dienheim all produce some good quality wines.

All Rheinhessen wines are sold in elongated brown bottles.

Liebfraumilch

This is not an area or a place on the map. It originally came from the Rheinhessia from the vineyards around a small church near Worms called Liebfrauenkirche (Church of our Lady). Now it is a blended wine from the Rheingau, Rheinhessen, Rheinpfalz or the Nahe. It may not now (since 1982) be a blend of wines from different areas; it must be a QbA wine from one of these four areas. It is a semi-sweet wine which is sold in elongated brown bottles.

Rheinpfalz

Although the Rheinhessen is the largest wine-producing area of Germany in terms of vineyard area, the Rheinpfalz (also known as the Palatinate), slightly smaller in vineyard area, is the largest in production. It is situated on the west side of the Rhine, the best vineyards being found on the lower slopes of the Haardt hills along the autobahn which is called the *Weinstrasse*. The southernmost extremity of the Rheinpfalz is the border with France, at a point just north of the Alsace wine-producing region. Müller-Thurgau accounts for 25 per cent of the vines, followed by Silvaner and Riesling. Ten per cent of the grapes are the red Portugieser.

Pfalz wines vary in quality but the best are truly great, being fuller bodied than the Rheingaus and less soft than the Rheinhessen wines. The bouquet is particularly full, and these wines are probably the best suited to being drunk with a meal. The finest wines come from the villages of Wachenheim, Forst, Deidesheim and Ruppertsberg.

All wines from this area are sold in elongated brown bottles.

Nahe

This area is, as its name suggests, situated along the Nahe which joins the Rhine just east of Bingen. The vineyards are planted with many varieties of grapes, but the Müller-Thurgau is the most common, followed by Silvaner and Riesling. These three account for 75 per cent of the plantings. The wines are therefore likely to be similar in style to the other Hocks; in fact they closely resemble the wines from Nierstein.

The two most important towns are Bad Kreuznach and Schloss Böckelheim, which give their names to the two *Bereich* of Nahe. Bad Kreuznach is the centre of the Nahe wine area both geographically and commercially. The wines of this area are becoming better known and respected.

Nahe wines are sold in elongated brown bottles.

Franconia

The area of Franconia is situated along the Main from Hörnstein, which is east of Frankfurt to about 18 miles (25 km) west of Würzburg. Much of this area is on steep slopes overlooking the river, and south-facing slopes are often the only usable sites. The main grape variety is the Müller-Thurgau, followed by the Silvaner (which used to be the dominant variety).

The best wines are produced from the vineyards around Würzburg, which is the centre of the Franconian wine trade. There are two outstanding vineyards – Stein and Leiste. Wines produced from the Würzburger Stein vineyards are permitted to be called Steinwein; other Franconian wines are not.

Franconian wines are medium dry to dry, full bodied and very suitable to accompany food. In good years *Prädikat* wines are made as in other areas. Franconian wines are sold in flat-sided flasks called *Bocksbeutels*.

Mosel-Saar-Ruwer

This area follows the Mosel and its tributaries the Saar and Ruwer from Koblenz, where it meets the Rhine, to the border with Luxembourg in the south. The vineyards are situated on very steep south-facing slopes. The soil contains large quantities of red slate which radiates heat on to the grapes during the day and night, helping to ripen them, increases drainage, and slows down the erosion of the soil from the steep slopes. It also adds its own character to the wine.

The most important grape variety is the Riesling, giving the highest quality wines and 50 per cent of the total production. The Müller-Thurgau is the next in importance and is on the increase. It is interesting that about 40 per cent of the vines are the original European vines, not those grafted on to American roots, as *Phylloxera* appears to dislike the slate soil.

The wines are low in alcohol, usually being between 8 and 10% vol, which gives them a lightness in the mouth. They are fresh and fruity medium wines with often more than a touch of acidity. They may have a slight prickle to them (*spritzig*), which is caused by a small amount of carbon dioxide gas being in the wine when it is bottled. This gives the wine a pleasant freshness. These wines are at their best when young, up to three years old, with the *Spätlese* and *Auslese* wines lasting a little longer.

The best villages on the Mosel are in the Bereich Bernkastel (Mittelmosel). These are Piesport, Bernkastel, Graach, Wehlen, Zeltingen and Brauneberg. The best in the Bereich Saar-Ruwer are Maximin Grünhause and Eitelsbach on the Ruwer and Wiltingen and Ockfen on the Saar.

Mosel-Saar-Ruwer wines are sold in elongated green bottles.

Ahr

This area on the Ahr is the second to smallest in Germany. It is best known for its red wines, which account for 60 per cent of the total production. The Pinot Noir (Spätburgunder) and the Portugieser, both black grapes, are the main varieties. High-class Riesling and Müller-Thurgau wines are sometimes made, but they are rarely exported.

Baden

Baden produces red, white and rosé wines. It is the third largest German wine-producing area. It runs from Franconia in the north, where the wines are almost identical to Franconian wines and which are permitted to use the *Bocksbeutel*, down through the Neckar valley and on to the main section from Baden-Baden to Basel. This part of the area is only separated from the

Alsace wine area by the Rhine. Nearly all Baden wines come from large co-operatives.

Many grape varieties are grown, but the Müller-Thurgau (35 per cent) is the main white grape followed by the Spätburgunder (Pinot Noir) (18 per cent), which is black. The wines are fuller bodied and higher in alcohol than the wines from the more northerly areas.

Mittelrhein

This area follows the north-eastern bank of the Rhine from Koblenz to the north of Linz, where the Ahr meets the Rhine. These vineyards are the steepest in the world. The Riesling grape accounts for over 75 per cent of the vines; the next most important is the Müller-Thurgau. Much of this wine is used for making sparkling wine (*Sekt*).

Hessische Bergstrasse

This is the smallest wine area of Germany, producing full-bodied white wines mainly from Riesling and Müller-Thurgau grapes. These are not exported.

Sekt

Sekt is the name for sparkling wine in Germany. There are two types:

Deutscher Sekt This is sparkling wine made from German wine.
Sekt This is made from imported wine which may or may not be blended with German wine.

The best *Sekt* wines are usually made by the *cuve close* (Charmat) process. Sparkling wine is very popular in Germany. It is presented and bottled in a similar way to Champagne.

Italy

Italy makes more wine than any other country. Each of its provinces (see Figure 4.9) produces wine. The majority is drunk in Italy, but since the DOC laws of 1963 (see Chapter 3) there has been a steady increase in the quantity of wine exported.

Piedmont

Piedmont produces a large quantity of high-quality red wines and also excellent sparkling wines. The best known sparkling wine is Asti Spumante, which is exclusively from the Moscato grape and is generally made by the *cuve close* (autoclave) method (see Chapter 5). It is normally sweet wine with a strong Muscat bouquet. It is made without any sugar or sweetening being added, and is light in alcohol (between 7.5 and 9% vol).

The red wines are much heavier:

Barbaresco DOCG (12.5% vol) Made from the Nebbiolo grape and named after the village. It must be aged two years in oak or chestnut wood. After three years it can be called *riserva* and after four years in wood *riserva speciale*.
Barbera (12.0–12.5% vol) Made from the Barbera grape and is in plentiful supply. It is usually dry but can be slightly sweet. After three years in wood it can be called *superiore* if it has 13% vol of alcohol.
Barolo DOCG (13% vol) A highly acclaimed strong deep red wine made from the Nebbiolo grape. It must be aged three years before bottling. After four years in wood it can be called *riserva* and after five years *riserva speciale*.
Gattinara (12% vol) Named after the town and made from the Nebbiolo grape. Very high quality dry red wine, lighter in colour and less strong than Barolo. It is aged four years before sale, two of which must be in wood. It often benefits from further ageing in bottle.

Figure 4.9 *Italy*

Veneto

Bardolino (10.5% vol)   Made from a blend of four grapes, this is a light red fruity wine. It may be termed *superiore* if it is aged one year in the district and reaches 11.5% vol of alcohol.

Prosecco (10.5% vol)   A white wine named after the grape which accounts for a minimum of 85 per cent of the blend. It varies from dry to sweet.

Prosecco Spumante (11% vol)   This is a dry sparkling wine usually made by the autoclave method (see Chapter 5).

Soave (10.5% vol)   Made from a blend of Garganega and Trebbiano grapes. It is a dry white, and probably the best known and most plentiful Italian white wine. When aged six months and 11.5% vol it can be called *superiore*. It is at its best when drunk young. *Classico* wines can be produced from an inner delimited area.

Valpolicella (11% vol)   Made from a blend of the same four grapes used in the production of Bardolino, but has a little more body. It is by far the most plentiful of Italian red wines and is one of the best known. It becomes *superiore* after one year's ageing and if it is 12% vol of alcohol, and like Soave is best drunk young. *Classico* wines can again be produced in an inner delimited area.

Recioto della Valpolicella amarone (14% vol)   This is a strong warm dry red wine full of fruit and flavour with a slightly bitter (*amarone*) taste. It sometimes has a slightly burnt flavour. Recioto della Valpolicella without the word *amarone* is semi-sweet. Both of these wines are made from the very ripest grapes (*recioto*).

Emilia Romagna

Lambrusco (11% vol)   This is a sparkling wine, the majority of which is red. It can be either sweet or dry. The sparkling red sweet wine has gained popularity in the UK off-sales market, particularly among party-goers.

Tuscany

Chianti

Chianti is the most celebrated of all Italian red wines and is certainly the best known in the UK.

Chianti DOCG (11.5% vol)   Chianti received DOCG status starting with the 1984 harvest. It is made from a blend of grapes within the following proportions: 75–90 per cent Sangiovese, 5–10 per cent Canaiolo Nero, and 5–10 per cent Trebbiano Toscano and Malvasia del Chianti (white grapes). Chianti cannot be released for consumption prior to 1 March of the year following the harvest. If the wine is aged for a minimum of three years from 1 January following the harvest, and it has a minimum of 12% vol of alcohol, it may be called *riserva*.

Chianti Classico DOCG (12% vol)   This comes from a defined area of this name which is in the middle of the Chianti region. The amount of Trebbiano and Malvasia grapes permitted in the blend is only 2–5 per cent. *Chianti Colli Fiorentini DOCG* and *Chianti Rufina DOCG* are two other Chianti subzones. These three Chiantis cannot be released for consumption prior to 1 June of the year following the harvest. If they are aged for a minimum of three years from 1 January following the harvest and they have a minimum of 12.5% vol of alcohol, they may be called *riserva*.

Governo process   The full title is *governo all'uso del Chianti*. It is a refermentation of racked wine with 5–10 per cent of must from grapes which have been dried up on *cannicci* or *castelli* (special wicker frames). This usually takes place before the end of the year of the harvest. It may be repeated in March or April, and this is called *rigoverno*. Governo is practised to increase the glycerol content, which makes the wine rounder and fresher.

Brunello di Montalcino DOCG (12.5% vol)   One of the very best Italian red wines, made from the Brunello grape. It is a strong dark red wine with plenty of tannin, and must be aged in wood four years before sale. After five years in cask it can be called *riserva*. This wine definitely matures with age.

Vino Nobile di Montepulciano DOCG (11.5% vol)   This wine is made from the same grapes as Chianti and it is similar in character. It was the first wine to be given DOCG status (perhaps because it was one of the first to apply). It is however an outstanding wine. It must be matured two years in wood, and after three years in wood it may be called *riserva*. After four years it may be called *riserva speciale*. Many well-informed experts consider that this wine might improve with bottle age rather than an extended wood age.

Umbria

Orvieto (12% vol)   Traditionally this was a sweet or semi-sweet (*abboccato*) white wine sold in a squat wicker-covered flask called a *pulcianella*. In recent years there has been a trend for drier and crisper wines. Orvieto is now more often made this way and sold in a Bordeaux-style bottle which is cheaper to make and easier to transport. It must be made from a minimum of 50 per cent Trebbiano grapes.

Torgiano (red 12% vol, white 11.5% vol)   More red wine than white is made, and the red is made from a similar blend of grapes to the Chianti of neighbouring Tuscany. When aged three years it can be sold as *riserva*. The white wine is similar to a dry Orvieto.

Latium

Frascati (11.5% vol)   This is the best known dry white wine from this area. A small quantity of semi-sweet, sweet and sparkling wines are also made. If the wine reaches 12% vol it may be called *superiore*.

Est! Est!! Est!!! (10.5% vol)   This wine owes its reputation more to an event in 1110 AD than to quality. It is a white wine made from the Trebbiano grape and some Malvasia. It is similar to Orvieto but is of a lesser quality.

Marche

Verdicchio (12% vol)   By far the best known wine from this region, and the only one of any significance for the UK market. There is a delimited part of this district which is entitled to use Classico on the wine label.

Campania

Campania is more famous for its volcano Vesuvius than for its wine, but there is plenty made here.

Vesuvio (11% vol)   Red and white wines are made, the whites varying between semi-sweet and dry.

Lacrima Christi (red 10.5% vol, white 12% vol)   Produced in the same district as Vesuvio, the slopes of Vesuvius, and is made in various styles – red, white, rosé and sparkling.

Apulia

This region of Italy produces more wine than any other. Nearly all of it is of a low quality, although 17 wines have been granted DOC status. It is best known for its *trulli*, which are small prehistoric buildings.

Sicily

Great changes in viticulture and vinification over the past 20 years have considerably improved the wines of Sicily. Wines bearing the letter Q meet official quality specifications (this also applies to Sicilian foods).

Corvo wines These wines are produced by a state-owned winery. They do not have DOC, as they are made from blends of grapes from many regions. However, there are red, white and sparkling wines of a good standard.
Marsala This is the best known wine from Sicily. It is a white, sweet or dry, fortified wine (see Chapter 5).

Sardinia

This island now produces some good quality wines, most of which come from the co-operatives.

Cannonau di Sardegna (13.5% vol) Cannonau is the name of the grape variety used; it is only found in Sardinia. The wine produced varies from strong rosé to deep red. The *riserva* wines have matured for a minimum of three years in wood.

Consorzi

There are many consorzi in Italy. These are voluntary organizations set up in many of the wine-producing regions in the 1930s to protect quality and to help market the wine. They have now really been superseded by the DOC law of 1963, but can still operate.

In Chianti, for example, the best known is the Consorzio Chianti Classico, which has a neck label for the bottle of the Gallo Nero or Black Cockerel. This is of course only for the Chiantis

made from grapes grown in the Classico zone. There is one very famous and outstanding wine from the Classico region which is not a member of the consorzio. It is Brolio Riserva, Chianti Classico. It is owned by the Ricasoli family, whose predecessor Baron Ricasoli developed the formula for the blend used to produce Chianti.

The consorzi organizations do not offer any official guarantee of quality.

Spain

Sherry (see Chapter 5) is the best known wine from Spain but, as is the case with port and Portugal, it forms a very small percentage of the overall wine production of the country.

Spanish wine production and labelling is governed by the Instituto de Denominaciónes de Origen (INDO), which is controlled by administrative growers committees or *consejos regulados*. There are 28 Denominaciónes de Origen, but many of these are unknown still in the UK. The most important are:

La Mancha
Montilla
Navarra
Penedés
Priorato (*rancio* wines)
Rioja
Tarragona
Valdepeñas

La Mancha

This is the largest demarcated region in Spain (see Figure 4.10) and produces one-third of all the light wines. They are high in alcohol and used extensively for blending with other wines throughout Spain. A large amount is also used for distillation into brandy and industrial alcohol. The region is better known for the quantity

Figure 4.10 *Spain*

produced rather than for the quality of its wines.

Montilla

Situated close to the Jerez region, this area produces strong white wines similar in style to sherry. Although usually unfortified, the alcoholic strength is 16–19% vol. The region gave the name *amontillado* to sherry, but cannot use this name for its own wines.

Navarra

This district is adjoining Rioja in the north, and produce 80 per cent red wines and 20 per cent white. The major grape variety is the Garnacho (related to Grenache), and this produces dark red wines high in alcohol, with some similarities to Côtes du Rhône wines. The reds are suitable to serve with pasta dishes, stews and roasts.

Penedés

Situated south of Barcelona, this region has a very high reputation for its sparkling wines. The best of these are made by the Champagne method (see Chapter 5) and are called *cava* wines. Of the wines of this region, 80 per cent are white, but red wine production is on the increase.

Priorato

This small region is 48 km inland from Tarragona. It produces strong dark red wines very high in alcohol (18% vol) which are used in blending. There are also some sweet white dessert wines which are slightly maderized (*rancio*: bitter, like Madeira).

Rioja

Named after the River Oja, this district is in the north of Spain astride the Rio Ebro. It is divided into three parts – Rioja Alta, Rioja Alavesa and Rioja Baja, in quality order. Red, white and rosé wines are produced.

The red wines may be of outstanding quality. They are matured in oak casks in the same way as claret, taking on an oak bouquet and taste. *Vino de crianza* on the label means that the wine has been matured in oak for a minimum of one year and has spent some months in bottle. It must be two years old before sale. *Reserva* on the label means that the wine has been matured in oak for a minimum of two years plus a further one year in bottle. *Gran reserva* on the label means that the wine has been matured in oak for a minimum of three years plus two years in bottle, or vice versa. Gran reserva wines must be seven years old before leaving the bodega.

White Rioja wines are also matured in oak for up to five years. These white Rioja wines may be dry or medium sweet.

Red Rioja wines are excellent when served with strongly flavoured dishes such as game, casseroles and roasts, and will also complement spaghetti bolognese. Light dishes are likely to be overpowered by the strong flavour of these wines. The red wines generally benefit from being opened well in advance of serving.

Tarragona

Situated on the coast south of Penedés, this region produces sweet red fortified wines high in alcohol, white and rosé wines.

Valdepeñas

This region is immediately south of La Mancha. It has red stony soil with a chalky subsoil; this retains water, thus making the region better for wines than La Mancha. Mostly red wines are produced; these are high in alcohol (12–13% vol) but are light, fresh and fruity. They are best drunk young, and accompany light meat dishes such as veal, poultry and lamb cutlets.

Vinos Espumosos

This is a national DO (Denominación de Origen) for sparkling wines (see Chapter 5).

Portugal

Although Portugal is best known for its port wine, this accounts for perhaps 2 per cent of the wine production of the country. The improved quality and control of Portuguese wines, together with their excellent value for money, is making them better known and more acceptable in the UK. However, the wine industry, other than one or two private companies, lacks organization and direction. The farmers receive very low prices for their grapes, insufficient to allow them to invest in new modern equipment.

The wines of Portugal, other than port, are governed by the Institute do Vinho e da Vinha. Wines complying with the standards laid down by this government body will receive a *selo de garantia* (seal of guarantee) if they come from a *região demarcada* (demarcated region), with a number and the name of the district. There are ten *Regiãos Demarcadas* officially recognized (see Figure 4.11). From north to south these are:

Vinho Verde
Douro
Dão
Bairrada
Colares
Bucelas
Carcavelos
Moscatel de Setúbal
Algarve
Madeira (island)

Other than Madeira (see Chapter 5) from the island of that name, whose wines are sold under the name of the grape, most of Portugal's wines are sold under the name of the region.

Vinho Verde

This region is mainly in the Minho province and is in the extreme north-west of Portugal. Its name derives from the fact that the grapes used are 'green', meaning slightly underripe. Red and white wines are produced. Although the white wines are better known in this country, red wines account for 70 per cent of Vinho Verde wines. There has been a massive increase in the popularity of these wines in the UK with sales increasing more than fivefold between 1980 and 1984.

The grapes are trained high off the ground on trellises or even on the branches of trees. This method of cultivation is called *enforcado* and allows the ground underneath to be used for crops while being shaded from the sun. Growing so high off the ground, the grapes do not benefit from reflected and radiated heat from the ground as do those grown in the normal way. They are therefore underripe at harvest time and contain a very high proportion of malic acid. This produces a strong malolactic fermentation which traditionally (although not always now) takes place in the bottle, giving a slight sparkle. This applies to the white and red Vinho Verde wines, and they should both be drunk

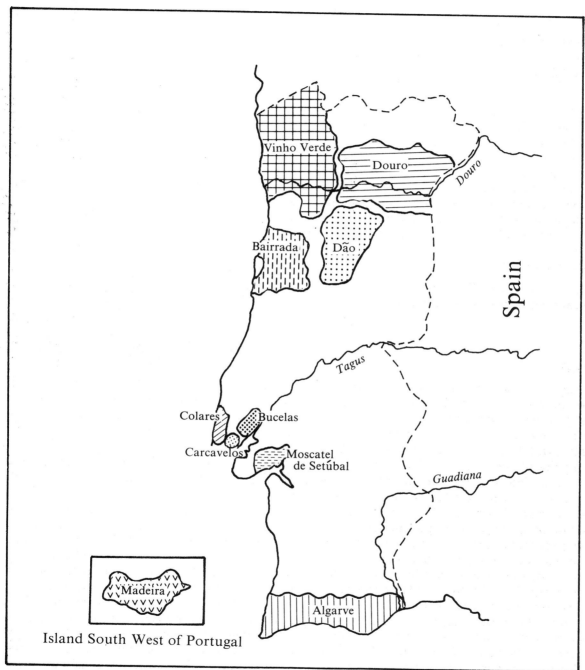

Island South West of Portugal

Figure 4.11   *Portugal's demarcated wine regions*

when young and fresh. They should both also be served chilled.

The white wines are highly acidic, dry, and low in alcohol, although some less dry and softer wines are being produced to suit the British palate. They are excellent served as aperitifs in hot weather. The white wines will accompany fish dishes or even Chinese meals; the reds will accompany stews.

Douro

Famous for its port, the Douro is responsible for making light red, white and rosé (*vinho rosado*) sparkling wines in far greater quantity. The semi-sparkling rosé wines are the most common and popular in the UK. The white wines are generally dry and are suitable with hors-d'oeuvres and chicken dishes; the reds have a deep colour and will accompany stews and offals, e.g. liver and bacon.

Dão

Just south of the Douro, Dão (pronounced 'down') is situated in the centre of Portugal. The 12 approved grape varieties are grown on terraced slopes of granite hills, producing 80 per cent red and 20 per cent white wines.

The red wines may be of a very high quality and mature in cask for a minimum of 18 months, but usually a lot longer. They are then matured in bottle, often for many more years.

The white wines are dry and light and should be drunk young, as they become flabby quite quickly. The white wines are suitable as aperitifs or served with light fish dishes, quiches, Chinese meals and chicken dishes. They should be served well chilled.

The reds may be strong powerful wines which are hard and full of tannin when young, but which mature into soft full-flavoured wines. They will accompany all roast meats and cheese.

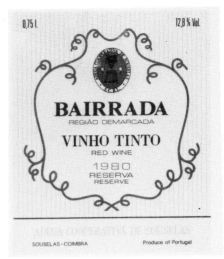

Bairrada

Bairrada is situated between the southern half of the Dão region and the west coast. This region became a *regiao demarcada* only in 1979. Its name originates from the local name for the clay soil, *barro*. It has been producing high-quality wines for a very long time.

The red wines are strong in colour, flavour and alcohol and must be matured for one and a half years in cask plus a further six months in bottle before sale. Many are matured in cask much longer, and the best Bairrada wines will mature in bottle for many years. They are suitable for service with strong meat dishes and will accompany game, roasts and strongly flavoured cheeses.

Most of the white wine produced here is blended with other whites and is made into Portuguese sparkling wine.

Colares

This small region situated on the west coast, north-west of Lisbon, is famous for its ungrafted Ramisco vines. These appear to be immune to the ravages of *phylloxera* owing to the depth of the sand 'soil', which reaches down 8–10 metres.

Red and white wines are produced. The reds are more well known. They are very dark in colour, best when aged in bottle for a few years, and suitable for service with the same dishes as the red Bairrada wines.

Carcavelos

This is a very small region on the coast just west of Lisbon, where sweet white fortified wines with an almond/nutty bouquet and flavour are produced. These wines are little known in the UK.

Bucelas

Just north of Lisbon, this small region produces a dry white wine from the Arinto grape which often ages well and will accompany fish, chicken and veal dishes.

Moscatel de Setubal

This region is a little further south and produces a famous fortified dessert wine (16–20% vol) which ages well in cask. The younger wines (five years old) are dark straw coloured and have a strong honeyed nose and flavour. The older wines (25 years old and upwards) are almost brown in colour and have a caramel taste.

The wine is suitable to serve with strong cheese or on its own at the end of a meal.

Algarve

Better known as a holiday resort, this area produces both red and white wines of average quality.

Other countries

America

The USA is the world's fifth largest wine producer, with the major areas being found in California and round the Finger Lakes in New York State. Other regions are being developed in Oregon and Washington, but by far the most important regions are in California.

In 1980 five general wine-growing areas were defined in California: North Coast, Central Valley, Sierra Foothills, Central Coast, and South Coast. Within these large areas there are smaller areas taking their names from their county, e.g. Napa and Sonoma, or from defined approved viticultural areas (AVA), e.g. Chalone and Livermore, both in the Central Coast area.

North Coast This is probably the best known area, made up as it is from the following counties: Lake, Mendocino, Sonoma, Napa, and Solano.

Central Valley This area produces 80 per cent of all Californian wine, but it is not recognized for its quality wines. It stretches from Sacramento in the north to San Joaquin in the south.

Sierra Foothills The following counties make up this area: Amador, Calaveras and El Dorado.

Central Coast This area is divided into three smaller areas: Bay Area, North Central Coast and South Central Coast. The Bay area is made up from Alameda, San Benito and Santa Cruz counties; the North Central Coast from Monterey, San Benito and Santa Cruz counties; and

the South Central Coast from San Luis Obispo and Santa Barbara counties.

South Coast   This area, which is to the east of Los Angeles, is in San Bernardino and Riverside counties.

European vines are grown extensively, producing wines sold under the name of the vineyard coupled with the grape variety (varietal) or varieties used to produce the wine. For many years European names such as Chablis and Burgundy were used to market the wines, but this is dying out.

Excellent Chardonnay, Sauvignon Blanc, Pinot Blanc, Chenin Blanc, Cabernet Sauvignon and Pinot Noir wines are produced. The local grape varietal of Zinfandel is now producing a large amount of white (blush-coloured) wine as well as the better known red. Many of these wines have a very strong fruity bouquet and are high in alcohol.

Quality *méthode champenoise* sparkling wines are also produced, particularly in Sonoma county and the Napa valley.

There are approximately 650 wineries in California. Some of the best are: Chalone for Pinot Blanc, Chardonnay and Pinot Noir; Robert Mondavi for Pinot Blanc, Chardonnay and Pinot Noir; Calera for Pinot Noir; Beringer; Pine Ridge for a remarkable French-style Cabernet Sauvignon blend and Chardonnay; and Hans Kornell for outstanding sparkling wines.

Argentina

This country is a very large producer of wine, but little at present is seen in the UK. Ordinary red wines are produced, with slightly less good white wines.

Australia

The Australian vineyards are situated in the Hunter River valley in New South Wales; the Great Western district in Victoria; the Barossa and Coonawarra valleys in South Australia; the Murray River vineyards in Victoria and South Australia; and the Swan valley and Margaret River valley of Western Australia.

The red wines tend to be strong flavoured and high in alcohol. The most popular grapes used are the Shiraz (Syrah) and the Cabernet Sauvignon, often being blended together. The Rhine Riesling has been the most popular for the white wines, but Chardonnay and Sémillon are now being widely grown.

This is a fast-developing wine-producing country which will offer some excellent wines in the future.

Austria

All the wines of any note are white. Grüner Veltliner, Kremser Veltliner, Schluck and Gumpoldskirchener are the best known. Much of the wine is made after the style of German wines, and the German terms *Auslese*, *Beerenauslese* and *Trockenbeerenauslese* are also used.

Cyprus

Cyprus is best known in the UK for its sherry, which is far removed from the taste of Spanish sherry. Red and white table wines are made, of which the red Commandaria is the best known.

England and Wales

In the variable and unpredictable climate of England and Wales, wines of from poor to good quality are made in the better years. Nearly all the wines (and certainly the better ones) are white. They are often similar in style to the German wines, which after all are produced in similar latitudes. Latitude 50.5°N passes through the vineyards of the Ahr and also through Torquay in the south-west of England.

Müller-Thurgau, Huxelrebe and Seyval Blanc are popular grape varieties, and there are many others being experimented with. English wines are usually rather highly priced in comparison with wines of similar quality from Germany.

Greece

The majority of Greek wine is produced for blending and local consumption. Less than 8 per cent is of controlled *appellation*, for which there are 29 designated regions.

Retsina   The best known wine from Greece is Retsina. This wine has had resin from the Aleppo pine (best) added to it so that it is really an aromatized wine. Originally, when wine was stored in *amphorae*, these vessels were sealed with resin to prevent oxidation of the wine. It was thought that as this wine was better than unsealed wine, the resin must contain some preservative qualities. Soon pine resin was added to the wine itself, and then to the must prior to fermentation. The Greeks became accustomed to this flavour and grew to like it. However, the flavour of Retsina has very little appeal to Western European palates. There are three controlled appellations for Retsina, for which 20 per cent of the Retsina made qualifies. Most Retsina is white, 10 per cent is rosé and a little is red.

Mavrodaphne (15% vol)   This is an AC wine. It is a sweet red dessert wine made from the grape of the same name. It is one of the best known Greek wines in the UK.

Samos (15% vol)   This is another AC wine. It is a sweet white dessert wine made from the Muscat grape on the island of Samos.

Château Carras   This is perhaps the best wine produced in Greece. The operation is modelled on a Bordeaux château and uses 50 per cent Cabernet Sauvignon and 50 per cent Cabernet Franc, producing an excellent red wine.

Hungary

Hungary produces red and white wines, the whites ranging from dry to very sweet. Egri

Bikavér (Bull's Blood of Eger) is the best known red wine, although an increasing amount of Cabernet is being produced.

Some of the best Hungarian wines are produced along the northern shores of Lake Balaton, the largest lake in Europe. Balatoni Riesling is a medium sweet, full-bodied white wine which is at its best when young. Balatoni Furmint is made from the Furmint grape and is a full-bodied sweet and luscious wine.

Tokaji (Tokay)

Tokay is a town in the north-east of Hungary close to the Russian border. The wines come in various styles, but they are all made from the Furmint and Hárslevelü grapes.

Tokaji Szamorodni   This is a full-bodied white wine which may be either dry or sweet. This will be stated on the label.

Tokaji Aszú   This wine is made from grapes from the same vineyards as Szamorodni. However, some grapes have been left on the vine to be attacked by *Botrytis cinerea* (giving noble rot); these grapes are picked separately and lightly pressed. The remainder of the grapes are pressed into a paste; this is added to the must in measures of 35 litres, the capacity of a *puttonyos* (a wooden bucket or tub). One *puttonyos* on the label of a Tokaji Aszú means that 35 litres of this strong mixture has been added to 140 litres of must. Aszú wines in the

UK are sold as either one, three or five puttonyos; the more puttonyos, the richer and sweeter the wine will be. This very rich sweet dessert wine is also slightly maderized (bitter, like Madeira).

Tokaji Eszencia This is even sweeter but is rarely produced.

The whole of the Hungarian wine production is controlled by the state authority Monimpex. This name appears on all Hungarian wines.

Luxembourg

The vineyards of Luxembourg are situated on the River Moselle and produce similar wines to the country's northern neighbour, Germany. The majority of the wine is drunk in Luxembourg but a little is now being exported. Most of the wine is still white wine; a small quantity of sparkling wine and some *pétillant* (*perlant*) is made.

New Zealand

Vines were introduced to New Zealand in 1819. Europeans emigrated to New Zealand and pioneered the wine industry, but it was not until the late 1970s that it really got on its feet. Today the majority of vineyards are on North Island, but an increasing number are appearing in the northern part of South Island.

Most of the well known European grape varieties are being grown here now, plus some lesser known varieties such as Pinotage which was developed in South Africa.

New Zealand could well be a wine country of the future.

South Africa

The vineyards are situated in the south-western Cape and along the Orange River further to the north.

A complete range of wines is produced here, mainly from French and German vines plus the Pinotage, which was propagated in South Africa. It is a cross between the Syrah and the Pinot Noir and was developed by the KWV (South African Wine Farmers Association).

South African sherry is now of a high quality and both the red and white table wines have also reached a high standard, particularly since cooled fermentation was introduced.

The control of origin, grape variety and vintage is shown on the bottle by a neck seal (Figure 4.12) granted by the South African Wine and Spirit Board to those wines which qualify. The lowest category qualifying for a seal signifies that the wine comes from a particular geographical area; the seal for this category has

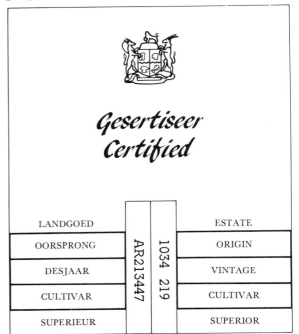

Figure 4.12   *South African seal*

a blue band on it with the word 'origin'. The highest category is designated 'superior'. There is a blue band for origin, a red band for vintage, a green band for cultivar (vine variety) and the words 'estate' and 'superior'. All or some of these may appear on the seal. These guarantee the words written on the label of the wine.

Soviet Union

Although very little Russian wine is seen in the UK, Russia is the third largest producer in the world. Red, white, rosé, sweet, dry, still, sparkling and fortified wines are all produced here.

Switzerland

Switzerland may be divided into three parts by language – French, German and Italian. The wine production of each part is influenced by the styles of these three countries.

Little Swiss wine is imported into the UK, mainly because of its high price. The best known wines are Dôle, a red wine made from the Gamay grape; Merlot, a red wine from the grape of that name; Johannisberg, a white made from the Müller-Thurgau; and Fendant, a white from the Chasselas grape.

Yugoslavia

Yugoslavia produces a large amount of red and white table wine. The best known in the UK is Lutomer Laski Riesling, a light white wine produced in the northern part of Yugoslavia close to the Austrian and Hungarian borders.

Bulgaria, Chile, Czechoslovakia, Algeria, Lebanon, Romania, Turkey, India and many other countries all produce wine in greater or lesser quantities.

Chapter Five

Sparkling and fortified wines

Sparkling wine

There are four methods of producing sparkling wine. The aim of all the methods is to produce a clear wine containing bubbles of carbon dioxide, but each has different characteristics.

The first and most complex process is that used in the Champagne region – *la méthode champenoise*.

Champagne and la méthode champenoise

The Champagne region
The Champagne region is 145 km north-east of Paris, and is the most northerly vineyard of France (Figure 5.1). It is situated on a base of belemnite chalk which has a very small layer of soil on top; the chalk gives good drainage while still retaining sufficient moisture for the vines. This chalk base is the main reason why the region is so suitable for the production of Champagne.

There are 120 communes in the Champagne region, which is divided into three areas: Montagne de Reims, Vallée de la Marne and Côte des Blancs. The main producers or houses of Champagne are in Reims, Épernay and Ay. The Marne flows through the middle of the area and was the route by which Champagne reached the outside world in its early days.

The Comité Interprofessionel du Vin de Champagne (CIVC) is the governing body for

Champagne and enforces all the AC regulations. It was formed in 1942, and comprises growers, producers, and government representatives. All stocks of Champagne and movements of Champagne are kept on records by the CIVC. This body also promotes the wines of this area.

The grapes used for the production of Champagne must come from the delimited area of Champagne. There are three permitted grape varieties: Pinot Noir (black), Pinot Meunier (black) and Chardonnay (white). Most of the black grapes are grown in the Montagne de Reims and the Vallée de la Marne, while most of the Chardonnay is grown in the Côte des Blancs.

The vineyards are graded from 100 per cent down to 50 per cent. For a vineyard graded 100 per cent the grower can sell his grapes for 100 per cent of the price fixed by the CIVC, and so on. Only three methods of pruning are permitted; *Guyot simple* or *double*, *taille Chablis*, and *cordon de Royat*. This is to ensure that the quality of the grapes is kept to a high standard.

La méthode champenoise
This is the method of producing a sparkling wine by inducing a secondary fermentation to take place in the bottle (see Figure 5.2). It is used to produce Champagne and other sparkling wines, but is the only method permitted by the CIVC for the production of bottles and magnums of Champagne. Sparkling wines other

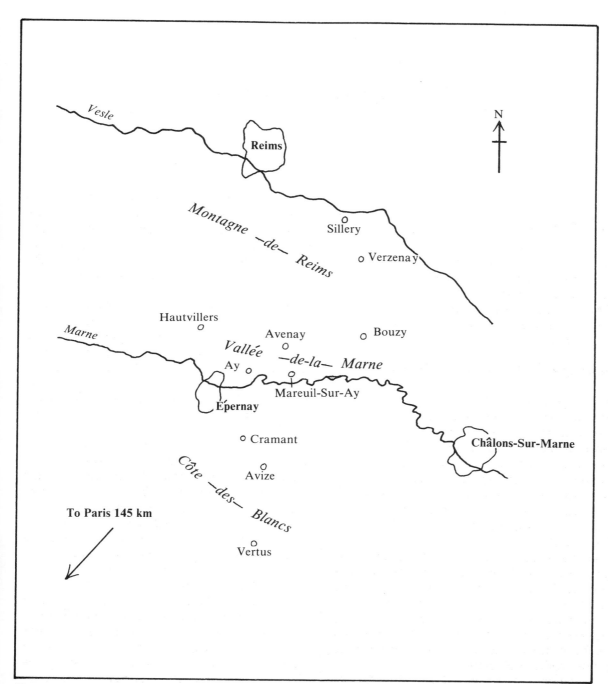

Figure 5.1   *Champagne*

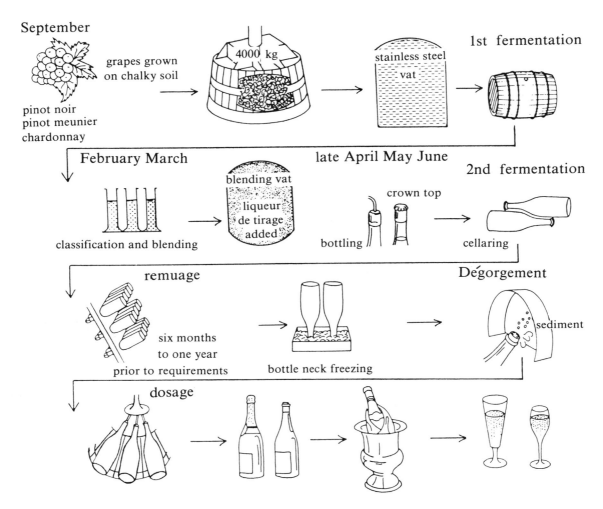

Figure 5.2   *The story of Champagne production*

than Champagne produced by this method may carry the words *la méthode champenoise* on the label. New regulations, however, state that this will only be permitted until 1994.

The quantity of must permitted to be extracted from the grapes is limited to 2666 litres from 4000 kg of grapes, or 100 litres from 150 kg of grapes. The standard size press in Champagne holds 4000 kg. The first fermentation takes place in large glass-lined or stainless steel tanks, with the exception of Champagne produced by the houses of Krug and Bollinger, who complete the first fermentation in oak casks in the traditional manner.

Four or five months later, in late February or early March, the *cuvée* is prepared. This is the blend, and is the hallmark of each Champagne house. Non-vintage Champagne blends contain on average 40–50 wines from as many as ten different years, whereas vintage Champagnes may be made from a blend of just one year. A small quantity of wine from other years is permitted in vintage Champagne to ensure that the correct balance is achieved.

The wine is now mixed with carefully measured quantities of liquid sugar, yeast, a little tannin and finings. This addition is called the *liqueur de tirage* and it produces a second fermentation in the bottle. If too much sugar is contained in this preparation, the bottles will explode owing to too much carbon dioxide being produced. The bottles are then sealed with a stainless steel crown top with a small plastic cup fitted into the top of the neck. The bottles are stored on their sides in underground cellars where during the first three to four weeks the second fermentation takes place, producing carbon dioxide and sediment. The wine is left to mature on the sediment for a minimum of one year for non-vintage Champagnes and three years for vintage. The better quality Champagnes are matured longer than this, averaging three years for non-vintage; Krug Grand Cuvée is matured six years. During this maturation period the carbon dioxide is absorbed into the wine, and the bubbles become an integral part of the Champagne.

The wine is now ready to undergo the *remuage*. This is the movement of all sediment of dead yeast cells caused by the second fermentation on to the crown top ready for removal. The traditional method of *remuage* is to shake the bottle thoroughly to loosen the sediment and then to place the bottles into *pupitres* (Figure 5.3) where, over a period of 12–20 weeks, the bottles are very lightly shaken and twisted to bring them to an almost inverted position. The sediment is now in the small plastic cup next to the crown top. A mechanical system of *remuage* is being pioneered called the gyro pallet. This may well replace the traditional manual system. The bottles are now upside down and can remain *mise en masse* this way for years.

Next the bottles are placed into a shallow

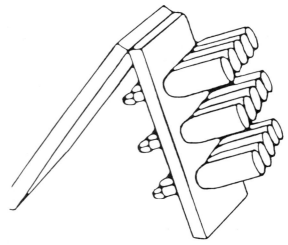

Figure 5.3 *Pupitres*

trough containing freezing mixture, which will freeze a small pellet of wine below the sediment. The house of Bollinger produce a marque called Bollinger RD (*récemment dégorgé*, or late degorged). The wine is often kept ten years before dégorgement takes place. The bottles are removed and the crown top is released, allowing the gas to force the ice pellet and sediment out of the bottle (*dégorgement*). The amount of wine which is lost is replaced by a measured amount of sweetened wine (*dosage*). At *dégorgement* the Champagne is completely dry, because all the sugar will have been used up during the second fermentation. The percentage of sugar syrup in the *dosage* determines the style of the wine, as follows:

Style	Syrup in dosage
Nature	None (usually small quantity)
Brut	1%
Extra sec, extra dry	3%
Sec, dry	5%
Demi-sec	8%
Demi-doux	10%
Doux, rich	10% upwards

The *dosage* is sometimes referred to as *liqueur d'expédition*.

The traditional Champagne cork is inserted and it is wired and dressed ready for sale. The wine is now kept for up to six months before shipment.

Champagne bottle sizes are as follows:

Quarter-bottle	185 ml
Half-bottle	375 ml
Bottle	750 ml
Magnum	2 bottles
Jeroboam	4 bottles
Rehoboam	6 bottles
Methuselah	8 bottles
Salmanazar	12 bottles
Balthazar	16 bottles
Nebuchadnezzar	20 bottles

Quarter-bottles, some half-bottles and the larger sizes of Champagne bottles are produced by the secondary fermentation taking place in magnums, followed by *remuage* and *dégorgement*. The wine is then transferred in a clear state to the larger or smaller bottles under pressure.

Non-vintage Champagne accounts for the vast majority of Champagne produced and reflects the style of the house more definitely than vintage Champagne, as this will vary according to the year. Good advice to all new students of Champagne is to drink a lot of non-vintage Champagne before splashing out on vintage.

Dom Pérignon, cellar-master at the Abbey at Hautvillers from 1670 to 1715, is credited with inventing *la méthode champenoise*. This abbey is presently owned by the Champagne house of Moët et Chandon, who have named their de luxe marque after Dom Perignon.

Blanc de Blanc

Blanc de Blanc Champagne is Champagne which is made entirely from the Chardonnay grape, which is white. This Champagne has a strong Chardonnay bouquet, is of a lighter style than the normal blends, and comes from the Côte des Blancs.

Rosé Champagne

Pink Champagne (or rosé Champagne, as it is more often referred to now) is still regarded by many as something of a novelty. Although this is undoubtedly what it was when it was first produced, it has been taken seriously by some producers and has improved considerably.

The house of Gosset has been producing rosé Champagne in clear glass bottles for decades, but until recent years mainly for the Italian market. Perrier Jouet and Laurent Perrier rosé Champagnes are two of the better known brands in the UK.

Rosé Champagne is made by blending red wine with white wine prior to bottling. It is the only AC wine for which this method of producing a rosé wine is permitted. The best red wine for making rosé Champagne is reputed to come from Bouzy.

Coteaux Champenois

This is the AC for the still wines of Champagne. Each year the *rendement* – the amount of grapes permitted to be used from one hectare of vines for the year – is set for the Champagne district by the CIVC. For example, this may be set at 9500 kg per hectare for AC Coteaux Champenois and 8500 kg per hectare for Champagne. This means that a maximum of 8500 kg per hectare can be used for Champagne, leaving 1000 kg per hectare for AC Coteaux Champenois. More of the 8500 kg could be used for Coteaux Champenois, with a corresponding amount less for Champagne.

Crémant

Crémant, when applied to Champagne, means that less yeast and sugar were added in the *liqueur de tirage* to produce a Champagne with half the normal gas pressure (about three atmospheres or 3.17 kg/cm^2). This is not the definition of *crémant* wines from other areas, although AC Crémant de Bourgogne must be made by *la méthode champenoise*.

Méthode champenoise wines from other areas

Aude Blanquette de Limoux, from Carcassonne.

Loire Saumur and Touraine produce some outstanding wines.

California Many regions produce these wines, in particular Napa and Sonoma.

Spain Penedés is the best known region. Spanish sparkling wines made by this method are called *cava* wines. If they are made by the *cuve close*, carbonation or transfer methods (see below) they are known as *vinos espumosos*.

Cuve close or Charmat process

These are the names which appear on labels of sparkling wine which have been produced by the bulk or tank method. The still wine is pumped into large tanks together with a measured quantity of sugar and yeast. The temperature is controlled to aid the secondary fermentation and the wine is circulated in the closed tanks by propellers. The fermentation is completed in a matter of days. Then the wine is drawn off through filters, still under pressure, and bottled.

This method is much quicker and cheaper than the Champagne method but is not permitted to be used for *appellation contrôlée* wines. It is permitted for *Qualitätswein* from Germany and *denominazione di origine controllata* wines from Italy. The bubbles are generally a little larger in these wines than in those made by the Champagne method and usually do not last as long in the glass. However, this method has been improved and developed to such a degree that it is sometimes difficult to distinguish between the wines made by the two methods on appearance. Examples of sparkling wines made by this method are Asti Spumante and Henkell Trocken Sekt.

Transfer method

In this method the second fermentation is carried out in the bottle as for Champagne, but the wine is then chilled and removed from the bottles, passed through a filter, treated with a *dosage* and rebottled under pressure in clean bottles.

Carbonation

This is the quickest and cheapest method of producing a sparkling wine. It is also the poorest in terms of quality. The wine is chilled in large tanks and is impregnated with carbon dioxide. The wine is then bottled under pressure. The resulting wine resembles a fizzy drink in the glass, with large flabby bubbles which do not last long, rather than an exciting sparkling wine fit for celebrating with.

Other sparkling wine terms

Vin de mousseux	French term for sparkling wine other than Champagne
Pétillant	French term, but used universally, meaning slightly sparkling
Perlant	French term meaning very lightly sparkling
Spritzig	German term meaning slightly sparkling
Schaumwein	German term for sparkling wine usually of lesser quality than *sekt*
Perlwein	German term referring to wine which has been deliberately made to be slightly sparkling
Sekt	German term for sparkling
Spumante	Italian term for sparkling
Espumante	Portuguese term for sparkling
Espumosos	Spanish term for sparkling

Fortified wines

Sherry

The name 'sherry' originates from the Spanish town of Jerez de la Frontera, which is situated in the heart of the sherry district (Figure 5.4). This district is in Andalucía in the south-western corner of Spain immediately round Cádiz. It covers an area about 50 km square.

Sherry is a fortified wine and a blend. Vintage sherry is not produced. The special characteristics of sherry are governed by the climate, soil and process of vinification. The wine is produced by the shippers rather than individual growers, although the shippers now own large vineyards themselves. The smaller growers are therefore only interested in the wine up to the pressing of the grapes. From then on the shipper takes over.

There are three types of soil in the district. The best is called *albariza*, which has a very high percentage of chalk in it and is very white. This chalky soil absorbs and holds moisture and reflects the sun, preventing the soil from drying up too much. This soil is planted with the white Palomino grape which is the principal grape for sherry. The other two grapes used are the Pedro Ximénez (PX) and the Moscatel, both of which are white. These two grapes are grown for blending purposes and for sweetening and colouring the sherry. *Arenas* soil is sandy and *barros* soil has more clay in it. They are planted with Pedro Ximénez and Moscatel.

Vinification of sherry
The steps in the vinification are as follows:

Harvest
Pressing
Fermentation
Fortification
Classification
Blending (by the Solera system)

The harvest takes place in mid-September. The grapes are picked and taken to the press houses. Before pressing the Pedro Ximénez and Moscatel grapes are dried on esparto grass mats, making these grapes very high in sugar. The grapes are not destalked before pressing. *Yeso* (gypsum) is added to the pressing, which makes the wine drier and more acidic and assists in clarification. Nowadays tartaric acid is often used in its place.

After the first three days of fermentation, when most of the sugar is converted into alcohol, the wine is drawn off into casks to complete its fermentation. The casks are not filled right up to the top, as it is an important part of the sherry vinification method to allow air to come into contact with the new wine. These casks are taken to the *bodegas* and kept in these casks while the fermentation is completed.

The wine is then fortified with grape spirit, but the quantity used varies according to the wine. Some will have turned to vinegar and will have to be distilled; some will have oxidized, taking on a toffee or nutty smell and flavour; and some will have been attacked by *flor*. The wines attacked by *flor* will make the best *finos* (dry sherries). This *flor* forms a covering on the wine like froth, preventing air from getting to the wine and oxidizing it; it is a type of yeast which lives on the wine, imparting a characteristic smell and flavour to it. The wines with *flor*

Figure 5.4 *The sherry district*

are fortified up to 15–16% vol of alcohol, while the other wines will be fortified up to 18% vol of alcohol to prevent further oxidation. The oxidized wines are usually made into *olorosos*, which are the sweeter sherries.

The wines are classified into four basic types:

Palma
Raya
Dos rayas
Palo cortado

Palma is the best and is used for *finos* and *amontillados*. *Raya* and *dos rayas* may be used for *finos* and *olorosos*, and *palo cortados* are used for the sweeter sherries.

Solera system
This is the system of blending sherry whereby old wine is constantly refreshed by the addition of younger wine of the same type (Figure 5.5). This procedure is followed because the wines vary so much from cask to cask. The wines are blended to form a palatable sherry and also to form a standard product to market. Sometimes a date, e.g. *solera* 1872, is found on the label of a sherry or on a wine list. This means that the *solera* was laid down in the year stated, not that the bottle was made in that year.

The number of *criaderas* or stages in a *solera* system will vary from shipper to shipper and from style to style. The example in Figure 5.5 shows seven tiers or stages (scales) before the sherry enters the bottom level, which is the *solera*. When sherry is drawn off from the *solera*, this cask is topped up from the no. 1 *criadera*, which is the next cask back in the system. This in turn is topped up from *criadera* no. 2, and so on up the scales until *criadera* no. 7. This is topped up with new wine. The new wine – *vino d'anada* (single-year wine), usually about two years old – is added to a suitable *solera* system.

Although the casks are stacked up high in the *bodegas*, the *criaderas* do not have to be stacked

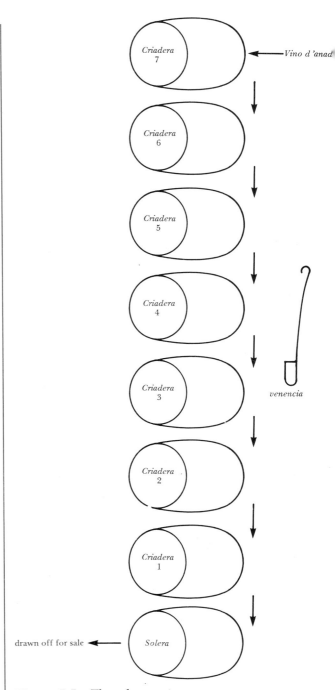

Figure 5.5　*The solera system*

above each other as shown. It is the order of replenishing that matters, not the height.

Extra care must be taken with those wines which have *flor* when transferring wine from one stage to another.

When wine is sold from the bottom level of the *solera*, no more than one-third is taken by law.

To make the sherry darker, *vino de color* may be added. This is made by boiling *mosto* from Pedro Ximénez and Moscatel grapes down to one-fifth or one-third of its original volume. To make the sherry sweeter, *vino dulce* may be added. This is made by adding brandy to current pressings of Pedro Ximénez and Moscatel grapes at an early stage in the fermentation, arresting the fermentation and leaving a lot of sugar in this wine. Pedro Ximénez grapes may be dried out in the sun until very little moisture is left in them, but they are very sweet and brown. These grapes are then pressed and the resultant juice is used to sweeten and darken sherry, particularly brown sherries. Caramel is used by some shippers to colour their sherries. *Dulce apagado*, made from the Palomino grape, is now being used to sweeten sherries.

Before sale, the sherry is fined with egg whites and white Spanish earth.

The *venencia* is a special cup used to take a taste of wine from a sherry butt through the bung hole. It was originally made from whale bone with a silver cup fixed to the bottom. The *copita* is the ideal sherry glass (see Figure 8.1).

It is generally agreed that the word 'sherry' on its own means that the wine is of Spanish origin. It if comes from anywhere else it must be preceded by the name of the country. On the label of one of these 'sherries', the name of the country of origin must be stated in letters of the same size or larger than those used for the word 'sherry', by law.

Types of sherry
From dry to sweet, the types are as follows:

Manzanilla This sherry is very dry and is produced from the vineyards of Sanlúcar de Barrameda, which are on the west coast. The wines are matured in cask, and it is said that the sea air imparts a slight salty tang to the wine.
Fino Very dry delicate wine, slightly less dry than *manzanilla*.
Amontillado Dry wine, but older. There are two types of *amontillado*. The commercial *amontillado*, which is medium dry, has added colour and sweetening and is of medium quality. The traditional *amontillado* is a matured *fino*, of high quality and more expensive.
Oloroso Less dry, more medium in style, but fuller. Some cream sherries are made from this by sweetening it. Some dry *oloroso* wine is now also being produced, but this is less common.
Amoroso Sweeter and softer than *oloroso* sherries. Often now called cream sherry.
Brown sherry Very sweet and dark.
Almacenista These are old original-style dry unblended sherries. They are not available in large quantities: they are more for the connoisseur than the average market.

Port

The name of port is protected in the UK. In 1703 the Treaty of Methuen gave preferential treatment to port over French wines, aiding its popularity. At this time it was not fortified. The quality of port is controlled by the *Instituto Do Vinho Do Porto*.

Port is a fortified wine produced from approximately 40 grape varieties, but there are eight or ten which account for the majority of wine produced. The vineyards are situated in the Douro *região demarcada* on the upper reaches of the River Douro, in north-east Portugal, between Régua and the Spanish border. The best vineyards are around Pinhão, 32 km up river from Régua. The grapes are grown on terraces which have been blasted out of the slate and granite. The vineyards are graded from A (the best) to F, according to the soil, location, grapes used and the concentration of the vines. The climatic conditions are severe, with temperatures ranging from well over 38°C in summer to below freezing in winter. In spring there is heavy rain; precipitation is up to 130 cm per annum.

The best port seems to be produced from vines with the smallest harvest. The grapes are picked in September and carried by hand to the press houses which are situated in the vineyards. The grapes are crushed and put into auto-vinificators, where the short fermentation (approximately 36 hours) takes place and the colour of the grape skins is extracted. The short-fermented must, low in alcohol but high in sugar content, is strained off into vats containing grape spirit (brandy) in the ratio of 10 parts brandy to 45 parts must. The brandy is in sufficient quantity to prevent further fermentation, thus ensuring that the wine remains sweet. The brandy, which must be bought from the government-controlled Casa do Douro (vinegrowers co-operative), is made from distilled Portuguese wine.

In the spring the wine is put into casks called *pipes* which hold 522 litres and is transported down to the port lodges at Vila Nova de Gaia, which is situated on the opposite side of the Douro estuary to Oporto. The port lodges are shippers' warehouses similar to the sherry *bodegas*. The port is further fortified, classified and blended.

Ruby port

This is the youngest and cheapest of the red ports. It is a blend of wines from more than one year, and is usually bottled and sold after approximately four years. It is an everyday port and is the one which should be used for such drinks as port and lemon. It is perfectly suitable to be drunk on its own, but it is not of the same quality and smoothness as the other ports. It is, as its name suggests, ruby red in colour. It is

sweet and may be a little fiery, and is ready for drinking as soon as it is bottled.

Tawny port

As with Amontillado sherry, there is a commercial tawny port and a traditional tawny port. The commercial tawnies are made by blending white port with ruby ports to produce a tawny colour. It is young and inexpensive – similar in price and quality to ruby port.

Fine old tawny ports are made by blending ports from several years and maturing them in cask for seven or eight years. Some tawnies are matured in wood for 10, 20, 30 or over 40 years, and this is stated on the bottle. This wood maturation causes the wine to become tawny in colour and to lose some of its sweetness. Fine old tawny ports are smooth, mellow and ready for drinking as soon as they are bottled. They are at their best slightly cool rather than at room temperature, and are very suitable to be served at the end of the meal.

White port

White port is made from white grapes. It is blended and matured in a similar fashion to ruby port and is a similar price. It varies between dry and sweet, and from a light straw to a golden colour. It is best served chilled, and the dry style is excellent as an aperitif.

Vintage port

A vintage year is declared by the individual shippers when they believe that their wine is of sufficient quality. Therefore in some years some shippers may declare a vintage, producing vintage port, while others may not.

Vintage ports are only made in these years from a blend of wines of this one year. The wine is matured in cask for two years and is then bottled. A white splash of paint is often put on the bottle to show which way up it has been stored so that the bottles may be put into racks in the same position. This ensures that the crust (sediment) which forms in vintage port is not disturbed. The corks are branded with the name of the shipper and the date of the vintage, and these are then often sealed in the bottle with wax to protect them. Labels are not usually put on the bottles until a later date, as they would probably rot or fall off over the long bottle maturation time. Vintage port will mature in bottle for 10–15 years and may continue to improve up to 40 years or more, depending on the vintage and quality of storage.

Vintage port is deep purple in colour, sweet, and full-bodied, with an alcoholic content of 20–22% vol. It throws a crust (sediment) in the bottle which may be very heavy, and it must be handled carefully so that this is not disturbed. All vintage ports must be decanted before service (see Chapter 8). They are very suitable for service with cheese or at the end of a meal, and they are very expensive. Less than half the production of a vintage year is made into vintage port.

Late-bottled vintage (LBV)

This is port from a single year, usually other than a declared vintage, which has been matured in wood for four to six years before being bottled. This allows the maturation process to be speeded up and the sediment to drop out of the wine. This port is ready for drinking when bottled and does not require decanting; thus it is very useful to the catering industry. It is a dark garnet colour. It has slightly less body, depth of flavour and bouquet than vintage port but is excellent value for money, being much less expensive. It carries the date of the vintage on the label.

OFF vintage

Many port companies are now producing vintage ports in years when they have not declared a vintage. These wines are made in the same way as vintage ports, but they are sold under other names, e.g. Graham's Malvedos Vintage

1969, Fonsecca Guimaraens Vintage 1962 and Taylor's Vargellas 1972. They should be matured in bottle and treated in the same way as vintage port. They are sometimes as good as vintage port, and have even been known to be better on occasions. They are less expensive than vintage ports.

Vintage character

This port is less expensive than vintage or late-bottled vintage port. It is a blend of good quality ports of more than one year, and it is matured in wood. It is intended to be similar in style to vintage port, but it is a long way from being its equal.

Since 1975 vintage ports, including those of an OFF year, LBV and fine old tawny ports, must all be bottled in Portugal.

Other fortified wines

Madeira

In Madeira the vines are grown on terraced hillsides on trellises similar to those for *vinho verde*, allowing other crops to be grown below them; there is a shortage of cultivated land on this volcanic island. The topsoil was enriched in the fifteenth century by a seven-year fire which burned all the forests, making the soil excellent for viticulture.

There are four main styles of Madeira wines drunk in the UK; each of them takes its name from the grape variety. They are all fortified, and almost all are blended by the *solera* system. There are vintage Madeiras, but these are rare.

The grapes are harvested and the mosto is fermented. The sweeter wines are fortified and then placed in their casks in an *estufa* (heating room); the drier wines are fortified after this process. The wine is warmed up gradually in the *estufa* to 45–50°C and then gradually cooled again. The process takes about six months. This makes the wine able to withstand extremes of temperature and to resist oxidation. It imparts a caramel flavour to the wine which is characteristic of Madeiras. The wine is then blended, usually by the *solera* system. Lower-quality Madeiras undergo heat treatment in a vat fitted with heating pipes. The wine is treated for a minimum of 90 days.

The four main styles of Madeira are:

Sercial This is a pale dry white wine, excellent as an aperitif or with consommé. Rainwater is a lighter style of Sercial, and not the name of a grape. It is not one of the four main styles of Madeira, but is exported to the UK.

Verdelho A darker, more golden, medium dry wine which is ideal as an aperitif or served with consommé and other soups.

Bual Slightly darker in colour but sweeter than Verdelho. Suitable to be drunk at the end of a meal or on its own.

Malmsey Malmsey takes its name from the Malvazia grape. It is sweet and luscious, and best suited to after-dinner drinking. It was in a butt of Malmsey wine that the Duke of Clarence drowned himself while imprisoned in the Bloody Tower in 1478.

Marsala

This is a DOC white fortified wine produced in Sicily, and it may be dry or sweet. Some slowly heated unfermented grape juice is added to it; this gives it a caramel flavour. The dry is suitable as an aperitif; the sweet is used in the UK more in cookery than as a dessert wine. Marsala All'Uovo is a mixture of Marsala and egg yolks.

Malaga

This is a sweet brown wine from the demarcated region of Malaga on the Mediterranean coast of Spain, 160 km from Gibraltar.

Vermouth

Vermouth is an aromatized wine and takes its name from one of its ingredients – *wormwood* (*Wermut* in German). It is made from a base of dry white wine (except for the rosé variety) with the addition of extracts of herbs, spices and other flavourings, plus a fortification of grape brandy.

Dry vermouths are called 'French' and sweet vermouths are referred to as 'Italian', although the two styles are made in both Italy and France. The Italian red (*rosso*) vermouth is coloured with caramel. The Noilly Prat brand of dry vermouth gets its golden colour from maturing in casks for two years in the open air. Chambéry, a small city in Savoie, produces an excellent pale and light dry vermouth.

There are four types of vermouth:

Dry This is light yellow to gold in colour and is dry.

Sweet Reddish brown in colour, sweet and full.

Bianco Straw coloured, sweet with a touch of vanilla in the flavour.

Rosé A blend of rosé wines forms its base; it is medium dry and light.

Muscats

Muscats and Muscatels are produced from the Muscat grape, which is found all over the wine-growing world. Apart from Muscat d'Alsace, the wines are all sweet and raisin-like with a strong Muscatel bouquet.

The most famous is AC Muscat-de-Beaumes-de-Venise. It is produced in Vaucluse in the Côtes du Rhône and takes its name from the village of Beaumes-de-Venise. As mentioned in Chapter 4, it is fortified before the fermentation is complete, thus leaving some of the unfermented sugar in the wine. This is a natural sweet wine – *vin doux naturel*. It is not sold under a vintage, and is at its best when young; it is not for keeping.

Sherry-type wines

The word 'sherry' on its own refers to the fortified wine produced in the Jerez region of Spain. All other sherry-type wines must include on their labels the name of the country of origin stated in letters no smaller than those used to write the word 'sherry', immediately in front of that word. Sherry-type wines are produced in South Africa, Cyprus and Australia.

British sherry

This is produced in the UK from imported must.

Saint Raphaël

An aromatized fortified red wine from France, Saint Raphaël has a predominant flavour of quinine. Its sweetness is counteracted by the bitterness of the quinine. It is served as an aperitif.

Chapter Six

Spirits, beers and other drinks

Spirits

A spirit is the distillate of a fermented liquor (wash). The most common base ingredients for potable spirits are fruit, cereals, molasses and vegetables. Distillation concentrates the strength and flavour of the liquor by removing most of the water.

Distillation of spirits

There are two types of still used to produce spirits – the pot still and the continuous still. The continuous still is also called the patent still or Coffey still (it was invented by Aeneas Coffey in 1832). Although there are two types of still, the process is basically the same.

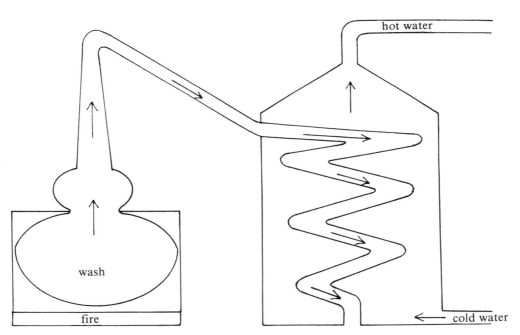

Figure 6.1 *Pot still*

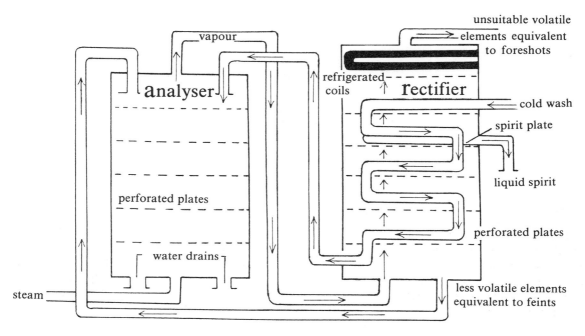

Figure 6.2 *Continuous still*

Pot still

A fermented liquor (wash) is put into a closed vessel and boiled (Figure 6.1). The first vapour which comes off is called the 'heads' or 'foreshots' and is not used. Alcohol boils at 78°C and so will vaporize before water. The vapour is passed along a closed pipe into a cold water tank where it is cooled; it condenses into a liquid, which is the spirit. This spirit will contain a high proportion of alcohol with some water and certain gases and flavouring oils which have been carried in the vapour. The gases and oils impart particular characteristics and flavours to the spirit. The residue left in the still is called the 'tails' or 'feints' and is not used.

Although a very pure spirit can be obtained by modern distillation methods, it would have no character and flavour. For this reason the pot still is used to produce the 'fine' spirits. Some whiskys, rums and brandies are produced in pot stills, and these are double distilled.

Continuous still

As its name suggests this is a continuous process, unlike the pot still. It produces a purer spirit containing fewer impurities.

The still comprises two tall columns (Figure 6.2). One column is the *analyser*, where the wash is vaporized, and the other is called the *rectifier*, where the vapours are condensed. The wash is heated in the analyser by superheated steam, whereas the pot still uses direct heat.

Continuous stills are designed specifically for the individual spirit required. For example, a grain whisky still will allow more flavouring to remain in the spirit than a vodka still.

Alcoholic strength

The alcoholic strengths of drinks are stated as the percentage of alcohol by volume (% vol) in the drink at 20°C: this scale is standardized by the Organisation Internationale de Métrologie Légale (OIML).

Table wines are usually between 9% and 13% vol and fortified wines are usually 18% to 26% vol. Spirits are normally sold at 40% vol in the UK, with vodka at 37.5% vol. There are higher strengths for some spirits.

Gin

Gin is a spirit distilled from a wash made from fermented grain, malted barley, maize or rye.

There are three main types of English gin:

London dry gin is made by adding a distillate of various flavourings to the base spirit. The flavourings used are juniper berries (*genévrier*), coriander, angelica root, orange and lemon peel, liquorice, orris root, cassia bark, cardamom, calamus root, fennel and almonds. These constituents are usually steeped in spirit and distilled in a separate run. The distillate is then used to flavour the spirit. Sometimes the flavourings are added to the grain mash and distilled in one process.

Plymouth gin is wholly unsweetened and is the correct gin for Pink Gin, which is a mixture of a little Angostura bitters and gin served with iced water. Plymouth gin is made by Coates and Co., Plymouth.

Old Tom gin is a sweetened gin, but is rarely seen now.

In addition there is Dutch gin, which is sold under the names of Geneva, Hollands, and Schiedam.

Gin is flavoured and coloured at will and is brought to the required strength by the addition of distilled water. It does not require maturing as do whiskies and brandies.

Vodka

Vodka originally came from Russia and Poland. It is colourless, and the best is filtered through charcoal filters to purify the flavour. The best is made from rye, although it is made from other grain. Genuine Russian vodka is distilled from wheat. It is odourless and flavourless and thus is ideal for mixed drinks and cocktails. Vodka is now made by British companies and in other Western countries. Flavoured vodkas are available from Russia and Poland.

Whisky

Whisky and its relatives – whiskey, rye and bourbon – are made from the distillation of malted barley, unmalted barley, maize or rye.

Scotch whisky
This is whisky which is made in Scotland. Its flavour and quality is governed by the type of cereal, the malting process, the peat used, the water, the distilling equipment used and the skill of the distiller and the blender.

There are two distinct types of Scotch. One is made from malted barley, double distilled in a pot still; this is called *malt whisky*. The other is made from barley and maize, usually unmalted and distilled in a continuous still; this is called *grain whisky*. The Scotch on the market is either straight malt or a blend of grain and malt whisky. The cheaper blends contain up to 70 per cent grain and the best as little as 30 per cent grain. There is one straight grain Scotch whisky made and sold as Old Cameron Brig.

Malt whisky may come from four districts:

The Highlands, which includes the famous River Spey and produces Glenlivet, Glenfiddich, Glen Grant and many other famous whiskys.

Northern Scotland, which produces Glenmorangie and Dalmore.

Western Isles Islay, Jura and Skye. These whiskies (such as Laphroaig) have a strong peaty smell.

Lowlands Bladnoch, Littlemill and Rosebank sell a small amount of straight malt, while all the rest is used for blending.

Malt whisky is made as follows. Barley is malted by steeping it in water and then spreading it out on a concrete floor in a warm atmosphere. The grains germinate, converting the starch to sugar. The germination is stopped by heating the grains over a peat fire. The peat smoke adds to the flavour of the Scotch. The malt is added to boiling water in a mash tun and the sugars and flavour are extracted. The liquid is drawn off and fermented with the addition of yeast. This wash is then twice distilled in a pot still.

Scotch must be matured in Scotland in cask for a minimum of three years by law. Ten years is a good age for high-quality malt, but in that ten years as much as 25 per cent may be lost by evaporation. The best casks for maturing Scotch are old sherry casks.

Irish whiskey

Irish whiskey is made in Ireland from a wash of malted and unmalted barley with some grain. Made by the pot still method, it is distilled three times but the majority is now made by the continuous still method. It is normally not sold until seven years old. 'Whiskey' is the Irish spelling, which is also used by the Americans for their whiskey.

Rye whiskey

This whiskey is distilled mainly from a wash containing a minimum of 51 per cent rye. The majority of rye whiskey is produced in North America.

Bourbon whiskey

Bourbon is an American whiskey which is made from maize, rye and malted barley. Bourbon takes its name from Bourbon County, Kentucky. It must contain at least 51 per cent maize spirit.

Rum

This is a spirit distilled from fermented molasses. Molasses is a syrup byproduct of the sugar industry from which crystalline sugar cannot easily be obtained by further refining. The type of yeast used in the fermentation has a great bearing on the resultant rum. Other factors are the method of distillation, the type and amount of caramel used for colouring, and the maturation. Rum can be matured in uncharred or charred oak casks. As with whisky, rum must be three years old before being sold in the UK.

White rum This was originally a Cuban rum, but now it is also produced in Puerto Rico and Jamaica. It is made by using the continuous still and maturing for just one year in uncharred oak casks. This rum is light in body, flavour and smell.

Dark rum This rum is rich and full-bodied. It is produced in Jamaica and is known as Jamaican rum.

Light rum This refers to the more aromatic rums which are produced in Martinique, Puerto Rico, Trinidad, Barbados, Haiti and Guyana. Demerara rum comes from Guyana, taking its name from the River Demerara.

Brandy

Brandy is the distillation of the fermented juice of fresh grapes without the addition of any other spirits.

Cognac

Cognac is produced in the delimited region of Cognac (see Figure 6.3). Grand Champagne is the best sub-region, followed by Petite Champagne and Borderies.

The quality of the brandy finally produced depends on the soil where the grapes are grown as well as on the distillation, maturing and blending processes. The more chalky soils are the best for Cognac. The AC allows just three grape varieties: St Emilion (Ugni Blanc), which accounts for 98 per cent of the vines, Folle Blanche and Colombard.

The names of the districts in order of merit are:

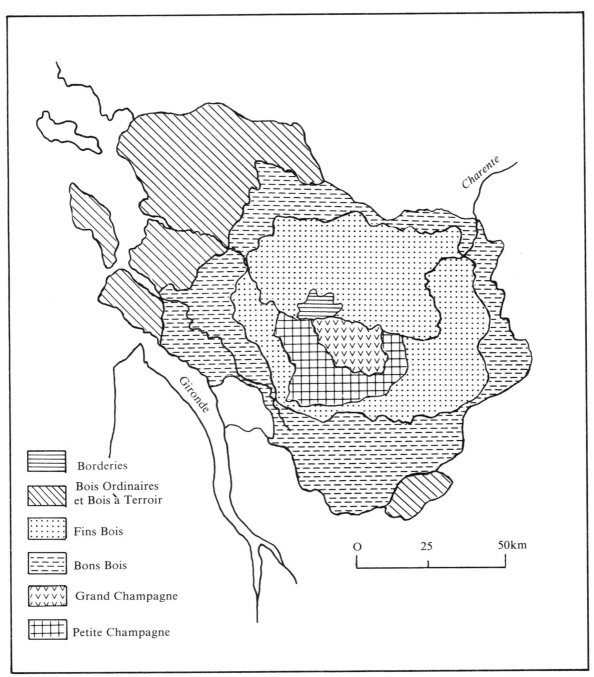

Figure 6.3 *Cognac*

Grande Champagne
Petite Champagne
Borderies
Fins Bois
Bons Bois
Bois Ordinaires, Bois à Terroir

The vineyards are picked in one go. The grapes are pressed and the must is fermented for 7–10 days. The wine produced is acidic and harsh and is between 8% and 10% vol of alcohol. The more unpalatable wine seems to produce the best Cognac.

Only copper pot stills are used for the distillation, which by law must be completed by 31 March of the year following the harvest. The distillation is done under French Excise supervision. The wine is heated slowly for two hours in the stills by open flames fuelled by coal or gas. At 78°C the alcohol vaporizes and travels through the coiled pipes in the cooling tank where it condenses into *brouillis*. This contains all the alcohol and some water plus other flavourings and trace elements. The *brouillis* is at about 30% vol of alcohol and is approximately one-third of the quantity of wine which was put into the still. The vast majority of what is left behind in the still is water. The still is cleaned out and the process is repeated with more wine.

When there are three lots of *brouillis* they are put together in a clean pot still and redistilled. This second distillation may take as long as ten hours. Only the middle portion of this distillation, which is called the *bonne chauffe*, is used. The foreshots or *tête* which is the earliest part of the distillate, and the aftershots or *queue* which is the end part of the distillate, are not used for Cognac; they are put in with another batch of wine for redistilling.

The *bonne chauffe* is run off into Limousin or Tronçais oak casks to mature. At this point the raw spirit is colourless and at 72% vol of alcohol – a strength which must not be exceeded if it is to be Cognac. It has taken approximately nine casks of wine to produce one cask of *bonne chauffe*.

During the maturation period (minimum three years by law) the Cognac absorbs tannin and some colour from the oak casks and loses some of its harsh and fiery taste. It evaporates at about 2–3 per cent per year, and this is called 'the angels' share'. The brandies are blended by the cellar master to produce house styles and qualities. Before they are sold the Cognacs are brought down to 40–45% vol of alcohol with distilled water and the colour is usually adjusted with a little caramel.

The finest Cognacs are:

Grande Champagne, Grande Fine Champagne These are made entirely from brandies produced from grapes grown in the Grande Champagne region.
Petite Champagne, Petite Fine Champagne These are made entirely from brandies produced from grapes grown in the Petite Champagne region.
Fine Champagne These are made entirely from brandies produced from grapes grown in the Grande and Petite Champagne regions, with a minimum of 50 per cent from the Grande Champagne region.

The age of cognac refers to age in cask before bottling. Cognac does not improve with age in the bottle. The terms used are:

Three Star (***) and *VS Cognacs* must be a minimum of three years old but in practice they are usually an average of five years old. These Cognacs may be drunk on their own, with mixers or used in cocktails.
VSOP and *VO Cognacs* VSOP stands for very special old pale. The Cognac law states that all Cognacs used in these blends must be a minimum of eight years old, but in practice the average wood age is much older.
XO, Cordon Bleu, Centeur, Antique These are terms used to denote very old brandies with an average age of 30 years upwards.

VSOP and older Cognacs are termed 'liqueur brandies' and should be drunk on their own with nothing added.

The word 'Champagne' used in the regional classification has no connection with the sparkling wine of that name. It is the old French word for field or country, and was originally used because the ground or soil is similar to that found in the Champagne region.

Vintage cognacs are very rare, as the law states that they must be 100 per cent from the year stated. Therefore they cannot be topped up with younger brandies to replace the part which has evaporated.

Armagnac
This brandy is produced in the delimited (1909) region of Armagnac, the majority of which is in the *département* of Gers in south-west France. It is situated 150 km south of the Charente area where Cognac is produced. There are three regions: Haut-Armagnac, Bas-Armagnac (the best) and Ténarèze. There are two ACs: AC Bas-Armagnac and AC Armagnac.

The main grapes used are the same as for Cognac – St Emilion (Ugni Blanc), Folle Blanche (Picpoul) and Colombard. The grapes are picked, many by mechanical means, and made into a very dry and acidic wine. The distillation must then be completed (by law) before the end of April following the year of the harvest.

The traditional method of producing Armagnac is by using the travelling continuous or rectifying still rather than the pot still. However, it is a different type of continuous still to that used to produce other spirits; it has a much shorter rectifying column. Because the rectifying part is smaller the spirit is nothing like as pure as gin, vodka or grain whisky spirit. The spirit comes over the still at only 53% vol alcohol compared with Cognac which averages 72% vol, so there is more flavour left in it. The two largest producers of Armagnac, Janneau and Samalens, distil all their own Armagnac, but the travelling still is very important as the area is made up of many other smaller producers.

Since 1973 the Cognac pot still, which is manufactured in Cognac, has been used in Armagnac as well as the old continuous still. The pot stills are fixtures and cannot travel, so they are confined to the larger producers. Some of the larger producers use a combination of spirits from both types of still. The same method as for Cognac production of a double distillation is used. The resultant distillate (the *bonne chauffe*) is approximately 70% vol alcohol.

After distillation the spirit is placed in black oak casks – so called because the leaves of the oak trees are black in summer. This oak is very sappy and causes the Armagnac to mature more quickly than Cognac. The casks are not kept completely filled as a small amount of oxidation is necessary to produce a true Armagnac. After 8–10 years in wood the Armagnac will have developed its taste. After 20 years Armagnac is well matured, but in some cases can improve further. No caramel or sugar is added to Armagnac as is done with some Cognacs, as it obtains all its flavouring and colour from the distillation and maturing processes.

Similar designations to Cognac are used to denote age: Three Star, VSOP, Vieille Relique, Tres Vieille Réserve and so on. Vintage Armagnac is made but it is only slightly less rare than vintage Cognac.

Other grape brandies
Grape brandies are produced wherever wine is made. Some countries (such as Germany) import wine to make it into brandy.

The qualities of these brandies vary considerably, but with a few exceptions they are considerably lower in quality and in price than Cognac and Armagnac. One such exception sold in the UK is Asbach, which is produced in Germany from wine imported from France.

Marc

Marc brandy is made by distilling the fermented liquor obtained from steeping the grape pips and skins left after the grapes have been pressed for the production of wine. These brandies usually have a slightly perfumed bouquet and are less smooth than Cognac and Armagnac. Marc de Bourgogne is produced in Burgundy. A small percentage of it is sold at the Hospice de Beaune wine auction, and this is stated on the label. Marc de Champagne is made by most of the top Champagne houses.

Grappa is Italian grape residue brandy.

Fruit spirits

Brandy is the best known fruit spirit, but there are many others.

Calvados Calvados is produced in the *département* of Calvados in northern France. It is made by distilling cider, which is made from fermented apple juice (see later). It is dry, apple flavoured and brown in colour. One limited area has an *appellation contrôlée* – Calvados du Pays d'Auge. This Calvados must be made by a double pot still distillation, must age a minimum of two years in wood and be sold between 40% and 45% vol. Other regions producing Calvados may use AC Calvados.

Framboise Framboise is made from the distillation of fermented raspberries and is colourless. It is usually French, German or Swiss.

Kirsch Kirsch is made from the distillation of fermented cherries and is colourless. It is used extensively in cooking, and in particular it is used with fresh fruit. It is usually French, German or Swiss.

Mirabelle Mirabelle is made from the distillation of fermented *mirabelles*, which are small yellow plums. This spirit is again colourless.

Poire William This fruit spirit is made from the distillation of fermented pears and is colourless. It is usually French, German or Swiss.

Slivovitz This is made from the distillation of fermented plums and is colourless. It is made in Hungary, Yugoslavia and Romania.

Quetsch is similar to Slivovitz but is made in Alsace.

All these fruit spirits except Calvados are aged in glass, not wood; that is why they are colourless (*alcools blancs*).

Other spirits

Aniseed-based spirits

Pernod is a spirit flavoured with aniseed.

Pastis and *Ricard* are spirits flavoured with aniseed and liquorice. These and Pernod are yellow in colour.

Ouzo is a Greek spirit flavoured with aniseed, and is colourless.

All these aniseed aperitifs are usually served with iced water. They all turn cloudy with the addition of water, with ouzo becoming milky.

Bitters

Bitters are spirits which have been infused with strongly flavoured plants, roots, bark, etc. They are served as aperitifs or used to flavour other drinks.

Angostura bitters Produced in Trinidad from rum, gentian, vegetable spices and vegetable colouring matter. It is brownish red in colour and used for the 'pink' in Pink Gin. It is 44.7% vol of alcohol.

Amer Picon This French bitters is orange flavoured and light red in colour. It is usually served as an aperitif.

Campari Well known Italian bitters served as an aperitif. It is flavoured with herbs and spices and is red in colour.

Fernet Branca Produced in Italy and France, it is particularly strongly flavoured. It is dark brown in colour.

Orange bitters Produced from spirit flavoured with Seville orange peel, it is used in cocktails and other mixed drinks.

Peach bitters Produced from spirit flavoured with peaches, it is used in mixed drinks and cocktails.

Sake

This is produced in Japan from fermented rice. It is a wine, not a spirit.

Schnapps and aquavit

This is a Dutch, Danish or German spirit made from the distillation of fermented grain. Aquavit is the national drink of Scandinavia; it is flavoured with caraway, but is a type of schnapps.

Tequila

This is a Mexican spirit which is made from the fermented juice of the cactus (*agave*).

Liqueurs

Liqueurs are sweetened flavoured spirits.

Advocaat A low-strength liqueur, yellow in colour, made from egg yolks and brandy. The best is produced in Holland.

Amaretto A brown coloured Italian liqueur flavoured with apricot kernels, tasting almost of marzipan.

Apricot brandy A golden coloured liqueur usually made from apricots and brandy, the best being flavoured with apricot kernels.

Bénédictine French golden coloured liqueur produced at the Monastery at Fécamp in Normandy. It is made from a mixture of brandy and a large number of herbs.

Chartreuse A high-quality French liqueur flavoured with herbs and produced by monks at Grenoble. There are two strengths: green Chartreuse at 55% vol and yellow Chartreuse at 43% vol.

Cherry brandy A reddish-brown cherry flavoured liqueur produced in many countries.

Chocolate liqueurs *Crème de cacao* is a brown or colourless chocolate flavoured liqueur produced in many countries. *Royal Mint chocolate liqueur* is a pale green mint and chocolate flavoured liqueur.

Coconut liqueurs Malibu is a colourless low-strength coconut flavoured liqueur, with a base of Jamaican light rum.

Coffee liqueurs Tia maria is a Jamaican dark brown liqueur made from rum, coffee and spices. Kahlúa is a Mexican brown liqueur made from rum and coffee. It is produced in Denmark under licence. There are many other coffee flavoured liqueurs made in various countries, e.g. *crème de café*.

Cointreau French, orange flavoured liqueur made in Angers. It is named after the family that produces it. It is colourless.

Cream liqueurs Baileys Original cream liqueur is a blend of Irish cream and Irish whiskey. Devonshire Royal cream liqueur is a blend of whisky, brandy and Devonshire cream. These are just two of the many cream liqueurs now on the market.

Curaçao Similar to Cointreau, this liqueur is made from spirit and orange peel. It is made in various colours – brown, red, blue and green. *Triple sec* is another name for the same product.

Galliano Italian herb flavoured yellow liqueur, owing its popularity in the UK to the cocktail Harvey Wallbanger.

Grand Marnier Orange flavoured liqueur using Cognac as its base, produced in France. There are two varieties, *cordon rouge* and *cordon jaune*, the former being of the higher strength. Both are golden brown in colour.

Kümmel Originating in Holland, it is a colourless caraway flavoured liqueur.

Maraschino A colourless cherry flavoured liqueur produced in Italy. It is made from the distillate of fermented maraschino cherries.

Mint liqueurs *Crème de menthe* is a mint

flavoured liqueur, either green or colourless. Freezomint is the name given to *crème de menthe* made by Cusenier.

Sambuca An Italian colourless liqueur with a flavour of liquorice and elderberry.

Scotch-based liqueurs These are liqueurs using Scotch whisky as their base. Drambuie, Glayva and Glen Mist are all golden coloured liqueurs produced in Scotland from Scotch whisky, herbs and honey. These whisky liqueurs must not be confused with liqueur whiskies which are old mature whiskies.

Southern Comfort This is another golden coloured whisky liqueur made from a base of bourbon whiskey, peaches and oranges.

Strega An Italian herb and bark flavoured yellow liqueur.

Beers: ales, stouts and lagers

All beers are brewed as shown in Figure 6.4. The various colours and flavours are obtained by the use of various types and colours of malt.

Malt is made by steeping barley in water for 48–72 hours until it begins to germinate. When this occurs the starches in the grain are converted to sugars. The grains are then dried by hot air in a kiln, which stops any further growth. The grain is then 'cooked' to the required colour and flavour. Light malt and crystal malts are used for light ales, bitters and lagers. Chocolate malt and black malts are used for mild ales and stouts.

Next the malt is 'cracked' in a mill, producing grist. This is mixed with hot liquor (water) at 65–66°C for two hours. The flavour has now been drawn out of the malt, and the wort (as the liquid is now called) is run off into a copper. Here it is boiled for 1¾ hours with sugar syrup and hops. The wort is then run off into the hop-back where it settles before being strained off into a paraflow (heat exchange) system, which cools it to 15–16°C. The wort is then moved on to the fermenting vessel. Yeast

(*Saccharomyces cerevisiae*) is added, and fermentation starts and continues for about seven days.

The beer now either goes into a storage tank for 3–21 days (lager is longer) to await bottling or kegging, or after two or three days is put into casks for cask-conditioned beer.

For lager production the yeast *Saccharomyces carlsbergensis* is used. This is a bottom fermentation yeast, working at the bottom of the fermentation vessel rather than at the top. The fermentation takes longer than for other beers because the temperature is much lower. The lager beer is then run off into storage tanks called lagering vessels for 10–24 weeks, where the beer is conditioned at a temperature of 1–3°C. The lager will withstand low temperatures after this without turning cloudy.

The majority of bottled beers are pasteurized and are therefore free of sediment. White Shield Worthington, Red Label (triangle) Bass and Guinness are beers which contain sediment, caused by yeast being left in the bottle to ferment. These beers must therefore be stored and served with more care.

The average strength of beer is approximately 4% vol of alcohol, but there may be as much as 10% vol of alcohol in the strongest beers. These very strong beers are normally sold in small bottle sizes of about 180 ml (6.3 fl oz).

Cider and perry

Cider is the alcoholic beverage obtained from fermented apple juice, or a mixture of apple and a maximum of 25 per cent pear juice. Perry is the alcoholic beverage obtained from fermented pear juice, or a mixture of pear and a maximum of 25 per cent apple juice.

After the cider apples are harvested in October/November, they are sliced or grated (the old method was to pound them) before pressing. The juice is then fermented at a temperature of 18–24°C for from four to six

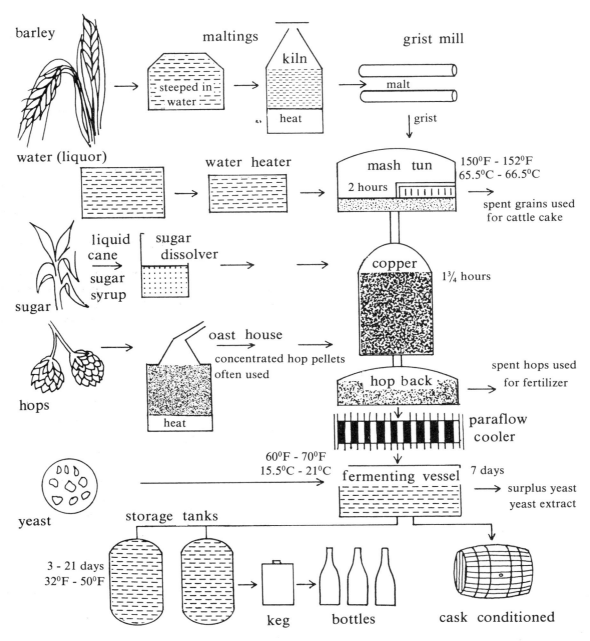

Figure 6.4 *The brewing process*

weeks. Sometimes the cider has carbon dioxide pumped into it, or is given a secondary fermentation by adding yeast and sugar to it. Perries are usually either carbonated or subjected to a second fermentation.

Cider has a strength of between 4% and 8% vol of alcohol. The legal limits for cider alcoholic strengths are 1.14%–8.5% vol.

Minerals

Natural mineral waters

Natural mineral waters must originate in a ground water body or deposit. All natural mineral waters which are intended for human consumption must be extracted from the ground through a spring, well or borehole.

Bottled natural mineral waters may be either still or sparkling. Sparkling mineral waters are labelled: either carbonated natural mineral water, naturally carbonated natural mineral water, or natural mineral water fortified with gas from the spring.

All natural mineral waters must be bottled at the place of origin without any additions or treatment other than filtration to remove iron or sulphur, and the addition of carbon dioxide.

Natural mineral waters contain mineral salts and have been proved to be beneficial to health.

Some of the better known mineral waters are given below.

Aerated waters and mixers

Manufactured aerated waters (often termed minerals) contain flavourings, for example lemonade, orangeade, cherryade, ginger beer and cola. All these are best served chilled. They are drunk on their own or mixed with other drinks, e.g. Cinzano and lemonade.

Mixers are the same as manufactured aerated waters but are considered more as mixing drinks, although they are also very popular drunk on their own. They are in styles and

Some well known mineral waters

Name	Origin	Mineral content	Style
Apollinaris	Ahr Valley, Germany	High	Sparkling
Badoit	Saint-Galmier, France	Low	Sparkling
Contrexéville	Contrexéville, France	High	Still
Évian	Évian, France	Low	Still
Perrier	France	Low	Sparkling
San Pellegrino	Italy	Medium	Sparkling
Vichy Célestins	France	High	Sparkling
Vittel	France	Medium to high	Still
Spar Reine	Belgium	Low	Still
Spar Marie-Henriette	Belgium	Medium	Sparkling
Vichy Catalán	Spain	High	Sparkling
Henniez	Switzerland	Medium	Still and sparkling
Buxton Spring Water	Buxton, England	Low	Still and sparkling
Malvern	Malvern, England	Low	Still and sparkling
Ashbourne	Ashbourne, England	Low	Still
Highland Spring	Blackford, Scotland	Low	Still and sparkling
Mountain Valley Water	Arkansas, USA	Low	Still

flavours which mix very well with spirits, e.g. gin and tonic. The most common mixers are:

Bitter lemon   Contains lemons and quinine.
Ginger ale (original dry ginger ale, American, and Canadian) Ginger flavoured, golden brown coloured.
Ruschian   Peach flavoured, rosé coloured.
Soda water   Colourless.
Tonic water   Contains quinine and is colourless.

Juices, syrups and cordials

Fruit juices

Fresh fruit juices may be extracted from fresh fruit in the bar with the juice extractor, but the most common bar fruit juice is bottled in 113 ml (4 fl oz) bottles.

Many bars use bottled lemon juice in their cocktails, but this often produces a different flavour to the original recipe.

The most common juices available are orange, lemon, grapefruit, pineapple, passion fruit and mixed fruits.

If freshly extracted juice is served, castor sugar should be offered with it, together with ice and straws.

Syrups

Syrups may be diluted to make a long drink or used in the preparation of mixed drinks and cocktails. Some of the more common ones are:

Name	Flavour	Colour
Cassis	Blackcurrant	Purple
Citron	Lemon	Yellow
Framboise	Raspberry	Red
Gomme	Sugar	Colourless
Grenadine	Pomegranate	Red
Orgeat	Almond	Colourless

Cordials

Cordials may be alcoholic or non-alcoholic. Lime juice cordial is the best known non-alcoholic cordial.

Alcoholic cordials are usually drunk in a combination with one or more other drinks. They are often added to spirits, e.g. rum and peppermint, or used in cocktail recipes. They have a long history in England; they were very popular in country districts and in particular in the West Country. Phillips of Bristol are one of the oldest and finest producers of cordials, and their range is listed below:

Green peppermint, white peppermint (5% vol) Mint grown at Mitcham in Surrey (known as Mitcham mint) is used to flavour these cordials. They can be drunk neat and are thought to be good for stomach upsets. The most common mixed drink is rum and peppermint.
Lovage (8% vol) This cordial is flavoured with celery, herbs and spices and is considered to be a good pick-me-up. Its recipe originated in Devon and it is still popular there. The most common mixed drink is brandy and lovage.
Shrub (6% vol) Shrub is flavoured with a blend of herbs and spices. Its recipe originated in Cornwall, and it is very popular in the West Country. The most common mixed drink is rum and shrub.
Aniseed (5% vol) The aniseed flavouring comes from the seeds of the anise plant. It is most commonly drunk mixed with spirits.
Pink cloves (7.5% vol) This is made from pink cloves produced in Zanzibar, and is used in any drink where the recipe calls for cloves, e.g. punches and cups. If added to vodka or gin it will not only flavour them but impart a pink flush.
Grenadine (8% vol) This red coloured cordial, like the syrup of the same name, has a pomegranate flavour. It is used in many cocktail recipes.

Chapter Seven

Taking beverage orders

Taking orders at the table

Wine list presentation

The host is the person who will give the drinks order to the sommelier. He or she may be identified as the person who has made the booking and, on arrival at the restaurant, the person who confirms his or her booking with the head waiter or restaurant manager. The head waiter or restaurant manager should inform the sommelier as to who is the host when the party has been seated.

If the customers are a chance party then the sommelier can approach the table and say 'Good evening, ladies and gentlemen, may I take your aperitif order?' The host normally takes charge and places the order; the sommelier will then know to whom he should offer the (opened) wine list. If the party is of two persons, a woman and a man, it is normal procedure for the sommelier to say 'Good evening, madam, sir, may I take your aperitif order?', addressing this request to the man. The 'Madam, sir' may be omitted from the greeting or, if the group is just women or just men, may be replaced by 'Good evening, ladies' or 'Good evening gentlemen.' The sommelier should then stand to the right of the host when taking the order.

The beverage list is the *shop window* for the drinks of the establishment. The sommelier must ensure that all these lists are clean and up to date. He must ensure that he has a working knowledge of all the drinks on the list and the composition of the dishes on the menu, so that recommendations may be made to customers. If any item on the list is temporarily unavailable the sommelier should point this fact out to the customer when the list is presented.

Recommending wines

When making recommendations the sommelier needs to judge the quality and price range with which the customer will be happy, and recommend accordingly. The sommelier must realize that it is the customer that has to be pleased with the choice, not the sommelier! Consequently the character of the wine must be made clear to the customer, e.g. whether the wine is red or white, still or sparkling, dry or sweet.

As a starting point for the sommelier when making recommendations, some general rules are:

1   Dry wines before sweet wines
2   White wines before red wines
3   White wines with fish and some white meats
4   Red wines with strongly flavoured meat dishes, red meats and game
5   Sweet still and sparkling wines with sweets

However, there is more to recommending than this.

Matching wine with food

Much has been written about matching wine with food, and people's ideas and preferences do vary as to which wines complement which dishes. No one person sat down and made rules; the classic marriages of wine and food came about by common usage.

Some writers have suggested that drinking the 'right' wine with the 'right' food is just snobbishness and not really necessary. However, consider the following:

1   Chablis served with curry.
2   Châteauneuf-du-Pape served with a poached fillet of sole with a white wine sauce.

In example 1 an excellent wine will be completely overpowered by the strong flavours in the curry, and thus wasted. In example 2 the reverse is the case, with the strong flavour of the wine overpowering the delicate flavours of the fish dish. It is apparent from these two examples that care should be taken when recommending wines with foods, in order to achieve the best combinations and enable the maximum enjoyment and value to be obtained from both the wine and food.

A perfect marriage of wine and food is when the wine tastes better when drunk with a certain dish, and the dish is enhanced when served with this wine. Ideally the enjoyment value of the wine and the dish together should exceed the sum of the enjoyment of the two components on their own.

When recommending or selecting a wine or wines, thought must also be given to what is to follow, so that an earlier wine does not spoil a later one. The following rules, some of which have already been mentioned, will help: dry wine before sweet; light wine before heavy; young wine before old; and white wine before red, except for the heavy sweet white wines which are served with the sweet or at the end of a meal.

Suggesting aperitifs

The purpose of the aperitif before a meal is threefold: to stimulate the palate for the meal to come; to satisfy a thirst; and to make the person drinking it feel relaxed.

Some suggestions for aperitifs are:

Champagne and other dry sparkling wines
Dry white wines such as white Burgundies, Soave, Muscadet, Sancerre, Vinho Verde, white Graves, Alsace Rieslings and Sylvaners
Sherries
Vermouths
Cocktails
Mixed drinks such as gin and tonic.

Recommendations for specific dishes

When recommending wines to accompany individual courses, remember that it is unusual for people to have a separate wine with each course of a long meal, and that customers invariably choose different dishes for different courses. It is often necessary therefore to recommend a compromise wine (or wines) which will satisfy all parties.

The following suggestions for wines with foods is meant to be a useful guide, and is not a full list of all the suitable wines.

Hors-d'oeuvres   Hors-d'oeuvres vary in content. Those containing vinegar should be served without wine as vinegar will kill wines. However, for most hors-d'oeuvres the following will be suitable: Chablis, Alsace Riesling, Sylvaner and Tokay Pinot Gris, Soave, Muscadet, Sancerre, Pouilly-Fumé, Mâcon Blanc, Vinho Verde, and other dry white wines.
Shellfish and other fish dishes   Recommend dry white wines similar to those for hors-d'oeuvres, plus the fuller-bodied white Burgundies, Mosel wines, some medium dry wines such as Vouvray, and Chenin Blanc wines from South Africa, California, and Australia. The stronger the flavour of the fish or the sauce, the stronger and more full-bodied the wine should be.

Chinese meals and quiches Try white Dão, white Graves, Vinho Verde, Soave, Hocks and Mosel wines, dry and medium Loire white wines, and Beaujolais.

Pasta dishes With spaghetti bolognese and other pasta dishes, suggest Chianti, Valpolicella and other red Italian wines, Navarra, Valdepeñas, Bairrada, Fitou, Corbières, and Côtes du Rhône reds.

White meat dishes and chicken Recommend light red wines such as Beaujolais, Touraine and Valpolicella; rosé wines; and Hocks, Mosels and other medium dry wines.

Grilled meats, roast meats, game, stews, casseroles, offals Suggest *crus* Beaujolais, clarets (particularly with roast lamb), red Burgundy, Red Dão, Côtes du Rhône red wines, Barolo, Barbaresco, Chianti and other red Italian wines, Pinotage, red Rioja and other red wines.

Cheese The wine served with the red meat course will accompany most cheeses. Thus the French take the cheese course directly after the main course, continuing with the same wine. Strong cheeses require strong wines, mild cheeses less strong wines. If a separate wine is to be served then try vintage port, late bottled and tawny ports, Barolo, Chianti, clarets and red Burgundies. In rare cases suggest heavy sweet wines, e.g. Château d'Yquem with Roquefort cheese, as offered at Château Yquem.

Sweets Wines with sweets, often referred to a little irreverently as pudding wines, are making a little bit of a comeback in popularity. The wine should be sweet and luscious, or medium to sweet and sparkling. Suggest Champagne, Asti Spumante, light red or rosé sparkling Italian wines such as Malvasia; or still wines such as *Spätlese* and *Auslese* Hocks and Mosels, Sauternes, Barsac, Coteaux-du-Layon and Muscat-de-Beaumes-de-Venise.

Coffee Serve with Cognac, Armagnac, liqueurs or port.

Writing the check

When an order has been taken by the sommelier, a check in duplicate or triplicate should be prepared. Some small establishments will use a single-sheet check pad, and this will be used by the person who prepares the bill.

The following should always be included on the check:

1 Date
2 Table number
3 Number of covers
4 Initials of the sommelier
5 Customer's room number if he is a resident of the hotel

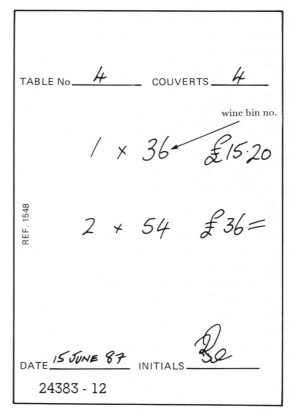

Figure 7.1 *Example of wine order*

6 Customer's signature (usually) if he is a resident

7 Name, quantity and price of drink required

The order must be clearly written, and if a wine is ordered it should be written on the check as the bin number shown on the wine list (see Figure 7.1).

The top copy should always be presented to the issuing department, i.e. dispense, cellar or bar. The duplicate should be used by the person who is preparing the bill. This copy will then be sent with a copy of the bill to the control office. It will be married up (matched) with the top copy which will have come from the issuing department.

Functions

Advance orders for functions should be entered on the banqueting memorandum, and a confirmation of this order should be sent in writing to the organizer.

Credit drinks sold during the course of a function should be authorized by the organizer and signed for at the end of the function. Where there is a request for a credit bar for before or after a meal, it is normal practice to agree a maximum cost. If this is to be exceeded, authorization should be obtained from the organizer before it is allowed to occur.

When taking liqueur and brandy orders at the table, it is sensible to make a sketch of the table and to write in the orders showing the position of the people who have ordered them (see Figure 7.2). If the sommelier cannot distinguish the drinks by appearance, he can place them on the tray in the same order as shown on the sketch.

Cash drinks at functions
Shortened wine lists are usually provided for functions. This will reduce the chance of a wine

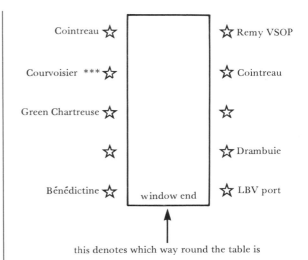

Figure 7.2 *Sketch of table for taking liqueur and brandy order*

running out. In addition the wines can be prepared with more confidence for service in advance, i.e. chilling white and sparkling wines, and ensuring that red wines are at room temperature.

Normally the majority of the cash wine orders are taken at a desk in the reception area close to the table plan, where orders may be placed by the guests. The staff taking the orders write down the customer's name, table number and the order before passing this on to the sommelier who is serving the table. The sommelier is therefore able to obtain and prepare the wine in advance.

The sommelier will write out a duplicate or triplicate check for the order. He will pass on one copy to the dispense bar or other issuing department, keeping the other copy or copies so that he may present one to the customer when the liqueurs and brandies have been served. If the triplicate system is used, one of the copies is available to be given to the customer as a receipt.

Taking orders at the bar

Suitable drinks for receptions

Most dry white wines and sparkling wines are suitable for aperitifs and reception drinks. Cocktails are also suitable for aperitifs, but not for a large number at a reception as they take time to prepare. An exception to this is a Champagne Cocktail, as this is easily prepared for large numbers.

Sherries, spirits and mixers, vermouths and many other drinks are excellent for these occasions. Soft drinks should always be offered, juices being universally popular.

If set wine is being served from a dispense bar for a function, as a general rule the bottles should have had their corks removed in advance.

Recording orders and sales

Orders should be made out on check pads and one copy should be presented to the dispense bar as described earlier for table orders.

In an open bar, sales should be recorded on an electronic or mechanical till and the correct cash value placed in the till drawer. The till drawer must always be kept closed when not being used for a sale. The till roll will record all sales as entered on the keys of the till. It is a sensible control to enter different categories of drinks under different keys so that an analysis can be produced at the end of the service, for example:

Key 1:   enter all cash drinks
Key 2:   enter all booked bar drinks
Key 3:   enter all booked wines
Key 4:   enter all bar snacks money

If the drinks are to be booked to a room number, the room number must be written clearly on the check and the customer's signature obtained.

These checks are entered on a summary sheet and sent with this sheet to the cashier.

When a note is offered for payment for drinks, state the value of the note and place it outside the till drawer (some tills have clips for this purpose) until the correct change has been taken from the till and checked. The note should then be placed in the till drawer and the drawer closed.

Credit cards should be checked against any list of stolen cards which is available. Check the date of validity and the name of the holder. The signature of the customer, which must be written on the voucher in front of the cashier, must be compared with the signature on the card. If the value required is high, a check on whether this amount of credit is available to the customer may be made by telephoning the credit card company. In addition, for room accounts follow the procedure described above.

Customer accounts should be prepared before the customer leaves the establishment, and they should be agreed and signed by the customer. A headed bill should be prepared and sent to the customer as soon as possible.

If cheques are to be accepted for payment, these must be accompanied by a cheque card. Confirm the following:

1 The dates of validity must be checked.
2 The name on the card must coincide with the name on the cheque.
3 The cheque must come from the same bank as the one stated on the card.
4 The value of the cheque must not exceed the limit stated on the card.
5 The signature on the card must match the one written on the cheque in front of the receiver. If there is any doubt as to the authenticity of the signature, the customer should be requested to sign his name again on the back of the cheque.
6 The cheque card number must be recorded by the receiver on the back of the cheque.

Chapter Eight

Serving beverages and tobacco

Choice of glasses

Glasses have evolved to enable the particular characteristics of different drinks to be appreciated to the full.

Whatever the shape or size of glass, it must be sound (with no chips) and highly polished when placed on a table or used for the service of a drink. If a major part of the enjoyment of a drink is the appreciation of its appearance and bouquet then a glass with a full bowl should be used, whereas for a drink such as gin and tonic or vodka and lime the size of the glass is a more important factor.

The shapes and sizes of glasses have changed over the years as more people have come to understand the best way to enjoy the various drinks. Glasses with coloured bowls should be reserved for ornaments; glasses for drinking should always have a clear glass bowl.

Sherries

The classic glass for the service of a sherry is the *copita*. The shape of this glass (Figure 8.1) concentrates the bouquet of the wine at the top of the glass. However, it is difficult to wash and polish and is liable to have a high breakage rate.

The next best glass for sherry is one which is large enough to be filled about one-third full by $\frac{1}{3}$ gill, which is the normal measure for sherry (Figure 8.1).

Various other glasses are used and many of

Elgin   Copita   Sherry

Figure 8.1   *Sherry glasses*

these are a measure in themselves when filled to the top. These do not allow the bouquet of sherry to be appreciated fully.

The commonest commercial sherry glass in the UK is the Elgin. This is not very suitable for the enjoyment of sherry, but is very economical and robust (Figure 8.1).

Another acceptable sherry glass is a stemmed glass with a small bowl, which is the type often found in homes (Figure 8.1).

Port

Port is often served in a glass just large enough to take a $\frac{1}{3}$ gill when filled nearly to the top. When a wine such as vintage port has been maturing for ten years upwards it is deserving of better treatment. A similar glass to the second glass suggested for sherry, or a 11–14 cl Paris goblet would be most suitable, once again allowing the bouquet to be fully appreciated. Fortunately for those who enjoy port, the present trend is towards this larger glass. Other fortified wines can be served in the same type of glass.

Still wines

Many shapes and styles of glass are suitable for the service of still wines. Once again the glass should be large enough for the appearance and bouquet of the wine to be appreciated.

It is becoming the practice to use a suite of glasses of different sizes for red, white, sparkling and dessert wines (Figure 8.2). The red and white wine glasses should be of a minimum capacity of 20 cl. If different sizes are used for red and white wines, then the red wine glass is now normally the larger glass; for example, use 20 cl for white and 25 cl or larger for red wine. Dessert wines are often served in smaller

Figure 8.2 *Commercial glasses*

glasses, as smaller measures of these wines are normally served when they are offered towards the end of a meal. A 14 cl glass would be the minimum satisfactory size.

German wines are traditionally served in tall green- or amber-stemmed glasses (Figure 8.3). Green stems are used for Mosel wines and amber stems for Hocks or Rhine wines. The light which is refracted through these stems and into the wine tends to accentuate the natural colouring of the wine. The highest-priced Hocks (Rhine wines) are sweet and amber in colour, whereas Mosel wines are a light straw colour with just a hint of greenness. The traditional German glass is the *Römer*, which is also either green or amber stemmed. This glass has a hollow stem and base which causes more coloured light to be refracted into the wine.

Wine served by the glass may be served in any quantity at present in the UK, although there is a code of practice (see Chapter 11) which recommends that the size of the measure of wine served should be stated and that the glass should have a line on it showing the level to which it should be filled. A useful measure

would be 12.5 cl, as this would give exactly eight glasses of wine from a litre bottle and six glasses of wine from a 75 cl bottle.

Sparkling wines

Much time and effort and not a little expertise go into the production of a quality sparkling wine. Therefore the glass used for its service must be one which offers the customer the maximum pleasure and enjoyment. The most suitable style of glass will be one which enables the customer to enjoy the wine's bouquet to the full, and the wine to show off its elegance and effervescence without losing its sparkle too quickly.

The best glass for these wines will have an elongated bowl of minimum size 22 cl, coming in towards the top, with a medium stem (Figure 8.4). Other glasses may be better suited to commercial establishments because of their ease of cleaning and polishing. If there are no tulip-shaped or tall glasses available, a Paris goblet is the next best glass to use.

Never use a saucer-shaped glass for the service of sparkling wine. The bowl is too shallow and too wide which causes the bouquet and effervescence to dissipate quickly.

Liqueurs

Liqueurs are often served in glasses which are the size of a measure, 1/6 gill or six out, which is very useful when serving large numbers quickly such as for a banquet. It also prevents loss of the liqueur through some of it adhering to the inside of a thimble measure (which would also need to be washed after the service of each liqueur). Liqueurs are usually quite thick and sticky, so again small glasses have an advantage over large ones in that less of the liqueur will get left in the glass sticking to its inside.

The Elgin shape is again very popular, the glass being the measure, and it does show off the appearance of the liqueur. Other glasses

Römer   Hock Mosel

green stem for mosel   amber for hock

Figure 8.3 *German wine glasses*

Champagne   Saucer   Cocktail   Brandy

Figure 8.4   *Champagne glasses*

(e.g. a small brandy glass) are not measures in themselves but allow the bouquet of the liqueur to be fully appreciated.

Cocktails

Cocktail glasses vary considerably like the drinks they hold, and are chosen for their shape and size to suit the cocktails being offered. Cocktails usually fill the glass, whereas wine should never do so; therefore a variety of sizes may be used in one bar (Figure 8.5). Many of the original cocktails were small quantities, usually about 5–6 cl or just over 1/3 gill; the modern trend is for larger cocktails, and consequently the glasses are now larger.

Beers

Draught beer glasses in this country are regulated in size. By law draught beer must be served in 1/3 pt, 1/2 pt or 1 pt measures. They must be government stamped and must be filled up to the brim or up to a line marked on the glass showing the correct level. The 1/3 measure is rarely used.

Bottled beers may be served in unstamped Worthington, Wellington, Paris or Slim Jim glasses, usually of 35 cl which allows for a head on the beer. Bottled nip beers are served in smaller glasses, e.g. 22 cl Paris goblets or the same size Wellington glasses (see Figure 8.5).

Brandies

Three-star brandy served with soda or ginger ale should be put into a 20 cl Paris goblet.

Brandy on its own should be served in a brandy balloon. These vary in size, but the most practical size for everyday use is 20–25 cl. Some brandy balloons are as large as 55 cl, but these are very expensive, take up a lot of shelf space and are liable to get broken more easily than the smaller ones. The brandy will cling to the inside of the glass and therefore more will be left behind in the larger glasses and wasted by the customer.

A good brandy balloon is made from thin glass to enable the drinker to warm the brandy in the glass in the palm of the hand quite quickly. Brandy balloons should not be warmed over a flame.

Figure 8.5 *Cocktail, beer and other glasses*

Other spirits

When whisky is served straight or with water it may be served in a 14–20 cl Paris goblet, club goblet, small tumbler, Old-Fashioned glass, or a highball glass. If it is to be served with a mixer such as dry ginger it should be served in one of these types, of minimum size 20 cl.

Gin, rum and vodka are served in similar glasses.

Minerals

Minerals may be served in Paris goblets, Slim Jims, tumblers and highball glasses.

Temperatures

Temperature ranges for the service of wine are open to much discussion and individual choice, but there are general rules of thumb which should be followed.

Red wines

Light-bodied red wines which are young often benefit from being served very slightly cooler than full-bodied reds – at about 13°C, which is slightly above a perfect cellar temperature. Some light red wines such as Beaujolais Nouveau are at their best served slightly cooler – at 10–13°C.

Full-bodied red wines should always be served *chambré*, which means at 18–21°C. To ensure that red wines are at the correct temperature for service, many establishments keep a stock of wines in a dispense area or in the restaurant itself. One problem of keeping the wine in the restaurant is that there is usually a great fluctuation of temperature over each day, which is bad for the wine and will cause it to deteriorate.

White wines

White wine should be served cool or chilled. Many wines are served too cold in the UK, thus preventing the full flavour of the wine to be enjoyed to the full. If a white wine is of a poor quality, it is best to chill it well; then its poor flavour will be masked by the cold temperature and not tasted.

The lighter and more delicate white wines should be served cool or, as the French say, *frais*. This is at 10–12°C. Heavy sweet white wines such as Sauternes and Muscat-de-Beaumes-de-Venise are at their best served cooler at 6–9°C. Sweet white wines should be served cooler than dry white wines.

Other beverages

Rosé wines are at their best when served cool – *frais*.

Sparkling wines contain carbon dioxide gas which expands when warmed and contracts when chilled. These wines are at their best when served chilled at 6–8°C. If the wine is too cold the flavours will be masked.

Dry sherries and the drier Madeiras are best served cool or slightly chilled at 10–13°C. A modern trend is to drink all sherries at this temperature. Sweet Madeiras, ruby and vintage ports should be served at 18–21°C. The better quality tawny ports are best served slightly cooler at 12–16°C.

Mineral waters should be served chilled at 6–7°C as for sparkling wines.

Beers Draught bitter beers and bottled light ales are best served at 12–14°C or cellar temperature. Draught and bottled lager is best served cooler at 9–11°C. Bottled brown ales and stouts are served at room temperature. Some people prefer bottled beers to be cooler than room temperature, so it is normal practice to keep some of each on a cooling shelf and to ask the customer which he prefers.

Serving wine

Identification of the host or hostess

The host or hostess should be identified when a party arrives in the establishment. He or she is usually the person who checks the reservation of the party (if previously booked) with the restaurant manager on arrival, or requests a table if they are chance customers. The host or hostess also usually handles the ordering of the meal. Chapter 7 further covers identification of the host and welcoming of customers.

Carafes

Carafes are open glass containers into which wine is poured for service of wine by the carafe. This is a method of serving 'house' wines, which are often in 1 litre or 1.5 litre bottles. The legally permitted quantities for service in carafes are 25, 50, 75 and 100 cl, and 10 and 20 fl oz; and the quantities which are being served must be clearly stated on the wine list by law. The

amount served must have an exact measure of one of the above quantities, so carafes now have a line marked on them showing how full to fill them. Unlined carafes may be used, but in this case the wine must be measured exactly before it is poured into the carafe. The shape of the carafe must be such that the carafe will empty of all its contents when tilted at an angle of 30° with the horizontal or 120° with the vertical (Figure 8.6).

Coolers and ice buckets

Coolers are open-topped double-walled plastic cylinders which keep prechilled bottles of wine cool at the table (see Figure 2.24). Most coolers do not cool the wine; they merely maintain its temperature, and then only for a short period. However, a variety of cooler is available which has two small freezer packs to insert to keep the wine cooler for longer.

Ice buckets (also called coolers) are filled with ice and water and are used to cool white, rosé

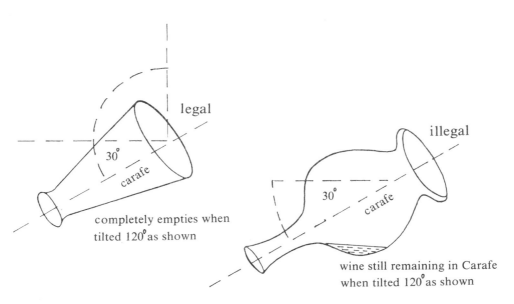

Figure 8.6 *Carafe design*

Figure 8.7 *Ice cooler and bucket*

and sparkling wine to the required temperature for service (see Figure 2.25). As much as possible of the bottle should be submerged in the ice and water to chill the wine effectively. Cold liquid remains below warm, so that if only the lower part of the bottle is in the ice and water the upper part of the wine will not cool down very quickly. It is therefore a wise precaution to slightly tilt the bottle when removing it from an ice bucket so that the wine in the top of the bottle will mix with the rest. Then when the customer is offered a taste he will be given wine which is at the temperature of the whole bottle.

If the wine bucket is to be taken to the restaurant table it should be placed either in a wine cooler stand on the floor to the right of the host, or on a plate or silver flat on the restaurant table. A crisp clean napkin should be draped over the top of the bucket in either case, which will enable the customer to serve himself if the sommelier is not available. It also improves the presentation.

When the wine has reached the required coolness it is sometimes advisable to remove the bottle, or part bottle if some has been poured from it, from the ice and to wipe the water off it. It should then be placed on either a coaster or a side plate on the restaurant table in front of the host. This will prevent the wine from becoming over-chilled.

Placing glasses on the table

If wine has been ordered in advance, which is often the case with functions, and where wine orders are taken in the bar before the customers enter the restaurant, the required glasses should be placed on the table before the customer arrives at the table (Figure 8.8).

The glasses should be arranged in a neat and tidy manner. They should be highly polished and placed upside down on the table until just prior to service. The glasses should be lined up with each other right along the table's length; this particularly applies when laying up tables for functions. Ensure that the bases of the glasses are highly polished as well as the bowls. Always carry glasses to and from tables on a salver. Handle them by the stem or base, *never* by the bowl.

If the wines are not ordered in advance then it is usual to lay up one or two glasses, one for water and one for wine. If the wine order is placed by the customer at the table then glasses for this wine should be placed on the table before the wine is presented for service.

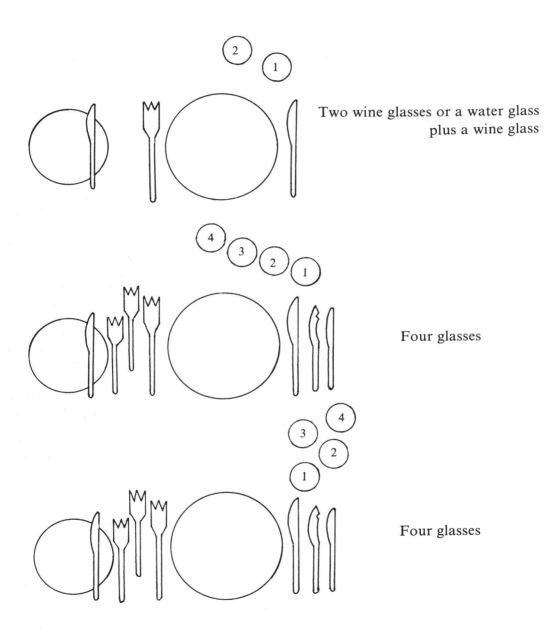

Two wine glasses or a water glass
plus a wine glass

Four glasses

Four glasses

Figure 8.8   *Placing glasses on the table*

Presenting and opening the bottle

When a bottle of wine has been ordered the sommelier should always present the bottle to the host on his right hand side, showing the label. This is to ensure that it is the wine which the host has ordered. There should be a cloth under the bottle; one hand is under the cloth, the other steadies the bottle (Figure 8.9a). It is a sensible precaution to say the name of the wine, as sometimes the customer is not fully concentrating on checking the wine, and many labels are similar. It is then prepared as necessary.

If the wine has been placed in an ice bucket, it should be taken out and wiped dry with a clean service cloth or clean napkin.

The capsule of the bottle must be cut *below* the glass ring on the top of the bottle and the part of the capsule above this point must be removed, otherwise small particles of dirt from under the capsule may get into the wine. The knife of the corkscrew should be angled up against this glass ring so that a clean straight cut is obtained (Figure 8.9b). The top of the neck of the bottle is then wiped clean with the clean service cloth or napkin.

The corkscrew must be inserted into the centre of the cork and screwed down enough for the screw to reach to the base of the cork, but not go through the bottom of it. Brace the lever of the corkscrew on the top edge of the bottle and lever the cork almost out of the bottle with the right hand, steadying the lever with the forefinger of the left hand and holding the neck of the bottle with the rest of the hand. The lever should be kept vertical during this part of the process (Figure 8.9c). The cork is finally removed by gripping the cork with thumb and forefinger and easing it out (without making a popping noise) (Figure 8.8d). The cork should then be removed from the corkscrew and the neck of the bottle wiped clean (Figure 8.9e).

If a small piece of cork breaks off and falls into the bottle of wine, the sommelier should remove this by giving the bottle a sharp flick into the cloth or over a sink if in a dispense bar or service area. The piece of cork should come out. If the cork or part of the cork gets pushed right into the wine in the bottle, it should be removed with a cork extractor (Figure 8.9f). This should be done at the sidetable, not at the customer's table. If it is impossible to remove the cork in this way, the bottle should be decanted or replaced.

Pouring the wine

After the cork has been removed and the neck of the bottle wiped the sommelier can smell the top of the bottle to ensure the wine is sound. A small quantity is poured into the glass of the host or hostess, from the right hand side of the customer, ensuring that the label is in full view. When the host has accepted the wine, the other guests on the table should be served with wine, finally topping up the host's glass. If there is a guest of honour, he should be served first; then the older women, younger women, older men and younger men. At a function, the chairman is served first and then the guest on his right, who will be the principal guest.

When pouring wine from a bottle, it should be held so that the label is uppermost and open to the customer's inspection. The wine should be poured firmly into the glass. When sufficient has been poured the neck should be tilted upwards and a small twist given to the bottle; this should cause any drips to be spread around the glass ring of the bottle instead of dripping onto the tablecloth (Figure 8.9g). The neck should then be wiped with the clean cloth behind the guest before pouring wine to the next customer. Glasses should be filled no more than one-half to two-thirds full, to enable the bouquet to be fully appreciated.

The bottle may be placed back into the bucket or cooler or placed on a plate or coaster on the table. The cork should be placed on the plate with the bottle. A doily should *not* be placed on the plate. Condensation on a cold bottle will cause the doily to stick to the bottle when it is picked up. After all, the plate is only a substitute for a coaster, which is usually made from a wooden base with a silver surround; coasters never have a doily put in them (Figure 8.9h). Ensure that the bottle or ice bucket is in a safe position and not likely to be knocked over.

Further service

The sommelier should keep an eye on the customers' glasses and refill as and when necessary, following the same order as before but without offering a taster to the host. Always serve the host last.

The sommelier should ask the customer if he would like a further bottle (of the same wine)

Figure 8.9 *Presenting and opening a bottle of wine*

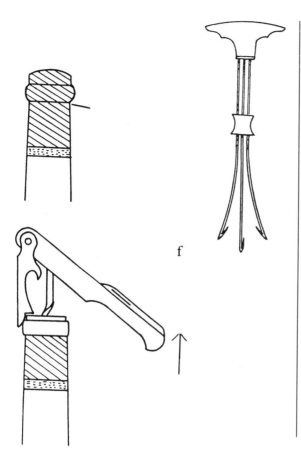

f

before the first one is emptied, if he thinks the customer might require one. He would then have time to prepare a second bottle for service.

The correct form of service for this second bottle would be to place fresh glasses in front of the host and each guest, and to present the bottle to the host and serve a taster to the host before serving the other guests at the table. It is common practice to offer just the host a fresh glass to enable him to taste it and to check its quality and condition, before topping up the other glasses.

The wine from the second bottle must not be mixed in the glasses with wine from the first bottle before it has been tasted and checked; it could be 'off', in which case it would ruin all the wine in the glass. In high-class establishments the sommelier would be expected to smell or even sample this second bottle to ensure that its condition and quality is correct.

The glasses should be removed from the table when they are finished with. If some of the wine served with an early course of the meal is left in the glass when wine offered with a later course has been served, the customer should be asked if he has finished with it, and it should be removed if this is the case.

drip of wine

g

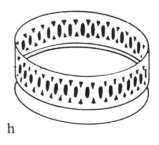

h

Figure 8.9   *continued*

Decanting

Wine is decanted for two basic reasons:

1 To remove wine from the sediment which has formed in the bottle
2 To allow the wine to take in oxygen – to 'breathe'

Wine which has sediment should be treated with great care so that the sediment does not get mixed up in the wine, causing it to become cloudy. If this should happen the wine should not be decanted but should be left unopened to allow the sediment to settle.

If sufficient notice is given by the customer, e.g. 48 hours, then the wine may be stood up. This will make the decanting process that much easier. Less than 48 hours notice may be sufficient for some wines, depending on the type of sediment.

Method of decanting

Remove the wine from the rack in the cellar with extreme care and place it in a wine cradle or basket. This should be presented to the customer, then taken to a table where the decanting will take place. In some establishments the wine is decanted on a table or trolley in front of the guest.

A glass decanter and decanting funnel should have been prepared by rinsing them both out with clean warm water. A piece of clean muslin is often placed into the top of the funnel. A lighted candle is made ready.

The capsule should be cut very carefully below the glass ring of the bottle, making sure the bottle is kept perfectly still in the cradle by gripping it with the other hand. The neck should be wiped with a clean service cloth or napkin. The corkscrew should be screwed into the cork, again holding the bottle steady in the cradle with the other hand. The lever is placed on the top of the neck of the bottle and the cork extracted in the usual way, carefully keeping the bottle still, and making sure the cork is eased out of the bottle so that wine is not sucked out with it.

The decanting funnel is placed into the decanter and a piece of muslin placed over the funnel if this is required. The bottle should be held steady with one hand while the cradle is removed with the other, and the wine is then poured steadily into the top of the funnel with the shoulder of the bottle held over the candle flame. If the bottle is held too close to the flame, soot may form on the underneath of the bottle, which will prevent the person decanting from seeing the sediment moving up the bottle to the neck. The pouring action should be continuous until the sediment reaches the shoulder of the bottle. At this point pouring must stop before *any* of the sediment passes into the decanter. If the cradle is one of the open silver varieties the bottle need not be removed for decanting as the sommelier will be able to see the light from the candle shining through the wine.

The bottle should be replaced in the basket with the cork for presentation to the host. Sometimes the cork is fastened to the neck of the decanter with an ornamental clip, or failing this an elastic band. The decanter stopper should be placed in the decanter.

The wine will be offered for service as for a bottle; the host is offered a taste, and then the guests are served. The decanter is then left on a coaster or plate on the table. When part-empty bottles or decanters are placed on the table they should be placed in front of the host. Remember to present the bottle and cork in the wine cradle when presenting the decanter.

If all bottles of a red wine requested are found to be too cold, it is sensible to ask the host if he would like the wine decanted. This will help the wine to come to room temperature more quickly. The glass decanter may be rinsed out with warm water, and this will speed up the process. It may also be suggested to the cus-

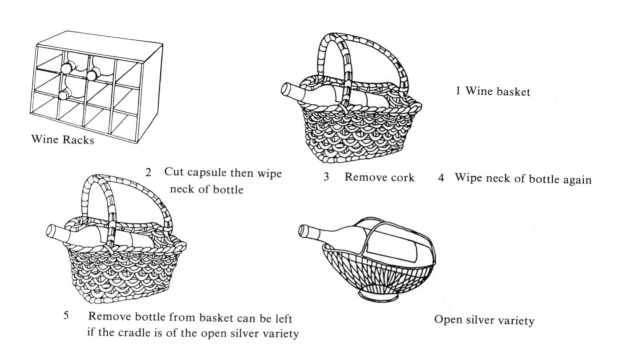

Wine Racks

1 Wine basket

2 Cut capsule then wipe neck of bottle

3 Remove cork

4 Wipe neck of bottle again

5 Remove bottle from basket can be left if the cradle is of the open silver variety

Open silver variety

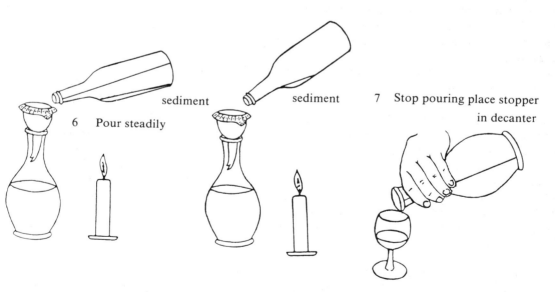

sediment

6 Pour steadily

sediment

7 Stop pouring place stopper in decanter

Figure 8.10 *Decanting*

129

tomer that he warms the glass of wine in his hands.

Note that the decanting basket was *not* designed for the service of wine at the table. To serve a red wine containing sediment from a basket will cause a quantity of the wine to be wasted; the wine will wash up and down the inside of the bottle as it is tilted up and down when pouring and lifted after pouring, thus causing the sediment to be disturbed. To serve a red wine which has no sediment in it from a basket just makes the service of the wine more difficult.

Dealing with faults in the wine

Corky wine

The real meaning of the term *corked* is that the bottle is sealed with a cork. However, when a customer uses this term to describe a wine he usually means that the wine is *corky* – that is, it has the smell and taste of cork. This condition is caused by a faulty cork.

The sommelier should apologize to the customer, remove the wine, check it himself, and if it is out of condition he should replace the bottle with another of the same type. If the wine is in the correct condition, it is prudent to offer a replacement wine of another type rather than have an argument about it. If the sommelier has detected this corkiness before serving the wine he should replace it with another bottle of the same type without offering the faulty one to the customer.

When the sommelier opens a bottle he should smell the wine, not the cork, and this will indicate to an experienced sommelier whether the wine is in good condition or not.

Broken cork

If a cork breaks and part falls into the bottle of wine, remove this with a cork extractor or decant the bottle. Do both away from the table.

Effervescent wine

If the wine is seen to be 'fizzing' or is slightly effervescent when it is known that it is a still wine variety, this will probably be caused by the wine undergoing a secondary fermentation. It is therefore out of condition and should be replaced. This condition will often make the wine smell yeasty. Always check that the replacement bottle is not in the same condition before serving it to the customer.

Serving spirits, beers and other drinks

When serving any drinks at either the table or bar, ensure that the correct glasses are used and that they are scrupulously clean (for the correct glasses, see earlier in this chapter). A careful check must be kept that the full correct measures are served, and that the drinks are served at the right temperatures and with the right garnishes where appropriate. *Never* refill glasses; serve each drink in a fresh clean glass.

Drinks should be carried to a lounge or restaurant table on a salver. The glasses should be placed to the right of the customer, and the barperson or sommelier should stand on the right of each customer when placing his drink. At a bar or lounge table the drinks are often placed on beer mats or flat paper 'coasters' which may be used to advertise specific drinks or the establishment. Where tankards or glasses with handles are served, the handle should be placed to the right of the customer. Where a spirit is being served with a *mixer*, the spirit should be placed in the glass and the mixer added in front of the customer, either at the bar or at the table, to enable the guest to have the quantity he requires.

Sommeliers and barmen should pick up glasses by the handle if there is one, or by the stem or the bottom half of the glass if there is not. The fingers of the hand must never be placed in or around the top of a glass, whether it is a clean one, a used one, or one containing a drink.

Mixed drinks and cocktails

Preparation methods

Mixing

Mixed drinks are prepared by gently stirring ingredients in the glass to be used for the service of the drink. An example of this type of drink is an Americano (see later in this section).

Shaking

Cocktails may be shaken in either a Boston or a standard shaker (see Figures 2.16, 2.17).

Assemble all the ingredients and make ready any garnishes required *before* commencing preparation of the cocktail. Once the ice has been placed in the shaker, it will start to melt. If some ingredients are placed in the shaker with the ice it will melt more quickly; if the barman then finds that an ingredient is not to hand, the drink will become diluted.

Plenty of ice should be placed into the shaker and any excess water should be strained off. The ingredients are then poured into the shaker on to the ice and the top is put on securely. Holding the top and bottom of the shaker together with both hands for the Boston shaker and with one or both hands for the standard shaker, shake vigorously so that the ice moves up and down the inside of the shaker quickly, cooling and thoroughly mixing the ingredients. The drink is then strained out of the shaker into the glass or glasses, which have been previously prepared.

Shaken cocktails are always opaque. This method of making a cocktail is used when ingredients of vastly different specific gravities are used together and when egg white, sugar or cream are among the ingredients.

A Boston shaker is used in conjunction with a Hawthorn strainer (see Figure 2.21) and is the best type when large quantities are being prepared. The standard shaker has a built-in strainer in its top and is more suitable for shaking a single cocktail.

Ingredients containing carbon dioxide, such as soda water, lemonade and cola, must *never* be shaken in a cocktail shaker, otherwise the shaker will burst open. If they are an ingredient of the cocktail they should always be added to the shaken mixture. These ingredients should not be used in a mixing glass or blender either.

Blending

Blended drinks are prepared by mixing the ingredients in a liquidizer. This method is very suitable for drinks which require a purée of fruit in them, long drinks and quantities. Crushed ice is usually used in the blender in place of ice cubes. Pina Colada is a drink which is suitable for this method of preparation (see later in this section).

Stirring

The ingredients for stirred cocktails are mixed together with a bar spoon in a mixing glass containing plenty of ice. The cocktail is then strained through a Hawthorn strainer.

Plenty of ice should be placed in the mixing glass and then any water strained off before adding any ingredients. As for shaken cocktails the ingredients, garnishes and glasses should be assembled before any ice is added to the glass to prevent loss of time and excess melting of ice, which will weaken the cocktail.

When the ingredients are all in the glass the bar spoon should be stirred round and round the inside of the glass vigorously, causing the ice to mix and cool the liquors. The spoon is removed and the Hawthorn strainer is placed in the top of the mixing glass, which is then tilted to strain the mixed drink into the cocktail glass. If the drink being prepared is for more than one person, half fill each of the glasses then top up each, so obtaining an equal strength of the drink in each glass. The prepared drink in the mixing glass becomes more dilute towards the end because of the continually melting ice.

Stirred cocktails are always clear, e.g. Dry Martini cocktail (see later in this section).

After a cocktail shaker or mixing glass has been used, the ice left in it must be thrown away and the equipment washed.

Ice

Ice is made in ice machines in various shapes and sizes. It must be clear and clean and plentiful in supply. For shaken and stirred cocktails and mixed drinks, small cubes or double chips are the most suitable. These are also the best shapes for regular bar drinks such as gin and tonics. Crushed ice is best for use in blenders, and this can be made by putting ice cubes through an ice-crushing machine. Always ensure that there is a plentiful supply of ice readily available.

When ice is put into an insulated container to stand on the bar, a splash of soda from a syphon will help to prevent the cubes of ice sticking together. Ice tongs or a spoon should be placed in or by the container.

When serving drinks which normally take ice with them, such as a gin and tonic or a dry vermouth, ask the customer if he would like ice; do not take it for granted and put it in without asking.

When preparing a stirred or shaken cocktail, at least half fill the mixing glass or shaker with ice. The mixing glass or shaker will be at the temperature of the bar and will therefore melt some of the ice while it cools down, so strain off any excess water before adding any ingredients of the cocktail.

Ingredients and accompaniments

Presentation of drinks is extremely important. However, although it is acceptable to dress up certain drinks, it should be remembered that drinks are for drinking. Do not over-decorate them with items which add nothing to the taste of the drink.

Lemon

Fresh lemons are an essential commodity in any bar. Remove any sticky labels and wipe the lemons thoroughly before putting them into the bar for use.

Lemon zest is used, twisted over drinks such as Dry Martini cocktails to extract the oils which will settle on the top of the drink, giving a delicate lemon smell and taste to it. Correctly the peel should not be put into the drink after extracting the oils (many barmen do put it in).

Lemon slices or half-slices are used as an ingredient of many drinks such as gin and tonic and Cinzano Bianco. As with ice, always ask the customer if he wants lemon; do not take it for granted and put it in automatically.

Fresh lemon juice is used in a large number of cocktails, e.g. Sours, White Lady and Collins. Bottled fresh lemon juice is available and is easy to use, but does not have quite the same visual impact as fresh lemons. Slightly warm lemons give more juice than cold. Never use lemon squash or drinks where lemon juice is required.

Cherries

Cherries bottled in a light maraschino syrup are used for cocktails and other mixed drinks and add colour and flavour. There are bottled maraschino cherries available which have their stalks left on, which adds to the presentation of some drinks where the cherry is more of a decoration.

Oranges

Remove any sticky labels from the oranges and wipe them thoroughly before putting them into a bar for use.

Orange zest is used in a few drinks in the same way as lemon zest.

Orange slices, half-slices and wedges are used for drinks such as Champagne Cocktails, Old-Fashioned and Campari.

Fresh orange juice is used in cocktails and on its own, and is prepared as for lemon juice. Slightly warm oranges give more juice than cold ones. Never use orange drinks or squashes when orange juice is stated in the recipe of a drink.

Mint

Fresh mint leaves are used as an ingredient of juleps, and sprigs of mint are used as a decoration to these and other drinks. As for fresh fruit used in drinks, it is essential that the mint is clean, and it should be washed in cold water before placing it in the bar for use.

Olives

Both black and green olives are used as ingredients in some drinks, as well as for table accompaniments in the bar.

Other ingredients

Other accompaniments or ingredients which should be available in a bar include:

Castor and cube sugars
Coffee beans
Cream
Eggs
Limes if available
Nutmeg and grater
Pearl onions
Salt and pepper
Tabasco sauce
Worcestershire sauce
Cucumber (for Pimms if offered)

Cocktail recipes

Cocktails are combinations of drinks and other ingredients which are mixed together in predetermined quantities according to set recipes. They should taste of a melange or mixture without any one ingredient predominating.

Cocktails are usually accepted as being short drinks of 5–12 cl. The majority are drinks which are suitable to be drunk as aperitifs, stimulating the gastric juices for the meal to come. Others are suitable as after-dinner drinks, such as a brandy Alexander. The many larger drinks which are in vogue at present are usually referred to as mixed drinks.

Cocktails fall into two basic categories:

1 Those prepared by shaking the ingredients together with ice, in a cocktail shaker, then straining the drink into a glass.
2 Those prepared by stirring the ingredients together through ice in a mixing glass, then straining the drink into a glass.

Although there are cocktails which are made up of just two ingredients the vast majority comprise three, and there are often more than three. These three parts usually are:

1 A base, usually of spirit
2 A sweetening, which may be a syrup, sugar or liqueur
3 A souring, often fresh fruit juice, bitters or other ingredients.

For example:

	Base	Sweet	Sour
White Lady	gin	Cointreau	lemon juice
Bronx	gin	vermouths	orange juice
Old Nick	rye whiskey	Drambuie	lemon juice, orange juice, orange bitters

This is a helpful way to remember the ingredients of recipes.

Both alcoholic and non-alcoholic cocktails may be prepared by shaking or stirring. Other mixed drinks are prepared by combining various ingredients together.

Americano
1 measure Campari
1 measure sweet vermouth
Soda water

An Americano is prepared by stirring equal quantities of Campari and sweet vermouth together in either a highball glass or Old-Fashioned glass half filled with ice, and topping this with soda water. Add a half-slice of orange or a twist of lemon zest and serve.

Bloody Mary
1 measure vodka
1 baby-size bottle tomato juice
2–3 dashes Worcestershire sauce
1 dash lemon juice

A Bloody Mary may be prepared by shaking, stirring or combining the ingredients together in the glass for service. The most suitable method is to stir it in a mixing glass. Serve in a highball glass or Old-Fashioned glass. Some people like Tabasco sauce, cayenne pepper and mill pepper added to this drink.

Champagne Cocktail
Glass of dry Champagne
1 teaspoon Cognac
1 cube of sugar
Angostura bitters

Place a cube of sugar in a Champagne glass and saturate it with Angostura Bitters. Add cold Champagne and top with approximately a teaspoon of Cognac. Finish with a half-slice of orange or a thick wedge of orange. This drink may be decorated with a maraschino cherry and a piece of orange, on a cocktail stick, resting on the top of the glass (Figure 8.11).

When preparing large numbers of this drink for a reception, the glasses, each containing an Angostura-soaked cube of sugar and a wedge of orange, may be half filled with Champagne a short while in advance and topped up with Champagne and Cognac as the guests arrive.

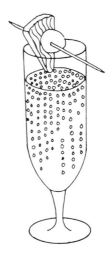

Figure 8.11 *Champagne cocktail*

John or Tom Collins
1 measure of London dry gin
Juice of 1 medium-sized lemon
1 teaspoon/bar spoon Gomme syrup
Soda water

Half fill a highball glass with ice. Add the gin, lemon juice and Gomme, then top up with soda water, stirring with a bar spoon. Decorate with a slice of lemon and serve with straws.

Cuba Libre
1 measure white rum
Juice of half a fresh lime
Cola

This drink is classed as a highball. It is made by adding the rum and lime juice to a highball glass half filled with ice and topping up with cola. Stir with a bar spoon and decorate with a thick slice of fresh lime. Serve with straws.

Fizzes
Fizzes are similar to the Collins except that all the ingredients except the soda water are shaken.

Gin Fizz is made from exactly the same ingredients as a Tom/John Collins. Shake the gin, lemon juice and Gomme together, strain into a highball glass and top up with soda water, stirring with a bar spoon.
Silver Fizz   As for a Gin Fizz with white of egg added to the cocktail shaker.
Golden Fizz   As for Gin Fizz with yolk of egg added to the cocktail shaker.
Royal Fizz   As for Gin Fizz with a whole egg added to the cocktail shaker.

Frappés
Frappés are made by pouring a measure of a liqueur into a 12 cl cocktail glass or short-stemmed glass filled with crushed ice, and serving with two half straws.
Two of the most popular *frappés* are:

Crème de menthe frappé (using green *crème de menthe*)
Cointreau frappé.

Harvey Wallbanger
1 large measure (1/3 gill) vodka
1 baby-size bottle orange juice
½ measure Galliano

This relatively modern, popular mixed drink is prepared by combining a large measure of vodka with a bottle of orange juice in a highball glass half-filled with ice. Half a measure of Galliano is poured on the top, and the drink is served with straws.

Highballs
Highballs are long drinks comprising a spirit and an effervescent mixer, and sometimes a third ingredient. They are all served in highball glasses.

Horse's Neck
1 measure brandy
Ginger ale
Peel of one lemon

Peel the skin off a lemon in one long spiral, placing one end in the bottom of a highball glass and the other over the top edge. Place ice into the glass, add the brandy and top up with ginger ale.

Rye Highball
1 measure rye whiskey
Ginger ale or soda water

A measure of rye whiskey is placed in a highball glass half filled with ice, and topped up with ginger ale or soda water, stirring with a bar spoon. A twist of lemon may be added.

A *rye and dry* in the UK is rye whiskey, ice and ginger ale.

Kir
Kir is a mixture of half a 1/6 gill measure of *crème de cassis* topped up with dry white wine and served in a wine glass.

Kir Royal is a mixture of half a measure of *crème de cassis* topped up with Champagne and served in a Champagne glass.

Manhattan
There are three types of Manhattan – sweet, medium and dry. They are all mixtures of rye whiskey and vermouth.

Sweet Manhattan
1½ measures rye whiskey
¾ measures sweet vermouth
1 dash Angostura bitters

Stir and strain into a small cocktail glass and add a maraschino cherry.

Medium Manhattan
1½ measures rye whiskey
⅜ measure sweet vermouth
⅜ measure dry vermouth

Stir and strain into a small cocktail glass, add a cherry and twist of lemon.

Dry Manhattan
1½ measures rye whiskey
¾ measures dry vermouth

Stir and strain into a small cocktail glass and finish with a twist of lemon.

Martini cocktails
There are three types of Martini cocktail – sweet, medium and dry.

Sweet Martini
1½ measures gin
¾ measure sweet vermouth

Stir and strain into a small cocktail glass and finish with a maraschino cherry.

Medium Martini
1½ measures gin
⅜ measure sweet vermouth
⅜ measure dry vermouth

Stir and strain into a small cocktail glass and finish with a twist of lemon.

Dry Martini
1½ measures gin
¾ measure dry vermouth (this will vary considerably with taste)

Stir and strain into a small cocktail glass and finish with a twist of lemon. A dryer version of the Dry Martini is sometimes referred to as an *American Dry Martini*. This is mixed in the ratio of five parts of gin to one part dry vermouth. It has become the fashion to drink Martinis very dry.

Old-Fashioned
1 large measure (1/3 gill) rye whiskey
Angostura bitters
Cube of sugar
Little water

A small cube of sugar is placed into an Old-Fashioned glass and saturated with Angostura bitters. A little water is added to dissolve the sugar, which is broken up with a bar spoon. Half fill the glass with ice, then add the rye whiskey. Decorate the drink with a half-slice of orange and a maraschino cherry. It is normal to serve a stirrer with this drink.

Pimm's
There are now only two types of Pimms:

Pimm's No. 1, which is gin based
Vodka Pimm's, which is vodka based.

Pink Gin
1 measure Plymouth gin
Angostura bitters
Iced water

The original Pink Gin was made with Plymouth gin, and this is still recognized as the correct ingredient. Angostura bitters are shaken into a spirit glass. The glass is twisted around to allow the bitters to coat the inside of the glass; any excess bitters may be emptied out. The gin is added, and the drink is served topped up with iced water.

Pink Lady
1 large measure (1/3 gill) gin
½ measure Grenadine
1 egg white

All the ingredients are shaken and strained into a small cocktail glass.

Pousse-Café
These drinks are made by layering syrups, liqueurs and spirits on top of each other in a narrow glass (Figure 8.12). The order in which the liquors are added depends on the specific gravity of each ingredient. Syrups are the heaviest, liqueurs are the next and spirits are the lightest.

The bottles of the ingredients should be lined up in order and a small quantity of each poured down the inside edge of the glass on to the open

Figure 8.12   *Pousse-café*

part of a small spoon, usually a coffee spoon or teaspoon, which is held against the inside of the glass and the opposite top inside edge (see figure).

Some people prefer to drink this through a short straw.

Screwdriver
1 measure vodka
1 baby size bottle of orange juice

The vodka and orange juice are added to a highball glass half filled with ice, and the drink is stirred with a bar spoon.

Sidecar
1 measure Scotch whisky
½ measure Cointreau
½ measure fresh lemon juice

Shake and strain into a small cocktail glass.

Sours
Sours are shaken cocktails of fresh fruit juice, a spirit and a sweetening (either a syrup or a

liqueur). The drink is usually enhanced by incorporating a little white of egg.

Whisky Sour
1½ measures Scotch whisky
1 measure lemon juice
½ measure Gomme
½ white of egg

Shake and strain into a large cocktail glass and decorate with a half-slice of lemon.

Tequila Sunrise
1 measure tequila
1 baby-size bottle orange juice
Little Grenadine

The tequila is combined with the orange juice in a highball glass half filled with ice. A little Grenadine is poured down the inside of the glass. Decorate with a half-slice of orange and a maraschino cherry, and serve with straws.

Pina Colada
1 large measure white rum
½ baby-size bottle pineapple juice
1 measure coconut cream or slightly less Malibu

The ingredients are blended with crushed ice and served in a highball glass or 28 cl Paris goblet. The drink is decorated with fresh pineapple and a maraschino cherry and served with short straws.

White Lady
1 measure gin
½ measure Cointreau
½ measure fresh lemon juice

Shake and strain into a small cocktail glass.

Non-alcoholic
There are many non-alcoholic drinks and cocktails. They can be made by using combinations of fruit juices, syrups, non-alcoholic cordials, milk, cream and eggs. These may be topped up

with soda water, lemonade or other non-alcoholic mixers.

A very popular drink with sportsmen and women is a mixture of fresh orange juice and lemonade.

The best known non-alcoholic cocktail is the *Pussyfoot cocktail*. This is a mixture of equal quantities of orange, lemon and lime juice, a dash of Grenadine and an egg yolk, shaken and strained into a large cocktail glass or highball glass.

Table and cocktail bar accompaniments

It is the practice in many establishments to put a few small snack items of food in dishes on the bar for the customers to consume while they are drinking.

Many of these items are intended to make the customer thirsty and thus buy extra drinks. An example of this was the introduction of potato crisps. They were not very popular until the manufacturer inserted a small bag of salt into the packet of crisps. They then became very popular with publicans because their customers did in fact drink more when eating them. They were of course generally sold to the customer, which also increased profits. Nowadays many crisps are ready salted or flavoured, the flavourings having a salty base to them.

Other items which are put out as cocktail bar table accompaniments or are sold in packets to the customers are:

Cheese cubes
Salted biscuits
Chipples, chipsticks
Cocktail gherkins
Dry roasted nuts
Plain nuts
Salted nuts
Olives – black, green, stuffed
Pearl onions
Pickled onions
Pork scratchings
Pretzels

Other proprietary cocktail snacks.

Cigars and cigarettes

Cigars

Cigars should be kept at a temperature of 15–18°C and a relative humidity of 55–60 per cent. However, this is not the normal environment of a restaurant or bar, so establishments do not usually keep great numbers of quality cigars in stock. Dry heat, drastic variations of temperature, damp and smells are detrimental to cigars.

Cigars which have become dry may be restored by putting them in their box for a few days in a damp cellar or atmosphere. Cigars should not normally be stored in these conditions, as if they get very damp they may go mouldy. If a white powder is seen on them this should be removed with a soft brush or handkerchief; it is a 'heat mould' and is not detrimental to the cigar. If boxes of cigars are to be kept for some time, store them upside down; this allows the cigars to breathe through the uncovered bottom of the cedar wood box.

Cigars are often kept and presented in humidor boxes. A humidor is a cabinet or box that has a flush fitting lid with a moisture pad in it. This will regulate the humidity by moisturizing the air if it is too dry. If the atmosphere is too damp then the pad must be used dry and it will then absorb any excess moisture.

Many cigars are individually packed in metal tubes. These are very good for establishments which are situated close to the sea, as salt air has a detrimental effect on a cigar. Inside the tube there is a thin piece of cedar wood around the cigar.

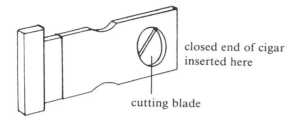

Figure 8.13 *Guillotine cigar cutter*

Cigars are usually offered at the end of a meal with the coffee. If there is a liqueur trolley the cigars would be presented from this. Before offering cigars or cigarettes make sure that there are sufficient ashtrays on the table. Cigars which are kept in a cedar wood box or humidor should be shown to the customer, who will choose the cigar he requires. The sommelier should then carefully remove the cigar, taking care not to catch the wrapper of any of the cigars in the box with a finger nail and thus break the outer wrapper. It is a good idea to place a cigar in the box in such a way that the customer can pick it up easily without catching another cigar, and possibly ruining it.

The sommelier should then offer to prepare the cigar for smoking. The closed end of the cigar has to be opened, and the best way to do this is to use a cigar cutter – either a flat guillotine cutter (Figure 8.13) or a V-shaped cutter. The cigar should not be pierced as this leaves an opening which is too small for the cigar to be enjoyed to its full potential. The cigar must be handled with great care to ensure that the outer wrapper leaf, which is very thin, is not broken. A cigar which is in good condition will be firm but yielding to light pressure from the fingers, so that it can be held firmly while cutting it. When cut the cigar should be tapped to remove any small particles left from the cutting operation. The cigar should be returned to the customer and he should be offered a light from a wooden match or gas lighter – never from sulphur or wax matches or a petrol lighter, as these will spoil the flavour of the cigar.

The practice of warming the cigar along its whole length with a lighted match is unnecessary. This came about years ago when an unpleasant tasting glue was used to secure the wrapper of the cigar. This is now no longer the case, so it is a redundant practice.

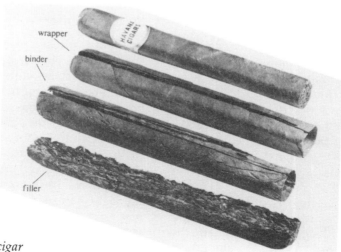

Figure 8.14 *A Havana cigar*

Although the taste and strength of a cigar cannot be judged from its colour, the following colour markings are often to be found on cigar boxes:

CCC *Claro*, a light brown colour
CC   *Colorado claro*, a little darker brown
C   *Colorado*, a darker brown still

Maduro or *colorado-maduro* is another less used colour grading, and means very dark brown. 'Green' cigars are not green in colour; the word is used to indicate that the cigar is very fresh and has been neither dried nor conditioned. These are usually sold in hermetically sealed glass jars. A Candela cigar is the name of a greenish-yellow cigar which is popular with Americans.

Havana or Habana cigars, which are produced in Cuba, are accepted as being the best, followed by Jamaican cigars. All boxes of Havana cigars have a green and white Cuban government label of guarantee on them. A Havana cigar is made in three parts (Figure 8.14):

1 The filler
2 The binder or bunch-binder
3 The wrapper

The wrapper is the most expensive part of the cigar and may be as much as two-thirds of the total cost of the cigar.

Cigars which are packed in cedar wood boxes of 25 are pressed cigars and appear to be slightly square in shape. Cigars tied in bundles of 50 are called 'cabinet selection'.

A *Corona* (14.5 cm) is a cigar with a closed rounded end. Petite Coronas and half Coronas are shorter cigars of the same shape.

Cigarettes

If a packet of cigarettes is ordered by the customer it should be presented to the customer on a silver or stainless steel salver, or failing this a plate. The Cellophane cover should be

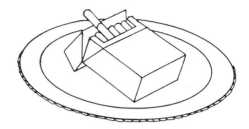

Figure 8.15 *Serving cigarettes*

removed from the packet. The top of the packet should be opened and the small piece of light foil removed from the inside, exposing the cigarettes. This is the correct service of cigarettes at a table in a restaurant or lounge (see Figure 8.15).

During the service of a meal, ashtrays which have been used should be changed for clean ones. The procedure to be followed is to approach the table with a salver holding a clean ashtray and something such as a coffee saucer or another ashtray to cover the dirty ashtray. The cover is placed over the used ashtray to prevent the ash from flying, and this is replaced with the clean ashtray; the used one is placed on the salver.

Speciality coffees

Speciality coffees are made by placing a measure of the chosen spirit or liqueur into a warmed speciality coffee glass or a Paris goblet, adding brown sugar to taste. Hot black coffee is poured into the glass to within 2.5 cm of the top, stirring all the time to dissolve the sugar. Double cream is poured gently over a teaspoon to float on the surface of the coffee (Figure 8.16).

The glass is served on a doilied sideplate with a teaspoon – in the centre of the cover, not to the right hand side. These coffees are usually prepared on a trolley or table in front of the customer.

Some examples of speciality coffees are:

Paris Goblet

Speciality Coffee Glass

Figure 8.16   *Speciality coffee*

Name	Liqueur or spirit
Calypso	Tia Maria
Caribbean	Rum
DOM or Monk's	Bénédictine
Gaelic or Highland	Scotch whisky
Irish	Irish whiskey
Prince Charles	Drambuie
Royal	Cognac, flamed
Rüdesheimer	Asbach brandy
Witches	Strega

A Viennese coffee has no liqueur or spirit added, but it is served in the same way with the cream floated on top and grated chocolate sprinkled over it.

Chapter Nine

Maintaining and increasing sales

Objectives of selling and merchandising

The objectives of selling and merchandising are:

1 Gaining customer confidence
2 Achieving customer satisfaction
3 Achieving and maximizing sales

Whenever customers enter a public house or a restaurant, they do so to purchase refreshment. It is therefore up to the beverage sales staff to satisfy the customers' requirements and to sell them as much as they will be happy to purchase. In most restaurants more profit is made on wine and other drinks per unit spent than on food.

To gain the confidence of the customers, the staff must greet them politely and in a welcoming manner, making them feel wanted. The sommelier is required to take drink orders, advising where necessary, and to serve these drinks at the correct time and in the correct manner. The basics of taking beverage orders have been described in Chapter 7.

Methods of maintaining and increasing sales

The beverage staff should be trained in food and beverage operations and should be encouraged to learn as much as possible about the products which they will be selling. In this way they will become confident and skilful in the service of drinks, and will have the ability to recommend drinks to the customers.

Good presentation of drinks in the restaurant and bar is of vital importance, as this will help to sell them. Many customers are also attracted to a bar by the showmanship of the bar person and their efficient and attractive service.

Customers like to be treated as individuals and to feel that their custom is valued?

Cleanliness and tidiness is always important, and should be maintained from opening right through the service time. This means wiping up spillages as soon as they happen, replacing used ashtrays, and ensuring that any tables and service surfaces are kept clean.

Glasses and glassware must always be sound (unchipped) and highly polished. Each time a drink is served in a bar a fresh glass should be used. Wine glasses should be placed in the correct position on the tables in a restaurant and for a function care should be taken to ensure that they are lined up. Good clean crisp linen shows off glasses well and should be used whenever possible, unless the tables are highly polished wood.

Wine lists must be attractive, well laid out, easy to keep clean and legible, with explanations where necessary to help the customers choose their requirements.

Descriptions of the wines which are printed on the wine list must be accurate and interesting. These descriptions are very important with the introduction of many lesser known wines to the market and the increase in price of the more traditional ones. Bin numbers should always be used on wine lists to identify the various wines; these enable customers to have confidence when ordering. If they feel embarrassed at not knowing the correct pronunciation of a wine, they will often order a different wine (usually a cheaper one) to hide their ignorance. Bin numbers will also reduce the chance of the wrong bottle of wine being sent up by the cellar or fetched by the sommelier.

Tent cards recommending particular drinks may be placed on the tables in the bar and restaurant. This is a proven aid to sales, as are displays of items you wish to promote. The display shelves in a bar should be used to *sell*; therefore they should be used for the display of drinks. They should not be used as a holding place for glasses which are to be used for service, as this is a waste of highly effective promotional space. Posters may be displayed recommending particular drinks, and examples of new drinks may be prepared and displayed on the bar, sometimes for customers to sample.

It is of major importance to the maximizing of sales that the sommelier and bar person have a good knowledge of the range of products on offer. They will then be able to make suggestions and recommendations for drinks to accompany courses and meals and to answer customers' questions. In addition, to maximize sales the beverage service staff need to be able to assess the spending potential of the customer so that they can suggest and recommend drinks which will be appropriate to their requirements.

Awareness and anticipation of customers' needs are two factors which come with training and experience.

Positive selling

Customers arriving for a meal should be asked what they would like to drink as an aperitif, e.g. 'May I take your aperitif order?'; alternatively a suggestion might be made to them. This approach does not give the customer the option of saying no quite so easily. If the aperitif glasses become rather low while the guests are in the bar or lounge areas, the staff should ask them if they require the same order again rather than waiting for them to make a request for more drinks.

The wine list should be presented to the customer with the menu. If the customer makes an order for wine which is obviously meant to accompany the main course, the sommelier could ask if he would like a wine with the starter course.

If a single bottle of wine is ordered by a party of six persons or more, then it would be sensible to ensure that a second bottle is prepared unopened. This will then be in the correct condition for service and can be offered for service when the first bottle is nearly finished. It is a good idea to mention to the customer that you will have a second bottle available if he should want it. Another approach which could be made when the first bottle is ordered would be for the sommelier to ask 'Two bottles, sir/madam?'

The sommelier should offer liqueurs, brandies or port at the end of the meal, just prior to the service of coffee. A liqueur trolley will certainly help sales, as will sweet wine and vintage port offered for sale by the glass and displayed on this trolley. If the restaurant is too small for a trolley, then other techniques can be used to maximize sales. For example, if a customer orders a brandy the sommelier could bring a range of three Cognacs and an Armagnac plus a thimble measure and glasses to the table on a salver. Very often the best quality and most expensive brandy is sold in this instance, and the customer will appreciate seeing a full measure being poured out in front of him. If a liqueur had been ordered as well then this would be brought on the same salver with a liqueur glass and would also be poured out in front of the customer at the table. Another positive approach would be to ask the customer if he would like a VSOP, and if he says yes to bring only VSOP brandies and older on the salver.

A form of positive selling is to use an initial approach which assumes that a sale has been made, and that the only decision to be made by the customer is which item to choose. An example when taking a wine order would be: 'Would you prefer a dry or medium dry wine with the prawn cocktails, sir/madam?' instead of 'Would you like anything to drink with the first course, sir/madam?' or 'Do you require wine with your meal, sir/madam?' To help explain this concept fully, the following is an example of negative selling: 'You won't require anything to drink with the first course, will you, sir/madam?' The positive approach is directing the customer as to his choice, whereas the negative approach is suggesting that no drink will be required. Customers may be encouraged into ordering by a positive approach when they might otherwise not have bothered.

It is vital for sales that any drink ordered is served in good time. The customer must not have to ask for his drink to be served once he has made the order. It is more obvious in a bar, but equally true in a restaurant, that while a customer is waiting to be served with a drink, sales are being lost. Therefore it is essential that sufficient and efficient staff are available who are alert and always keeping an eye on the customer.

Properly run bonus schemes can be an incentive to staff to increase sales.

Chapter Ten

Staff practice and customer relations

Personal presentation and hygiene

All people involved in the service industries, and in particular those concerned with the service of food and drink, must be totally acceptable to the customer. This includes such things as a good standard of personal hygiene, appearance and politeness.

Good health is an essential requirement for a bar person or sommelier. These two jobs entail many hours of walking and standing.

Appearance and personal hygiene must be of a very high standard. Body odour and bad breath are both unacceptable. It can be most unpleasant for a customer to be served by someone suffering from one of these problems. Staff should wash frequently with soap and water, shower or bathe at least once a day, and clean their teeth regularly. An anti-perspirant should be used by the service staff.

The following rules should also be adhered to:

1 Hands and nails must be clean, there must be no nicotine stains on the fingers, and nails must be well manicured and short. Nail varnish should not be worn.
2 Hair must be kept clean, neat and well groomed. If it is long it should be tied back.
3 Staff must wash their hands after visiting the toilet, by law (see Chapter 12). They should also wash their hands after doing any dirty jobs such as bottling-up shelves or polishing silver.

4 Staff should not touch their hair, nose or mouth, and then handle glasses or food.
5 Staff must not serve food or drink when suffering from diarrhoea, food poisoning or infectious diseases.
6 Staff must not cough, spit or sneeze over food or drink.
7 Staff must *not* smoke or take snuff in a food or drink area.
   NB It is also an offence for a barman to smoke behind the bar.
8 Staff suffering from cuts, burns or abrasions must cover these with waterproof dressing to reduce the chances of infection.
9 Heavy perfume should not be worn as it will detract from the food and wine and may offend the customer.
10 The service cloth must be changed when soiled and it must *never* be put under the arm.

In general, staff should practise good hygienic standards and habits. They must comply with the Hygiene Regulations (see Chapter 12).

Clothing which is worn outside the working area should be either changed or covered with a uniform. This must be clean, well pressed and well fitting.

Shoes must be comfortable, well fitting and highly polished.

Ear-rings, bracelets, rings other than wedding and signet rings, and hanging jewellery are all unacceptable in the working environment.

Attitudes and behaviour

Staff should be positive in their movements. They should stand without leaning on a table, bar or sideboard, and should appear smart and alert at all times.

It is important that service staff enunciate clearly so that the customer is able to understand them, bearing in mind that a restaurant or bar is a pretty noisy place at any time. Staff should speak at a medium pace. If the words are garbled, the customer will become impatient if he is unable to understand.

It is important that staff never use bad language, even away from the customer, as the spoken word usually carries farther than is anticipated.

Staff should greet customers with a smile and welcome them to the establishment. They should show a readiness to oblige the customer. Customers are not paying the staff to be discourteous to them. The customer should be treated pleasantly and politely; in this way he will become relaxed more quickly and feel at ease. *Civility* means being pleasant and courteous, and must be practised by the service staff. This must not be confused with *servility*, which means to cringe, to 'bow and scrape'. This behaviour must *not* be practised.

To be tactful is to be diplomatic and to be able to say the right things when the customer has a complaint or problem. It is also a requirement when conversing with other staff. It is important to be patient with customers and other members of staff. Cheerfulness and good humour produce a happy atmosphere and can help when dealing with difficult situations. These are essential attributes of all good food and beverage staff.

The customer is entitled to be served by a person with a pleasant and cheerful manner. The meal experience should be a pleasurable occasion for the customer, and the attitude and demeanour of the service staff are major factors in achieving this.

Employees in this service industry should be fully aware of the importance of punctuality and reliability. When a member of staff is late or absent from work, the restaurant or bar will still open and the same number of customers will walk into the premises to be served. This will mean that the remaining staff will have to work harder. The late arrival for work of a hotel manager will not usually cause a great problem, but the late arrival of a barman could cause loss of revenue. Unlike many office jobs, 'the show must go on'.

Self confidence comes with knowledge, training, practice and experience, and is a requirement of any salesman. He must believe in his own ability and his recommendations to the customer, and he must project this belief to the customer. A lack of confidence on the part of a barman or sommelier may lead to a loss in sales and may be the cause of accidents.

On occasions a customer can be very difficult to serve. He may complain unnecessarily and may appear to be objectionable to a member of staff. The staff member must always keep an even temper and be polite. Usually the customer will then calm down. If a situation is arrived at where the member of staff is unable to cope with the problem, he or she should ask a superior to deal with it.

Social skills are about getting on with people. To do this fully it is necessary to understand how other people think and react to certain situations. It is necessary on occasions to think before speaking to ensure that unintentional offence is not given. In particular, people who live in a multiracial society as we do must give consideration to the cultures of people from countries and backgrounds other than their own.

Teamwork and communication

When information is received, ensure that it is passed on in the correct form to the necessary people. A customer may arrive and give you some detail about their party which is booked for dinner, e.g. that there will be two less for the dinner, or that somebody's birthday is being celebrated. This information must be passed on immediately to the restaurant manager.

If a telephone message is taken, the date and time that it was received must be recorded on the message slip. The person to whom it is intended should be clearly shown plus the name of the person who received it.

To create a pleasant and efficient working atmosphere, staff should work together and help each other. A simple example is when a member of staff fetches a piece of equipment which he requires and at the same time fetches a similar piece for another member of staff, which will save the other person either forgetting it or having to fetch it. This is achieved without doing anything extra at all, but is an example of teamwork or working together to get something done.

A pleasant and efficient working atmosphere will only be achieved by people thinking of others rather than just themselves, and by staff looking around (when they are not busy) for things which need doing or for ways in which others can be assisted.

Staff should be polite and respectful to supervisors and should follow their instructions. If the section is running as a team with the objective of creating a pleasant and efficient environment for the service of customers, any criticism given is probably meant for the good of the operation, and is really meant to help rather than to criticize. Staff who can accept criticism and act upon it will become better at their job and get more job satisfaction.

If staff are to do a good job, they must be motivated. To be friendly but firm with subordinates is a very important contribution to their motivation. They need to feel that you are really interested in them and that you are trying to help them. It is important to offer praise when things are done well. Give credit where credit is due, rather than take credit oneself when others have earned it. Offer advice and encouragement should a member of staff find difficulty with a task. This can be done with a smile and a joke so that the person feels at ease.

When giving directions or instructions to subordinates, make sure that they are clear and unambiguous, and that the person to whom they are given understands them.

The whole establishment as well as the food and beverage service section must work as a team, so it is essential to co-operate with other departments and to give them information which may be useful to them. Often an occasion will arise when you receive information which will be useful for another department to know about. For example, the barman may notice that a party of 22 persons has arrived when he knows the restaurant is expecting 19. He should pass this information on immediately. The restaurant manager would then pass this same information immediately to the head chef.

Recognized procedures

Telephone practice

Telephone enquiries should be received in the following manner:

1 The telephone should be answered as promptly as possible. Remember that it is a person calling to speak to you rather than a machine.
2 Lift the receiver, say 'Good morning/afternoon/evening', announce the name of the bar or restaurant, then say 'May I help you?' Speak steadily and clearly and speak directly into the mouthpiece of the handset.
3 Never lift the receiver off and put it down on the side without speaking to the caller; this is extremely rude and frustrating for the caller.

4 Never lift and replace the receiver, thus cutting the caller off.

5 When receiving enquiries for bookings, note the date and time the customer wishes to book for, the name of the caller, their telephone number, and the number of persons they wish to book for.

6 Note any other details, e.g. ruby wedding celebration with the names of the two principal people.

7 If you have to leave the phone to obtain some information, tell the caller and keep the time away from the phone as short as possible.

8 When putting the phone down while the person is still connected, avoid banging it as this will be uncomfortable for the person on the other end of the call.

9 Never leave the receiver dangling on the end of the wire while you go to fetch some information.

10 Remember that all noise and spoken words will be picked up by the receiver and transmitted to the caller.

11 At the end of the call, thank the person for calling and place the receiver back in position.

Personal enquiries

Enquiries received from customers in person should be treated in much the same way as telephone enquiries. Any queries received from customers should be dealt with as quickly as possible and in a polite manner.

Compliments

Compliments offered by customers should be received with courtesy and the customer should be thanked politely. The compliment should then be passed on to the persons or section concerned if it is for someone other than or in addition to yourself. For example, a customer may compliment you on the quality of the wine which you have served. This information should be passed on to the person responsible for preparing the wine list and ordering the wine.

Elderly, children and disabled

Due consideration must be given to elderly customers, children and handicapped persons.

Elderly people may require a little more time and patience.

Very young children may require immediate attention. They are usually less of a problem to the parents and the establishment when they have been served with a drink of fruit juice, lemonade etc.

Disabled customers like to be treated in as normal a way as possible. They generally make light of their disability.

Complaints

Complaints received from customers are very important and must be recorded. Many establishments keep a complaints book where these are noted down. All complaints should be reported to the management who should speak directly to the customer concerned.

Action should then be taken to ensure that the same thing does not occur again. In particular, when next this customer comes into the bar or restaurant, special care must be taken to ensure that everything goes smoothly.

Drunken customers

Customers sometimes arrive on the premises under the influence of alcohol or become inebriated while on the premises. The law clearly states that such customers should not be served with any more alcohol.

If either of these situations should occur, the management should be called to deal with the problem. It is often at this point that the customer will become unpleasant and abusive. This can be very disruptive to other guests, and a good manager will usually speak to the customer concerned in a quiet but firm manner. Sometimes the manager will be able to conduct the conversation away from the main public area.

If a customer does become drunk while on the premises it is advisable to have as little contact as possible with him.

Fire and bomb warnings

In the case of a fire or bomb warning, the procedures laid down for the establishment must be immediately followed (see Chapter 12). Reassure customers and help them to evacuate the premises in an orderly manner. If you discover the fire or suspected bomb yourself, you should raise the alarm immediately.

In the event of fire, after alarm and evacuation, close all windows and doors and attack the fire with fire-fighting equipment. It is important to use the correct type of extinguisher for the fire. There is a colour code for British-made fire extinguishers indicating for which type of fire each is suitable (see Chapter 12).

Customer illness or accident

Every effort should be made to prevent accidents taking place. Accidents occur unexpectedly and can result in damage to a customer's belongings and person, or damage to the property of the establishment.

If an accident causes damage to the customer's belongings the matter must be reported to the restaurant manager or general manager, who will note all the particulars and take any action which is thought to be necessary. If a customer is injured or taken ill, it will depend on the extent of the injury or the seriousness of the illness as to the procedure to be followed. In any case the restaurant manager or bar manager must be informed.

Very often a customer who feels unwell is helped by being moved to a cooler and quieter place, e.g. from the bar or restaurant to a private room or a vacated reception bar area, and given a glass of water.

If there is a severe problem, a doctor should be called. If the customer is very ill or injured badly and cannot be moved from a public room or area, screens should be placed round the table and a member of staff should remain with the customer until the doctor arrives. Whichever of these situations occurs, the details must be carefully recorded.

Theft or loss of customers' property

It is necessary to display a printed notice declaring that the management of the bar or restaurant will take no responsibility for the loss of any property belonging to a customer. If accommodation has not been booked in the establishment there is no liability on behalf of the proprietor unless negligence can be proved. In this case the establishment is held to be liable.

If coats are taken by the establishment and hung up in a cloakroom then liability does exist. Under the law of bailment, if property is handed to and received by another person he is duty bound to return it in the same condition as he received it.

If theft or loss is reported by a customer the manager must be notified. He or she will take down all particulars and will probably notify the police.

Apologies to customers

If it is necessary to apologize to a customer, this must be done in a respectful, courteous and sincere manner.

Anticipating and satisfying customer needs

Welcoming

When a customer arrives in an establishment he must be noticed and welcomed, not left standing about. Staff should greet the customer in a pleasant and courteous manner on their first contact with him or her. The attitudes and behaviour of staff have been discussed earlier in this chapter.

Depending on the relationship between the customer and the staff of the establishment, the form of address will vary. The normal form of address for an evening would be 'Good evening, sir; good evening, madam', or 'Good evening, ladies and gentlemen' if there are more than one of each.

Some correct forms of address
The following list of forms of verbal address is not intended to be comprehensive, or indeed a toast-master's 'bible'. It is meant to be an accurate guide as to the correct way to speak to the persons mentioned as customers.
The Queen One should not begin a conversation with the Queen. On answering her, use 'Your Majesty' in the first instance and 'Ma'am' afterwards (pronounced Mam).
Royal princes and princesses Once again a conversation should not be begun by a member of staff. On answering, use 'Your Royal Highness', and afterwards 'sir' or 'Ma'am'.
Dukes and duchesses are formerly addressed as 'Your Grace'.
Peers and peeresses below duke and duchess are addressed as 'My Lord' and 'My Lady'.
Archbishops are formerly addressed as 'Your Grace'.

Bishops should be addressed as 'My Lord' or 'My Lord Bishop'.
Cardinals are addressed as 'Your Eminence'.
Lord Mayors and Lady Mayoresses Address them as 'My Lord' and 'My Lady'.
Mayors (male and female) Address them as 'Your Worship' or 'Mr Mayor'.
Mayoresses Address them as 'Mayoress'.

For a comprehensive list of the correct modes of address, consult *Debrett's Correct Form*.

Treating customers

The approach of staff to treating customers has already been mentioned earlier in this chapter.

Customers should always be spoken to in a polite manner and treated with respect. Staff should converse with customers to discuss their requirements, their choice and often other things such as local information. Be prepared to listen and to talk to customers if they want to, but do not force yourself on to them or interrupt their conversations. Staff should never repeat conversations which they have overheard.

Ensure that customers do not have to wait for you to serve them because you are holding a long conversation with another customer.

Customers' departure

When customers leave the bar or restaurant, say for example 'Goodnight, sir, madam (ladies and gentlemen), I hope to see you again soon', or 'I hope you have enjoyed your evening'. Ensure that they have taken all their personal belongings with them by scanning their tables and chairs and surrounding areas.

Chapter Eleven

Licensing and quantities

Licences

To legally supply and sell alcoholic drinks to the public, it is a requirement of the Licensing Act of 1964 (England and Wales) and the Licensing Act 1976 (Scotland) that a licence should be held.

Off-licence

This licence is required for the sale of liquor for consumption off or away from the premises. There are two types of off-licence:

1 For the sale of all types of liquor
2 For the sale of beer, cider and wine only.

All sales made under an off-licence must be in closed containers.

Full on-licence (England and Wales)
Public house licence (Scotland)

This licence is required for the sale of liquor for consumption on or off the premises to any person permitted by law to purchase alcoholic beverages. It is possible to restrict this to the sale of beer, cider and wine only. Other differences which may be obtained are:

Six-day licence This permits sales from Mondays to Saturdays. Only residents may be served on a Sunday.
Seasonal licence This licence is obtained for only part of the year where there is a heavy seasonal trade and little local custom out of season.

Residential licence

This licence allows for the sale of all liquor to residents of a hotel. The residents may also purchase drinks for their guests at their own expense.

Restaurant licence

This licence allows for the sale of all liquor to persons taking a meal where the drink is an ancillary to the meal, and where the meal is served in a proper restaurant.

Residential and restaurant licence

This is a combination of the above two, allowing for the sale of liquor to residents and also to non-residents partaking of a meal.

Occasional licence

This licence allows for alcoholic drinks to be served on a premises which is normally unlicensed. It can only be obtained by a licensee who holds a full on-licence applying for a special occasion.

Occasional permission (Licensing Act 1983)

This may be obtained by a person who does not hold a full on-licence and who can be an ordinary member of the public, on behalf of an organization, e.g. a local parents and teachers association. This gives the same permission as an occasional licence, and is intended for an individual event. Only four occasional permissions may be obtained by an organization in any period of twelve months.

Permitted hours

These are the hours in which licence holders may serve alcoholic liquor. They may vary from area to area, but must not exceed 9½ hours per day on Mondays to Saturdays inclusive. There must be a minimum single break of two hours during the afternoon. These permitted hours may not begin before 10.00 a.m. or finish later than 11.00 p.m. If 10.30 p.m. closing is chosen, then the permitted hours may add up to 9 hours only. On Sundays, Good Friday and Christmas Day, the permitted hours are from 12.00 noon to 2.00 p.m. and 7.00 p.m. to 10.30 or 11.00 p.m.

From 2 May, 1987 a new Act, the Licensing (Restaurant Meals) Act 1987 came into force. It applies to establishments which comply with section 68(1)A of the Licensing Act 1964 and hold a certificate under section 68 from the licensing justices. It is intended for establishments which are habitually used for the provision of substantial refreshment (meals) for which the sale of alcohol is an ancillary. This new act permits the sale of alcoholic drinks as an ancillary to meals between 3.00 p.m. and 5.00 p.m. (the hours the Licensing Act 1964 stipulated that the sale of alcoholic drinks would not be permitted). A notice must be displayed in a conspicuous position in the restaurant stating the effect of the 68(1)A extension order and the subsequent 1987 Act amending it.

Extensions to permitted hours

Extensions to hours and special orders of exemption may be obtained for premises covered by a full on-licence, restaurant licence, or residential and restaurant licence.

Conditions and regulations

Premises

There are certain conditions laid down concerning gaming and the provision of music and dancing on licensed premises for which licences may have to be obtained.

It is illegal to allow prostitutes to use the premises to obtain business, and it is illegal to allow the premises to be used as a brothel.

It is illegal to harbour thieves on the premises or to hold stolen goods there.

Official entry

The police and Customs and Excise officials have right of entry to licensed premises. This does not apply to registered clubs.

In England and Wales a police officer may enter any licensed premises during permitted hours, and half an hour after the morning or evening session and during any extension, in pursuance of his duty. He may also enter a premises during the period it is licensed by an occasional licence.

In Scotland he may enter licensed premises at any time other than an off-licence, unless he is reasonably certain that a crime is being or has been committed on the premises of the off-licence.

In England, Wales and Scotland, it is an offence to knowingly permit a police officer on duty to remain on the premises longer than is required for him to perform his duty. It is also an offence to supply him with liquor or any other refreshment unless a senior officer has authorized it.

Local authority trading standards officers and environmental health inspectors may also enter any catering premises.

General regulations

All employers and employees on licensed premises must abide by the Weights and Measures Act 1963, the Hygiene (General) Regulations 1970 (England), the Food Hygiene (Scotland) Regulations 1959 (as amended), the Trades Description Act 1968, the Race Relations Act 1976, the Sex Discrimination Act 1975, the Licensing Act 1964 (England and Wales), and the Licensing (Scotland) Act 1976.

Service and dispensing

It is an offence under the Licensing Act to serve a person who is drunk. It is an offence for a licensee to allow drunkenness and violent or disorderly conduct on the premises.

It is an offence for an employer and employee to serve beer, cider and certain spirits by the incorrect measures (see later in this chapter). It is also an offence to mix or dilute liquors without expressly informing the customer of the dilution or mixing. The customer would have to be *informed of* the resulting strength of the dilution.

All optics and non-drip measuring instruments must be sealed with a government seal. They must be exact measures, they must be kept clean and they must not be tampered with.

Employers and employees must not serve any customer after the termination of permitted hours or any extension which has been granted. A period of 10 minutes (England and Wales) or 15 minutes (Scotland) is permitted for the customer to consume his drink after the termination of the permitted hours or extension. If the drink was served with a meal then the period allowed for 'drinking up' is 30 minutes. After these periods have elapsed the employer and employee are responsible for the removal of all the glasses whether they are empty or not.

Age restrictions

It is an offence to give a child *under five* years old any intoxicating liquor at any time except with the authority of a doctor or for a medical case of extreme urgency.

Children *under fourteen* may not be allowed to enter a bar of a licensed premises during permitted hours except to pass through to another part of the establishment when there is no other way. If the bar is just an ancillary to a hotel lounge or restaurant then a child under fourteen is permitted in the room.

Over fourteen years a young person is allowed into any bar to which the licence permits them, but they may only buy or consume non-alcoholic drinks.

Between the ages of *sixteen and eighteen* young persons may purchase beer, cider or perry to accompany a meal in a room set aside for the service of table meals. In Scotland they may also purchase wine to accompany the meal.

Providing that an accompanying adult purchases it, a young person or a child may consume beer, wines or spirits with a meal if it is served in a room set aside for the service of meals.

A person over the age of *eighteen* may purchase any intoxicating liquor.

A licensee and his staff must not serve intoxicating liquor to anybody under the age of eighteen apart from the above exceptions.

Legal measures of alcoholic beverages

Spirits

Gin, whisky, rum and vodka may only be served in a bar in measured quantities of 1/6, 1/5 or 1/4 gill or multiples of these. A gill is 1/4 pint or 4 fluid ounces.

The chosen size of measure must be used in all bars and restaurants in the establishment, and a sign must be displayed indicating this measurement. There are no legal measurements for spirits other than those mentioned, so it follows that other spirits may be served in any quantity by law. However, the customer will expect to be served the same measure of brandy in particular as is used for the regulated spirits.

Wines

There are no legal restrictions concerning the quantity of wine sold in a closed container or bottle except that it must be as stated on the bottle or container.

Wine sold in a carafe is subject to the conditions of the Sale of Wine Order 1976. This states that wine sold in an open container can only be sold in measured quantities of 25, 50, 75 and 100 cl (1 litre), or 10 and 20 fl oz (see also Chapter 8).

Wine served by the glass is subject to the conditions of the Capacity Measures (Intoxicating Liquor) Regulations 1983. These regulations apply to the sale of still wine by the glass. They allow the licensee to choose between either serving any measure of wine into an unmarked glass *or* serving an exact measure and advertising the size of this measure to the customer. This measure must be able to be proved.

Code of practice

A code of practice has been agreed by the trade associations with the Department of Trade and Industry. A licensee who chooses to adopt the code of practice will specify the amount and advertise this to his customers.

Either metric or imperial measures may be offered, but not a mixture of the two. A maximum of two sizes may be offered on one premises. If two measures are offered there must be a difference of either 50 ml (metric) or 2 fl oz (imperial). A verified dispenser must be used. This can be a government-stamped spirit measure; a government-stamped measuring thimble except for 125 ml, 150 ml and 175 ml; a stamped wine meter; or a glass bearing a government stamp or an approved manufacturer's mark. This glass may also be used as a measure, and the wine may be poured from this glass into a plain unmarked glass for service.

Although this code of practice is voluntary at the time of writing, there is a considerable amount of pressure on the government to standardize wine glass measures and to make it obligatory for a licensee to clearly state the measure that he is using.

Beers

Under the Weights and Measures Act 1963, draught beer and cider may only be sold in measured quantities of 1/3 pint, 1/2 pint, or multiples of 1/2 pint, unless it is being offered for sale as part of a mixed drink such as shandy. The 'gas' which is contained in the head of a glass of beer is not counted towards the measured volume (Weights and Measures Act 1979).

Draught beer and cider must be served in a government-stamped glass of the quantity required or through a government-sealed beer meter.

Chapter Twelve

Health and safety

This chapter gives an outline of the main conditions of the various laws and acts which affect food and beverage sales and service, but it should not be taken to be a complete work on these areas. For a fuller understanding the author suggests that a book devoted to the law should be consulted, e.g. *Hotel and Catering Law in Great Britain* by David Field (Sweet & Maxwell 1982).

Health and Safety at Work Act 1974

The Health and Safety at Work Act 1974, as amended by the Fire Precaution Act 1971, in effect making it obligatory for any premises used for the sale of food and drink to obtain a fire certificate.

The employer (hereafter referred to as 'he') must take reasonable precautions to ensure the employees' health, safety and welfare, as far as is reasonably practical, while they are at work. He must provide a safe place of work and take all reasonable precautions to see that it remains safe. He must also ensure the health and safety of customers and guests as far as is reasonably practical. This includes the safe structure of the building; electrical and gas installations; safe floor and stair coverings (e.g. no frayed or turned up carpet edges); and dry and uncluttered floors.

All fire and emergency exits must be kept clear.

The employer must provide equipment which is safe when used correctly, and which must be correctly installed and maintained. He must provide adequate training for staff so that they know the correct methods and techniques of using the equipment.

He must provide safe methods of access to all rooms.

In establishments with more than five employees the employer must provide a written health and safety policy which is shown to the employees.

A record must be kept of any accident to an employee causing him to be unable to work for three or more days. Serious accidents or occurrences regarding dangerous situations must be reported to the environmental health officer immediately. All accidents to employees which occur at their place of work must by law be recorded. A standard accident book is available from HMSO.

Although the employer is held responsible for any act of negligence causing loss or injury to a customer, an employee must exercise reasonable care and skill in the performance of his duties and could be held liable for any loss or injury to a customer. The employee must safeguard the health and safety of colleagues as well as his self.

No person shall intentionally or recklessly interfere with or misuse anything provided in the interests of health, safety or welfare.

Offices, Shops and Railway Premises Act 1963

This Act covers persons employed in the sales and service of beverages in hotels and restaurants, but excludes employees of registered clubs and purely residential hotels.

It requires that the work and public areas are kept clean, clear and well lit. Non-public work areas must be kept at a minimum of 16°C.

Drinking water and cups, or a drinking fountain, must be available for employees. Sufficient toilets and washing facilities must be available which are suitable for the requirements of staff of both sexes. A place must be provided for the employees' outdoor clothing.

Staircases must be well lit and must have handrails. Equipment which is in any way dangerous must have its dangerous parts guarded. Employees must not be asked to lift loads which are liable to cause them injury.

First aid boxes must be available, and one member of staff must be in charge of and be competent in first aid. Other employees must not tamper with or interfere with these first aid materials.

The environmental health officers have right of entry and inspection at their convenience.

Food Hygiene Regulations

Many of the points covered under the Offices, Shops and Railway Premises Act are also dealt with under the Food Hygiene (General) Regulations 1970, and Food Hygiene (Scotland) Regulations 1959, as amended. Beverages are regarded as food under these regulations, so beverage sales and service activities are governed by them.

Food and beverage business premises must be sanitary, and all equipment which is likely to come into contact with food and drink must be able to be kept clean and free from contamination. This equipment must then be kept clean. The work area must be kept clear of accumu-

lated refuse. Food must be kept at least eighteen inches (450 mm) from the ground, but this does not include items such as bottles of beer which are in sealed bottles. All food rooms must be kept in a good state of repair and must be properly lit and ventilated.

Spare gas cylinders, whether empty or full, should be stored in the open air with the valves uppermost and closed. Safety caps where provided must be in place. The storage area must be well away from buildings, drains, cellars or basements, and combustible materials.

Clean toilet facilities must be provided away from food areas, and wash basins, water, soap, nailbrushes, and hand drying facilities must also be provided. Notices must be displayed in the toilet areas telling employees to wash their hands after using the toilet.

All beverage sales and service staff must keep themselves and their clothes clean. All cuts and abrasions must be covered. Staff must not smoke, spit or take snuff in a beverage service area with open food. It is an offence under these regulations to smoke behind the bar. Employees suffering from certain diseases and illnesses must not work near food.

Accidents: causes and prevention

There are two main categories of accident:

1 Those caused by human error
2 Those caused by unsafe or defective equipment and/or working areas

Human error

Many accidents are caused by employees drinking on or off duty. It is a fact that alcohol slows down the human reaction time considerably, and increases errors of judgement. Persons who have taken drugs may have the same problems. Remember that medicines prescribed for common illnesses are drugs and may have adverse effects, including drowsiness.

Fatigue is a major cause of accidents.

Comfortable well made solid shoes which give protection to the top of the foot should be worn, and they should be kept in good repair. Badly worn, open toe and high heeled shoes are very dangerous and are unsuitable for this type of work.

Other accidents are caused by using the wrong equipment for a task, or by the incorrect use of equipment. These may be due to a lack of instruction or supervision; over-familiarity; laziness, which is a form of carelessness; untidiness, which may be caused by pressure of work, poor storage and worktop facilities; and carelessness, e.g. carrying too many glasses on a tray.

Broken glass in a sink and broken bottles in beer crates or skips can cause serious cuts. Dirty glasses should be washed in glass washing machines. Chipped or cracked glasses should be thrown away, and care should be taken when emptying bottle skips and full beer crates. Always wrap broken glass in plenty of paper.

Many accidents end with a person falling, and falling is in fact the most common cause of injury on licensed premises. The two most common types of fall are those caused by tripping over items such as flexes, wires, boxes, frayed carpets and other obstructions, and those caused by people falling off pieces of equipment, chairs or tables on to which they have climbed instead of a ladder, or straight falls from ladders and stairs. It is therefore imperative to keep all corridors, passageways, staircases and work areas clear of boxes, crates, bottles, litter and other obstructions; they must also be kept well lit. Always use a proper set of steps rather than chairs, tables, boxes or other pieces of equipment.

Equipment and working areas

Poor lighting, heating and ventilation all cause accidents. Uneven, slippery and cluttered floor areas, badly maintained or broken equipment and furniture, unguarded dangerous equipment, unclean equipment and work area, and unsafe and untidy storage of commodities and equipment are other causes of accidents.

All crates and empties must be stored neatly and tidily.

Remember that under the Health and Safety at Work Act the employer is responsible for the safety of the public as well as the staff, so if delivery of liquor entails the use of a hatchway, trapdoor, lift or hoist, inside or outside the premises, a person must be designated to guard these areas to protect staff and public from accidents.

Many accidents can be avoided by employers and employees taking just a reasonable amount of care.

The employer must ensure that employees are aware of possible dangers. They must be encouraged to report faulty equipment, problem areas or any potential hazard which becomes apparent. They must be trained to keep all areas clean and to clear up spillages as they occur.

Posters and notices should be displayed reminding employees of potential hazards and how to deal with them. The correct use of machinery and equipment instructions should be posted up by the respective items.

As the Health and Safety at Work Act states, employees as well as employers must take every precaution to safeguard the health and safety not only of themselves but also of their colleagues.

All employers and employees must know what action to take in the event of fire (see later in this chapter).

Electric shock

Accidents involving electricity usually cause electric shocks to people and may also result in a fire.

All electrical equipment must be installed by a qualified electrician, as many accidents are caused by faulty installations.

It is important that the correct fuse is used for each piece of equipment and that the plug is wired up correctly (see Figures 12.1 and 12.2). Many accidents are caused in the hotel and catering industry by faulty or damaged plugs, wires or flexes.

Any electrically operated piece of equipment is usually quite safe when used correctly and well maintained, but it is a potential hazard to health and safety and must be checked frequently. Electrical heaters are sometimes used to dry bar cloths by draping them over the outlet of the hot air. This practice is extremely dangerous and will quite likely lead to a fire.

Water and other liquids are good conductors of electricity and will make any electric shock worse if associated with any electrical fault. Therefore electrical equipment must *never* be touched with wet hands, and wires and flexes should be kept away from water and areas which often get splashed with water.

Flexes and wires should be kept out of the way so that staff and customers cannot trip over them. Counter mountings and display material in bars must have a low voltage supply, *never* mains voltage (consult a qualified electrician if in doubt). Lights should be switched off before attempting to clean them. It is dangerous to use multiplug adaptors in bar areas.

Electrical equipment should be switched off at the mains before dealing with any fault.

Procedure in the event of electric shock

The electricity supply must be switched off immediately. If this is not possible, pull the person clear without touching the person's skin, and do not stand in water.

Call for medical help, and attempt resuscitation if the person has stopped breathing.

A card clearly explaining the correct treatment for electric shock should be displayed in any area where electrical equipment is used.

Fires

Fires are very dangerous and cause loss of life. However, it must be recognized that smoke and fumes actually account for more deaths, so it is important to consider this when furnishing or decorating a room. The smoke produced when modern furniture burns is highly poisonous and often fatal.

Fire procedures

To cause a fire there needs to be a combination of a combustible material or substance, oxygen (usually air) and heat. Once the fire has started it will provide its own heat. Open windows and doors will supply air and a draught to fan the flames.

If a small fire has started, the fire alarm should be sounded, any fuel supply switched off and the fire attacked with the correct type of fire extinguisher. Any combustible material nearby should be moved away from the fire, thus isolating it from further fuel.

All members of staff should be instructed in what they should do on the outbreak of a fire. The employer must prepare a fire routine for the establishment. Notices detailing this procedure should be displayed in staff quarters, public rooms and (for hotels) in the guests' bedrooms as well (Figure 12.3). Proficiency in operating this procedure should be maintained by carrying out regular fire drills and instruction.

The employer must ensure that the fire alarm system, emergency lighting and fire fighting equipment provided in the premises is checked at regular intervals by a competent person. A suitable record must be kept of the dates of the routine inspections together with the signature of the person carrying out the inspection (Figure 12.4).

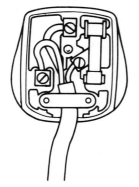

Figure 12.1

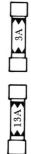

Selecting the right fuse

Each 13 amp plug has its own individual cartridge fuse which is simply pressed into position. The illustration shows such a plug with its protective cover removed, clearly showing the position of the fuse.

Fuses can be obtained in two ratings, 3 amp and 13 amp and for maximum safety the fuse must be selected to suit the particular appliance connected to the plug.

How to wire a plug

Any new appliance purchased now should be connected as shown in the diagram:

Green and yellow wire (earth) to terminal marked E or ⏚
Brown wire (live) to terminal marked L
Blue wire (neutral) to terminal marked N

However some older appliances may have flexes which use the old colour code and should therefore be connected: Green (earth) to terminal marked E or ⏚. Red (live) to terminal marked L. Black (neutral) to terminal marked N.

The large earth pin of a 3 pin plug should always be connected to the green or green and yellow wire as this helps prevent you suffering a shock if an electrical fault develops in the appliance. Always make sure that there are no loose wires and that the cord grip is holding the flex firmly.

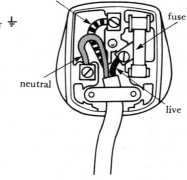

Figure 12.2

The colour code for fire extinguishers is as follows:

Extinguisher type	Colour	Main uses
Water	Red	Wood, paper, fabrics
Foam	White or cream	Petrol, oil, fat and paint
Vaporizing liquid	Green	Electrical and electronic equipment
Carbon dioxide	Black	Liquids, gases, electrical and electronic apparatus

Fire prevention

Many outbreaks of fire are caused by smoking, by unextinguished cigarette ends being put into waste bins, and by accidents while using a naked flame such as a lighted match. Self-extinguishing bins should be used in bars, and care should be taken when emptying ashtrays, particularly at the end of a service, to ensure that all cigarette ends are extinguished. Paper and combustible materials must not be allowed to accumulate.

Lights and shades must be well maintained; faulty electrical equipment and wiring, and

notice for display at fire alarm callpoints

FIRE ROUTINE

1   If you discover a fire, immediately raise the alarm by operating the nearest fire alarm callpoint.

2   On hearing the fire alarm (continuously ringing bell) leave the building via the nearest available escape route and assemble at
    * ....

3   Do not use the lift/s.

4   Do not stop to collect personal belongings.

5   Do not re-enter the building until told it is safe to do so.

NB Make yourself familiar with the escape routes from the building NOW.

notice for guest bedrooms

FIRE ROUTINE

1   If you discover a fire immediately raise the alarm. The nearest alarm callpoint to your room is * ....
    ....

2   On hearing the fire alarm (a continuously ringing bell) leave the building via the nearest available escape route and assemble at
    * ....

3   Do not use the lift/s.

4   Do not stop to collect personal belongings.

5   Do not re-enter the building until told it is safe to do so.

NB Make yourself familiar with the escape routes from the building NOW.

notice for display in staff areas

FIRE ROUTINE

IF YOU DISCOVER A FIRE

1   Immediately operate the nearest fire alarm callpoint.

2   Attack the fire, if possible, with the appliances provided but without taking personal risks.

ON HEARING THE FIRE ALARM

3   .... * will call the fire brigade immediately (Dial 999 — ask for FIRE BRIGADE).

4   Leave the building via the nearest available escape route and report to the person in charge of the assembly point at
    .... *

5   .... * will take charge of any evacuation and ensure so far as it is possible, that no one has been left in the building.

6   Do not use lift/s.

7   Do not stop to collect personal belongings.

8   Do not re-enter the building until told it is safe to do so.

* (Note: Complete as appropriate)

Figure 12.3

FIRE EXTINGUISHERS – RECORD OF TESTS AND INSPECTIONS

Date	Location or Number	Inspected or tested?	Satisfactory Yes/No	Remedial action taken	Signature

FIRE INSTRUCTIONS AND DRILLS – RECORD OF WHEN GIVEN

Date	Instruction Duration	Fire Drill Evacuation Time	Person/Department Receiving Instruction/Drill	Nature of Instruction/Drill	Observations of Instructor etc	Signature of Instructor etc

Figure 12.4   *Fire prevention log book headings*

electric lights in contact with lamp shades, cause fires. All gas appliances should be well maintained and faults promptly rectified. Care should be taken when changing bottled gas cylinders. Spare and empty cylinders should be stored outside the main building.

Fire prevention is the responsibility of both the management and the staff. Before leaving a public room or premises at night or at the end of a service, a routine should be followed. Empty all ashtrays, check carpets and furniture for dropped cigarettes, switch off all electrical equipment and remove power plugs. Check that gas taps are turned off, and close all doors to all rooms and staircases. This procedure is absolutely essential.

Pest infestation

Insect and/or rodent infestation is likely to occur in even the most hygienically run operation, although a high standard of hygiene will reduce the likelihood of this happening.

Although many infestations, such as cockroaches and rodents, should be treated by a professional pest control company, successful individual spot treatments can be carried out on some of the most common pests. Only materials which have been cleared by the Pesticide Safety Precaution Scheme should be used.

The following pests are the most common to be found in a beverage sales and service area.

Ants Ants will infest food and drink areas, particularly in the summer. Ensure that all bottles are securely sealed. If the nest can be identified it should be treated with a proprietary ant control product. If it cannot then the point of entry of the ants should be traced back and this point plus the ant run within the establishment should be treated.

Silverfish Treat the infected areas such as cracks and crevices and the inside of cupboards with a proprietary crawling insect killer.

Flies Pyrethrum or pyrethroid fly sprays are particularly effective for use in bars and service areas, but all items of open food must be covered when they are used and for a short time

Why you should practise correct handling and lifting

Because you then use those muscles best fitted for the job.

Because it takes the strain out of handling and helps you to carry out handling movements more easily.

Because it protects you from sudden injury by strain and rupture, or ill health arising out of unconsciously using bad handling methods. Such bad methods are often responsible for what we call 'rheumatism', 'fibrositis', or 'slipped disc'.

Because it enables you to finish the day fresh to enjoy your leisure.

Because every job can be made easier by correct handling.

These points are essential for smooth and easy handling of all kinds

1 CORRECT GRIP
Use the palms and roots of the fingers and thumb.

2 STRAIGHT BACK
Lift with the legs and relax the knees.

3 CHIN IN
Raise the top of the head and tuck the chin in.

4 CORRECT FEET POSITIONS
Stand with feet apart, but no wider than the hips, with one foot forward in the direction you intend to follow.

5 ARMS CLOSE TO THE BODY
This enables you to use the body muscles correctly.

6 BODY WEIGHT
Use your body as a counterbalance. Its weight can reduce the muscular effort necessary.

Figure 12.5 *Handling and lifting loads*

afterwards. In areas other than public rooms, an ultraviolet fly control unit may be most suitable.
Cockroaches Apply an insecticidal lacquer aerosol or a proprietary crawling insect killer to cracks, crevices and other affected areas. It is advisable to seek the services of a professional pest control company.
Rodents Seek the services of a professional pest control company.

The most satisfactory method of pest control in hotels and catering establishments is to employ a professional pest control company on a contractual basis.

Lifting and carrying loads

Do not attempt to lift a load which is too heavy. As a general rule these are loads over 20 kg, but this weight depends on the shape and size of the load and the strength of the lifter.

Where possible use a sack barrow to move beer crates. This can also be used to move beer kegs if a keg trolley is not available.

When lifting an item from the ground, squat down with the knees apart (Figure 12.5). Take a firm hold on the load using a full palm grip. Keep the back straight and upright. Bend the knees and let the legs do the work. Keep the arms straight and close to the body. Do not twist the body whilst lifting; avoid sudden movements and twisting of the spine. Take account of the centre of gravity of the load when lifting.

If a load is too heavy, call for assistance. Do not rush into lifting a heavy load; try the weight cautiously first. Plan the move to avoid unnecessary lifting. Move a load by the simplest method. Clear all obstacles from the area and from the place you intend to deposit the load.

Be careful not to cause injury to other persons. Avoid wearing rings and bracelets. Wear protective gloves to avoid injuries from sharp edges.

Appendices

Appendix 1: 1855 classification of the Médoc

Where a château has altered its name, the new name is quoted.

Premiers crus

Vineyard	Commune
Château Lafite	Pauillac
Château Margaux	Margaux
Château Latour	Pauillac
Château Haut-Brion	Pessac, Graves district
Château Mouton-Rothschild (upgraded to first growth 1973)	Pauillac

Deuxièmes crus

Château Rausan-Ségla	Margaux
Château Rauzan-Gassies	Margaux
Château Léoville-Las-Cases	St Julien
Château Léoville-Poyferré	St Julien
Château Léoville-Barton	St Julien
Château Durfort-Vivens	Margaux
Château Gruaud-Larose	St Julien
Château Lascombes	Margaux
Château Brane-Cantenac	Cantenac and Margaux
Château Pichon-Longueville Baron	Pauillac
Château Pichon-Longueville Comtesse de Lalande	Pauillac
Château Ducru-Beaucaillou	St Julien
Château Cos d'Estournel	St Estèphe
Château Montrose	St Estèphe

Troisièmes crus

Château Kirwan	Cantenac and Margaux
Château d'Issan	Cantenac and Margaux
Château Lagrange	St Julien
Château Langoa-Barton	St Julien
Château Giscours	Labarde
Château Malescot-St-Exupéry	Margaux
Château Cantenac-Brown	Cantenac and Margaux
Château Boyd-Cantenac	Margaux
Château Palmer	Cantenac and Margaux

Château Lagune	Ludon
Château Desmirail	Margaux
Château Calon-Ségur	St Estèphe
Château Ferrière	Margaux
Château Marquis d'Alesme Becker	Margaux

Château Haut-Bages-Libéral	Pauillac
Château Pédesclaux	Pauillac
Château Belgrave	St Laurent
Château Camensac	St Laurent
Château Cos Labory	St Estèphe
Château Clerc-Milon	Pauillac
Château Croizet Bages	Pauillac
Château Cantemerle	Macau

Quatrièmes crus

Château St Pierre	St Julien
Château Talbot	St Julien
Château Branaire-Ducru	St Julien
Château Duhart-Milon-Rothschild	Pauillac
Château Pouget	Cantenac and Margaux
Château La Tour-Carnet	St Laurent
Château Lafon Rochet	St Estèphe
Château Beychevelle	St Julien
Château Prieuré-Lichine	Cantenac and Margaux
Château Marquis de Terme	Margaux

Cinquièmes crus

Château Pontet-Canet	Pauillac
Château Batailley	Pauillac
Château Haut-Batailley	Pauillac
Château Grand-Puy-Lacoste	Pauillac
Château Grand-Puy-Ducasse	Pauillac
Château Lynch-Bages	Pauillac
Château Lynch-Moussas	Pauillac
Château Dauzac	Labarde
Château Mouton Baron Philippe	Pauillac
Château du Tertre	Arsac

Appendix 2: Classification of Graves 1953

Crus classés (rouges)

Château Haut-Brion (also classified in 1855
    Médoc)
Château La Mission-Haut-Brion
Château Haut-Bailly
Domaine de Chevalier
Château Carbonnieux
Château Malartic-Lagravière
Château Latour-Martillac
Château Latour-Haut-Brion
Château Pape-Clément
Château Smith-Haut-Lafitte
Château Olivier
Château Bouscaut

Crus classés (blancs)

Château Carbonnieux
Domaine de Chevalier
Château Couhins
Château Olivier
Château Laville-Haut-Brion
Château Bouscaut

Appendix 3: 1855 classification of Sauternes and Barsac

Grand premier crus

Vineyard	Commune
Château d'Yquem	Sauternes

Premiers crus

Château La Tour-Blanche	Bommes
Château Lafaurie-Peyraguey	Bommes
Château Haut-Peyraguey	Bommes
Château Rayne-Vigneau	Bommes
Château Suduiraut	Preignac
Château Coutet	Barsac
Château Climens	Barsac
Château Guiraud	Sauternes
Château Rieussec	Fargues
Château Rabaud-Promis	Bommes
Château Sigalas-Rabaud	Bommes

Deuxièmes crus

Château Myrat	Barsac
Château Doisy-Daëne	Barsac
Château Doisy-Dubroca	Barsac
Château Doisy-Védrines	Barsac
Château d'Arche	Sauternes
Château Filhot	Sauternes
Château Broustet	Barsac
Château Nairac	Barsac
Château Caillou	Barsac
Château Suau	Barsac
Château de Malle	Preignac
Château Romer	Fargues
Château Lamothe	Sauternes

Appendix 4: 1954 classification of St-Emilion

This classification of 1954 is being reviewed. A new classification made in 1984 will be operational from the 1984 vintage, but at the time of writing this new classification has not been ratified.

Premiers grand crus

Category A
Château Ausone
Château Cheval Blanc
These two wines are agreed by all to be superior to other St-Emilion wines.
Category B
Château Beauséjour (Duffau-Lagarrosse)
Château Beauséjour (Bécot)
Château Belair
Château Canon
Château Clos Fourtet
Château Figeac
Château La Gaffelière
Château Magdelaine
Château Pavie
Château Trottevieille

Grands crus

There are 72 vineyards entitled to use this classification.

Self-assessment questions

Chapter 1

1 The hotel and catering industry employs
between
(a) 1 and 1½ million
(b) 1½ and 2 million
(c) 2 and 2½ million
(d) 2½ and 3 million.
2 How much of each £1 spent by customers in
the hotel and catering industry goes to the
government in taxes?
(a) 12p
(b) 16p
(c) 20p
(d) 24p.
3 The HCTB is an organization
(a) which protects the wages of workers in the
    hotel and catering industry
(b) which promotes training within the hotel
    and catering industry
(c) of hotel and catering teachers
(d) of hoteliers and caterers.

Chapter 2

1 The Hawthorn strainer is used
(a) to decant old wines containing sediment
(b) to strain fresh fruit juices
(c) in conjunction with a standard cocktail
    shaker
(d) in conjuction with a mixing glass.
2 Carbon dioxide may be fed into casks of
traditional cask-conditioned beer to
(a) increase the speed of service
(b) improve the quality of the 'head'
(c) prevent spoiling bacteria contacting the beer
(d) speed up the conditioning of the beer.
3 Which of the following is a legal method of
dispensing whisky in a public house?
(a) straight from the bottle into the glass
(b) through an unsealed and unstamped optical
    dispenser
(c) using a government-stamped thimble mea-
    sure
(d) using a lined glass.
4 Coasters are used to
(a) carry wine bottles on the table
(b) strain cocktails
(c) decorate drinks
(d) put round the neck of a bottle to prevent
    wine dripping.
5 Muddlers are used to
(a) take the gas out of sparkling wines
(b) stir drinks
(c) make crushed ice
(d) relieve hangovers.

6 A shive is correctly described as the
(a) round piece of hard wood used as a bung in the top of a cask
(b) round piece of hard wood used as a bung in the tap hole
(c) connector which is attached to the top of a keg of beer
(d) tapered piece of wood used to vent new casks of beer.

7 Detergents should not be mixed together because
(a) they may give off poisonous fumes
(b) the strength will be too high
(c) they might counteract each other's cleaning qualities
(d) it will be very expensive.

8 The correct way of removing a smear on a glass while polishing it for the table is to
(a) breathe on it, then polish it with a dry cloth
(b) hold it over very hot water, then polish it with a dry cloth
(c) polish it with a damp cloth
(d) rub the smear with a finger then polish it with a dry cloth.

9 Glasses are frosted by
(a) placing them in a trough of ice cubes
(b) placing them in a refrigerator
(c) placing them in a deep freeze
(d) dipping the rim in egg white and sugar.

10 The most suitable temperature for a beer cellar to be kept at is
(a) 7.2°C
(b) 10°C
(c) 12.7°C
(d) 15.6°C

11 Ullage is described as
(a) the stand in the cellar on which casks of beer are placed
(b) the charge made by a hotel on bottles brought in by the customer
(c) any out of condition wine which has to be returned to the supplier
(d) non-alcoholic beer.

12 A bursting disc is found on
(a) kegs of beer
(b) carbon dioxide cylinders
(c) cask-conditioned beers
(d) the top of spirit bottles.

13 A kilderkin of beer will contain
(a) $4\frac{1}{2}$ gallons
(b) 9 gallons
(c) 10 gallons
(d) 18 gallons.

Chapter 3

1 Vines are grafted in order to
(a) improve the quality of the wine
(b) help attract *Botrytis cinerea*
(c) increase the yield
(d) counteract *Phylloxera*.
2 Which of the following grapes will produce a wine with a spicy bouquet and flavour?
(a) Chardonnay
(b) Chasselas
(c) Gewürztraminer
(d) Muscat.
3 Which of the following grape varieties is important to the production of Hermitage?
(a) Cabernet Sauvignon
(b) Gamay
(c) Grenache
(d) Syrah.
4 The tannin found in wine comes from the
(a) grape pips
(b) grape skins
(c) malolactic fermentation
(d) juice of the grape.
5 The liquor obtained from the skins and pips left after pressing grapes is called
(a) marc brandy
(b) vin de goutte
(c) vin de presse
(d) Ratafia.
6 Which of the following alcohols is found in wine?
(a) Butanol
(b) Ethanol
(c) Methanol
(d) Pethanol.
7 *Pelure d'oignon* is a term used to describe
(a) Spanish sparkling wine
(b) German sparkling wine
(c) rosé wine
(d) old Sauternes.
8 Bitterness in wine is tasted
(a) in the centre of the tongue
(b) at the sides of the tongue

(c) at the front of the tongue
(d) at the back of the tongue.
9 Which of the following ACs is considered to be the best?
(a) Bordeaux Supérieur
(b) Haut-Médoc
(c) Médoc
(d) Pauillac.
10 An *Anbaugebiete* is
(a) a wine-growing area for *Qualitätswein*
(b) a quality wine
(c) an official control number
(d) a wine growing region for *Tafelwein*.
11 *Spätlese* wine is made from
(a) late-gathered grapes
(b) specially selected bunches of grapes
(c) individually selected grapes
(d) frozen grapes.

Chapter 4

1 Which of the following could be found on the label of a sweet wine from Alsace?
(a) *Sélection de grains noble*
(b) *Passe-tout-grain*
(c) Edelzwicker
(d) *Réserve Spéciale*.
2 Sancerre is produced in
(a) Anjou
(b) Central Vineyards
(c) Nantais
(d) Touraine.
3 Which of the following is a sweet wine?
(a) Muscadet de Sèvre-et-Maine
(b) Coteaux de la Loire
(c) Bourgeuil
(d) Bonnezeau.
4 Pauillac is a
(a) commune of Sauternes
(b) good-quality wine from Côte de Beaune
(c) high-quality wine from Pomerol
(d) commune of the Médoc.
5 Which of the following is a DOCG wine?
(a) Asti Spumante
(b) Bardolino
(c) Chianti
(d) Orvieto.
6 The Spanish demarcated region which produces high quality *cava* wines is called
(a) La Mancha
(b) Rioja
(c) Penedés
(d) Valdepeñas.
7 Commandaria is produced in
(a) Austria
(b) Cyprus
(c) Greece
(d) South Africa.

Chapter 5

1 Which of the following produces the carbon dioxide in a bottle of Champagne?
(a) *Dégorgement*
(b) *Dosage*
(c) *Liqueur de tirage*
(d) *Remuage*.
2 Coteaux Champenois is correctly described as
(a) Champagne with half the usual gas pressure
(b) the range of hills south of Reims
(c) still white wine from Champagne
(d) a Premium brand of Champagne.
3 Sherry fermentation is carried out in
(a) *bodegas*
(b) *criaderas*
(c) *estufados*
(d) *soleras*.
4 The term *venencia* refers to the
(a) new wine of a single year
(b) sherry tasting glass
(c) town where *fino* sherries mature and take on a salty taste
(d) long-handled cup used to extract samples from a sherry cask.
5 *Vin doux naturel* is a
(a) sweet unfortified wine
(b) the sweetening used to sweeten sherry
(c) sweet fortified wine
(d) wine produced without the use of chemicals.

Chapter 6

1 Irish whiskey is made from
(a) barley and other grain, and distilled twice in a pot still
(b) maize only, and distilled twice in a continuous still
(c) barley and other grain, and distilled three times in a pot still
(d) maize only, and distilled once in a continuous still.
2 The part of the distillate from which Cognac is finally produced is called
(a) bois Ordinaires
(b) *bonne chauffe*
(c) *brouillis*
(d) bons Bois.
3 Fine Champagne is made entirely from grapes which have been grown in the
(a) Grande Champagne
(b) Petite Champagne and Borderies
(c) Grande Champagne and Fins Bois
(d) Petite Champagne and Grande Champagne.
4 Which of the following spirits would *not* be correctly referred to as *alcool blanc*?
(a) Calvados
(b) Framboise
(c) Mirabelle
(d) Poire William.
5 Angostura bitters is produced in
(a) Antigua
(b) Cuba
(c) Puerto Rico
(d) Trinidad.
6 Which of the following has a flavour of caraway?
(a) Amaretto
(b) Galliano
(c) Kümmel
(d) Sambuca.
7 The mash tun is used in the production of beer to
(a) steep barley in to encourage growth
(b) boil the hops, wort and sugar together
(c) extract the flavour from the malt
(d) grind or crack the grains of malt.
8 Apollinaris is produced in
(a) Belgium
(b) France
(c) Germany
(d) Italy.
9 Which of the following mineral waters is produced in France?
(a) Vichy Catalán
(b) Henniez
(c) Spar Reine
(d) Vittel.
10 Quinine is one of the ingredients of
(a) Bitter lemon
(b) Ginger ale
(c) Ruschian
(d) Soda water.

Chapter 7

1 Which one of the following combinations should prove to be the most satisfactory?
(a) Barolo with grilled dover sole
(b) Fitou with spaghetti bolognese
(c) Californian Chenin Blanc with roast rib of beef
(d) Châteauneuf-du-Pape with a selection of hors-d'oeuvres.
2 Which one of the following drinks is most suitable to serve as an aperitif?
(a) Red Dão
(b) Schloss Johannisberg Riesling Auslese
(c) Soave
(d) Bairrada.

Chapter 8

1 Which style of glass would be the most suitable to serve a lager beer in?
(a) Thistle
(b) Titan
(c) Sleever
(d) Pilsner.
2 Which one of the following cocktail ingredients must never be shaken in a cocktail shaker?
(a) Angostura bitters
(b) Cream
(c) Egg white
(d) Soda water.
3 Which of the following drinks contains Campari?
(a) Americano
(b) Bloody Mary
(c) Sidecar
(d) Pink Lady.
4 A White Lady cocktail contains
(a) fresh orange juice
(b) fresh lemon juice
(c) a cube of sugar
(d) vodka.
5 Havana cigars should be kept at a temperature of
(a) 10–12.8°C
(b) 12.8–15.6°C
(c) 15.6–18.3°C
(d) 18.3–21.1°C.
6 A Corona cigar is best prepared for smoking by
(a) warming it over its whole length with a lighted match
(b) cutting the sealed end with a guillotine cutter
(c) piercing the sealed end with a cigar piercer
(d) crackling it between the fingers.
7 The wood associated with cigars is
(a) Apple
(b) Cedar
(c) Chestnut
(d) Oak.

8 Prince Charles coffee is prepared with
(a) Cognac
(b) Drambuie
(c) Glayva
(d) Scotch whisky.
9 When a second bottle of the same wine is ordered by a party of four, the sommelier should present the bottle to the host then
(a) provide clean glasses to all the customers and pour the wine
(b) provide clean glasses to all the customers, offer the host a taste, then pour the wine
(c) pour the wine into the existing glasses
(d) supply the host with a clean glass, offer him a taste then pour the wine.
10 If the customer complains that the wine is corked, the sommelier should apologize, check it himself, then
(a) decant the wine
(b) pass the wine through muslin
(c) change the wine for another bottle
(d) remove the cork.

Chapter 9

1 Which of the following would be the best approach to a customer who has ordered a wine which is suitable for his main course?
(a) Would you like a wine before this one, sir?
(b) Would you prefer a dry or medium wine with your first course, sir?
(c) Would you like anything to drink with your first course, sir?
(d) You don't require a drink with your first course then, sir?

Chapter 10

1 If a member of staff is having difficulty performing a task, his superior should
(a) take over the task
(b) offer advice and encouragement
(c) upbraid the person for not being efficient
(d) make a written report and give the member of staff a warning.
2 The correct form of address for a duke is
(a) My Lord
(b) My Lord Duke
(c) Sir
(d) Your Grace.
3 The correct form of address for a bishop is
(a) My Lord
(b) Your Worship
(c) Your Eminence
(d) Your Grace.

Chapter 11

1 The period that a bottle of wine may be left on a customer's table in a restaurant after the end of permitted hours, or an extension if one has been obtained, is
(a) 10 minutes
(b) 15 minutes
(c) 30 minutes
(d) 1 hour.
2 What is the minimum age that a child may be legally given a glass of wine by an accompanying adult to be drunk with a meal in a room set aside for meal service?
(a) 5 years
(b) 14 years
(c) 16 years
(d) 18 years.
3 It is a requirement of the law to display a sign stating the size of the measure used when serving
(a) Brandy
(b) Gin
(c) Sherry
(d) Wine.

Chapter 12

1 The minimum number of people that an employer may employ without having to provide a written health and safety policy which is shown to the employees is
(a) 2
(b) 5
(c) 10
(d) 20.
2 The minimum temperature permitted in a non-public work area is
(a) 10°C
(b) 12.8°C
(c) 16°C
(d) 18.3°C.
3 Which is the correct way to wire a plug?
(a) Blue wire to terminal L, brown wire to E, green/yellow to N
(b) Brown wire to terminal L, blue wire to E, green/yellow to N
(c) Blue wire to terminal L, green/yellow to E, brown to N
(d) Brown wire to terminal L, green/yellow to E, blue to N.
4 Which colour of fire extinguisher is the correct one to use on a computer which is on fire?
(a) Green
(b) White
(c) Red
(d) Black.

Answers to self-assessment questions

Chapter 1
1 c
2 d
3 b

Chapter 2
1 d
2 c
3 c
4 a
5 b
6 a
7 a
8 b
9 d
10 c
11 c
12 b
13 d

Chapter 3
1 d
2 c
3 d
4 b
5 c
6 b
7 c
8 b
9 d
10 a
11 a

Chapter 4
1 a
2 b
3 d
4 d
5 c
6 c
7 b

Chapter 5
1 c

2 c
3 a
4 d
5 c

Chapter 6
1 c
2 b
3 d
4 a
5 d
6 c
7 c
8 c
9 d
10 a

Chapter 7
1 b
2 c

Chapter 8
1 d
2 d
3 a
4 b
5 c
6 b
7 b
8 b
9 c
10 b

Chapter 9
1 b

Chapter 10
1 b
2 d
3 a

Chapter 11
1 c
2 a
3 b

Index

Numbers in *italics* refer to the City and Guilds 717 syllabus section.

Index

Speciality coffee, *(5.12)*, 140
Spile, *(02)*, 11, 18, 20, 21
Spirits, *(3.12)*, 99–106Spritzig, *(3.2, 3.5a)*, 68, 89
Spumante, *(3.5a)*, 70, 89
St Croix du Mont, *(3.2b)*, 48
St Emilion, *(3.2b)*, 48, 101, 104
St Joseph, *(3.2b)*, 59
St Peray, *(3.2b)*, 59
Ste-Foy-Bordeaux, *(3.2b)*, 49
Stein, *(3.4w)*, 68
Still, *(3.12)*, 99
Stillion, *(02)*, 12, 18
Stocks, *(02)*, 16
Storage, *(02)*, 16
Strega, *(3.15u)*, 107
Superiore, *(3.4p)*, 69–71
Sur lie, *(3.2b)*, 59
Sweetness, *(3.4m)*, 38, 87
Switzerland, *(3.2c)*, 83
Sylvaner, *(3.2b, 3.3, 3.4)*, 25, 65–8
Syphons, *(02)*, 7
Syrah, *(3.2b, 3.3)*, 26, 59–61
Syrups, *(3.17d)*, 110

Tafelweine, *(3.2b, 3.4a)*, 36, 63
Taking orders, *(4.2a, b, 6.1)*, 111–15
Tank beer, *(02)*, 19
Tannin, *(03)*, 33
Tapping casks, *(02)*, 18
Taps, beer, *(02)*, 13, 18, 21
Tarragona, *(3.4y)*, 73, 76
Taste, *(3.2a)*, 32, 33
Tavel, *(3.2b)*, 61
Tawny Port, *(3.6b)*, 94
Telephone practice, *(7.4)*, 147
Temperatures, *(5.2)*, 121, 123
Tequila, *(3.14e)*, 106
Thrawl, *(02)*, 12
Tia Maria, *(3.15i)*, 106
Till, *(02)*, 12, 17
Tokaji, *(3.2c)*, 81
Tongue, *(3.2a)*, 33
Touraine, *(3.2b)*, 56, 89
Transfer method, *(3.5a)*, 89
Treaty of Methuen, *(3.6a)*, 93
Trebbiano, *(3.2b)*, 71
Triple sec, *(3.15l)*, 106
Trocken, *(3.4m)*, 38, 66
Trockenbeerenauslese, *(3.2b, 3.4g, 3.4p)*, 36, 66, 80
Tuscany, *(3.4x)*, 71

Ugni Blanc, *(3.12d)*, 101, 104
Ullages, *(02)*, 17
Umbria, *(3.2b)*, 72

Valdepenas, *(3.4y)*, 73, 76
Valpolicella, *(3.2b, 3.4x)*, 71
VDQS, *(3.4c)*, 34, 37

VO, *(3.12e)*, 103
Veneto, *(3.4x)*, 71
Venezia, *(3.6a)*, 92, 93
Verdelho, *(3.6a)*, 96
Verdicchio, *(3.2b)*, 72
Vermouth, *(3.7a)*, 96
Vesuvio, *(3.2b)*, 72
Vila Nova de Gaie, *(3.6b)*, 94
Vin de Paille, *(3.2b)*, 34, 63
Vin de goutte, *(3.3)*, 29
Vin de mousseux, *(3.5a)*, 89
Vin de pays, *(3.4b)*, 33
Vin de presse, *(3.3)*, 29
Vin de table, *(3.4a)*, 33
Vin doux naturel, *(3.7)*, 96
Vin Fou, *(3.2bh)*, 63
Vine, *(3.3)*, 28, 29
Vinho Verde, *(3.4z)*, 76
Vinho rosado, *(3.4o)*, 78
Vinification, *(3.3)*, 29–31
Vino Espumoso, *(3.5)*, 76, 89
Vino Nobile de Montepulciano, *(3.2b, 3.4x)*, 72
Vino d'anada, *(3.6a)*, 92
Vino da tavola, *(3.4a)*, 37
Vino de Criaza, *(3.4p)*, 75
Vino de color, *(3.6a)*, 93
Vino dulce, *(3.6a)*, 93
Vino tipici, *(3.4a)*, 37
Vintage, *(3.4j)*, 37
Vintage Character, *(3.6b)*, 95
Vintage Port, *(3.3.6b)*, 94
Viticulture, *(3.3)*, 29
Vodka, *(3.12b)*, 100
Voignier, *(3.3)*, 59
VQPRD, *(3.4)*, 37
VS, *(3.12e)*, 103
VSOP, *(3.12e)*, 103

Wales, *(3.2c)*, 80
Weinbaugebiete, *(3.2b, 3.4w)*, 63
Weinstrasse, *(3.4w)*, 67
Whisky, *(3.12c)*, 100, 101
White Port, *(3.6b)*, 94
Wine cooler, *(02, 5.2)*, 10, 123
Wine cradle, *(02)*, 9, 128
Wine definition, *(03)*, 23
Wine lists, *(02, 6.2d)*, 16, 111
Wine production, *(03)*, 23–31
Würtemburg, *(3.2b, 3.4w)*, 63
Würzburg, *(3.4w)*, 68

XO, *(3.12e)*, 103

Yeso, *(3.6a)*, 90
Young persons, *(8.2)*, 153
Yugoslavia, *(3.2c)*, 83

Zinfandel, *(3.2c)*, 80